OMNI

(combined form): UNIVERSAL, ALL

ARE EXTRATERRESTRIALS STEERING US TO A ONE-WORLD RELIGION THROUGH CROP CIRCLES?

By
Dee Finney & Joe Mason

Delores Finney 1938 —
Joseph Mason   1939 —

Library of Congress Control Number: 2004093199

ISBN# 0-9745434-7-0

COVER ART: The Electric Wigwam

Printed in the United States of America
Publishing Services Provided by:

Write to **Print**
P.O.Box 1862
Merrimack, NH 03054
www.writetoprint.com

Address All inquires about this book to:

C/O Great Dreams Publications
P.O. Box 570
Waterford, CA 95386

Table of Contents

INTRODUCTION
By Joe Mason

We have been studying the phenomenon of crop circles almost since their inception in England in the late 1970's. My formal studies started in 1990. There were some crop formations in earlier times, but there wasn't the notice then that there is now. Researchers have looked through photographs taken by airplane since WWI and no crop formations were seen in any photo.

I wrote a list of ideas in 1992 about the earthchanges, which have become quite predictive, about a very great change coming to our world. In many cases dreams were involved, not only mine but by others as well. Often coincidences occurred, usually the accidental finding of a similar concept elsewhere, such as in myths or the dream of another person. We have a very large stack of material supporting these ideas as well as much data published on the internet. Our hope is that others will find more connections and verifications to some of the ideas through their own dreams, inspirations or studies.

I made up the following list of predictions in 1992 and sent them to several crop circle researchers around the world:

1. Truths will slowly be revealed that will drastically change the world-view. Many are ancient teachings. There will be resistance to this, but eventually the symbols will be newly understood and fit into scientific discoveries.

2. The change in world-view toward unity and love will completely transform our world in unbelievable ways.

3. We will learn that we are creating the reality here and have the power to have it as we wish. We are the Demiurge, the craftsman/builders, a sub-deity. This is depicted sometimes as a swastika with a 'builder' symbol (right-angled square) in each quarter. Counter-clockwise represents a negative-creation, and clockwise (going east) is positive. Similar symbols are four couples around a square, the octopus, which is negative, and the eight-pointed star, which is a positive, unity symbol.

4. Our thoughts and beliefs create the reality. They are prime movers of the 'orgone' or low-energy fields that form patterns around which physical matter coalesces. Time and cause/effect are part of the creation here. On a higher level of reality, this creation can be viewed as an eternal now; each moment created through rapid vibrations. The new beliefs involve a conquering of fear and belief in evil. Simply by believing that our existence is blessed and good, will lock-out evil, or negative activity. This is the 'giant' or "Titan" that will be defeated. The battle of good over evil is a question of what we choose to believe. Symbolically this is shown as a tree individually, or a great tree collectively. The Tree of Knowledge represents the beliefs that create the Tree of Life, that is, the reality.

5. Our Oversouls, or Higher Selves, are involved in the creation. Each of us are reincarnational, or focus personalities of the Oversoul. Our other personalities exist in the past and future from our viewpoint. The Oversoul, a very powerful consciousness unit, is symbolized as a circle of interlocking rings that resembles a flower. Each 'petal' is a focus personality.

6. The order of consciousness is a hierarchy. This can be viewed as a pyramid, with humans at the base, oversouls above, on up to the One, or God at the top. The entire structure is God and Her/His manifestions, thus "All-That-Is" is a more true concept of God. (Ephesians 4:6)

"And because ye are sons, "God hath sent forth the Spirit of his Son into your hearts, crying Abba, Father".

7. All-That-Is is within each unit of consciousness and matter. Each unit is like a seed, containing the pattern of the All within it. The Creator manifests as dual, or male/female. This is across scales from subatomic to macrocosmic. The Feminine aspect generates, or gives birth to the Masculine. The Masculine is radiated out into space-time. The physical reality is the male aspect or a part of it. The Spirit reality is the Generating, or Female aspect. Each aspect has a part of the other, that is, each male has part of the female and vice versa. The Yin Yang myth is true.

8. In the creation of mankind, the relative balance of the dual aspects creates the Son, in a Trinity, or three-part relationship. This is the meaning of The Barbury Castle crop formation in 1991.

YIN YANG

BARBURY CASTLE - 1991

It's the subatomic consciousness unit, or smallest particle of matter in our creation. Larger gestalts of consciousness and matter are built up from these units. The central circle represents the One Deity. The two rings are the Dual aspects. These are the invisible energies creating the triangle, or three-sided pyramid.

The north circle, a male/sun symbol, is the Masculine aspect within us. The southwest circle is the feminine aspect, or Holy Spirit. Adam and Eve are the equivalents; they are one, and within us. The ratchet spiral represents the son in a cycle of time. In dreams and myths the relationship of the aspects is often shown as mating or marriage. This is the meaning of the Virgin Birth and is symbolized by the "Y" within the triangle. I saw this in a dream as the part of the woman's body where the legs meet. It's the Generating world giving birth to this one.

Applicable myths are the Pythagorean Tetraktys, Tao Teh Ching 42, the Christian Trinity and similar teachings found world-wide. Ancient glyphs show this as a circle with ring inside a triangle, a "Y"-shape, Eye in a triangle, the letters "AUM" in a triangle representing "the Father and Mother engendered the son, Man." The animal symbol is the face of the bison or ox. The horns represent the dual aspects, like antennas. (see Psalms 92:10) The Salvador Dali painting "Christ of St. John of the Cross" has this symbolism.

Psalms 92:10 "But 'my horn' shalt thou exalt like the horn of an unicorn: I shall be anointed with fresh oil."

9. The great change involves a change in the Duality balance. This is multidimensional and all encompassing. It's part of a universal, pre-ordained Plan. It is considered an evolutionary leap for mankind. We are going from a male dominant to a more balanced condition of the two aspects. Our "lost aspect" is a question of "forgetting." It was there all along, but we "forgot" it for a purpose for a cycle of time. The change involves an "awakening," or "remembering" of the lost aspect.

In terms of the human mind, rational, analytical thinking is a male attribute. Intuitive, psychic abilities are a feminine attribute. The change will increase the feminine abilities, bringing new knowledge about the nature of reality. A joining of the realities, spiritual and physical, will be achieved.

10. We will learn that the dream-reality is essential in the creation of daily reality. Events here in the physical realm are planned there in the spirit realm. Infinite idea potentials exist there that can be manifested here. We unknowingly operate in the

Christ of Saint John of the Cross

spirit realm nightly, planning individual and collective events. The great change will involve coincidence or simultaneities that seem accidental. They are planned in the dream-state and contain symbolism. As we begin to learn the symbolic language of the dream-world, we will understand the meaning of events in daily life. An ancient symbol of our collectiveness is the spider, as placing a thread between each of us. The modern dream symbol of this is the computer, with each of us hooked up to the central control system.

11. This world of ours has been involved with an experiment of consciousness for a cycle of time. We have been working with the Father, or Masculine aspect; the aggressive, thrusting outward attribute, that can become negative and violent. The great change involves a transmuting of this warring-attribute to the positive. This is accompanied by the death of the Male War Gods, or a belief in them, and an awareness of the Mother/Father Deity. The ancient symbol of the Dual deity is a circle bisected by a line, which has appeared in many crop patterns. Major symbolic numbers are nine and multiples thereof: (18, 36, 54, 72, 108, 144) also (432, 28 and 128).

12. The warring-cycle, on a large scale, probably started with Sargon I of Akkad, (now southern Iraq) about 4,320 years ago. (432 is a cycle of time number) Babylon is a symbol of disunity.

13. A period of stress on a global level started with WW1 in 1914. This was the beginning of the apocalyptic cycle. A symbolic event preceded this in 1912 with the sinking of the Titanic.

14. Another pair of symbolic events occurred in the late 1960's; the moon landing and the great leap of Bob Beamon in the Olympics in Mexico City. They symbolized the great evolutionary leap for mankind. The Gulf War also contained symbolism.

15. The film "2001: Space Odyssey" symbolically portrayed the great change. An unknown intelligence, represented by the obelisk, controls evolution from apes to man, developing rational intelligence. When the obelisk is found on the moon millions of years later, it communicates to space that it is time for the next evolutionary step. The computer, HAL, represents the collective-selves not connected; an artificial intelligence with no heart. The astronaut Dave's experience represents the lone spiritual

journey. He goes to the heart of the craft and disables HAL. The computer breaks down and sings, "Daisy, Daisy - on a bicycle built for two." The Daisy is a symbol of the Oversoul and the bicycle, the aspects balanced. Daisy-like crop patterns appeared in 1991, along with a flower-profusion in England. Bicycle-like crop patterns appeared, such as those at Pepperbox Hill and the "insectograms." The film ends with Dave transformed into a baby in a bubble heading back to earth. A new cycle of evolution begins.

NOTE: Oddly enough, in 2001, on 9/11 the terrorist attack occurred. We believe this marks the beginning of the real odyssey to discover our real origins. It is primarily a journey inward - inner space - rather than outer.

16. East is the direction of enlightenment. When you awake from the dreaming and things "dawn" on you, the sun is rising in the east and the morning star, Venus, shines for awhile. The two lights are the symbolic equivalent of Adam and Eve, that is, a large male/rational aspect, and a small female/intuitive one.

In the film, "2010," the sequel to "2001," the earth receives two suns. Symbolically, this is the balancing of the aspects involved in the great change.

17. There may be an actual equivalent to the obelisk. Recent satellite photographs revealed a perfect ring of circles at the Yucatan. They are the Sacred Cenote holes, or natural wells. The wells are now thought to mark the spot where the great meteorite struck 65 million years ago that caused the extinction of the dinosaurs and other large species. Core samples revealed crystalized quartz 1,100 meters below ground.

Scientist J.J. Hurtak claims to have had a spiritual visitation in 1973. He wrote "The Book of Knowledge, The Keys of Enoch," telling of a great evolutionary leap for mankind. A map of the Yucatan is shown in the book, called "The Sacred Grid". Lines are drawn between megalithic sites revealing a three-part triangle. It's quite similar to the Barbury Castle pictogram. Dr. Hurtak was told that this area had triangular grids of crystal and is a communication point with the heavens. It will be involved in a grid shift and alignment effecting the changes here.

Some dowsers say that the energy grid is associated with naturally sited, underground quartz. There may be a seven-mile wide crystal underground at the Yucatan functioning like a radio oscillator, effecting the energy grid.

NOTE: Our DNA is shaped like a radio-tuning coil. Therefore the DNA within our cells may be acting like antennas as they are sensitive to the vibrations of the energy grid. This is considered a cellular communication. Dreams seem to be showing this by the symbol of the telephone, especially the cellular phone. There will be a grid-shift and alignment with a greater grid within the solar system. The effect of which will be a great improvement in our ability to use our inner cell-phones.

18. The Pleiades and Orion are major symbols in the great change. (see Job 38:31) The Pleiades, commonly called the Seven Sisters, has six readily visible stars, with a dimmer seventh, known as "the Lost Pleiad." This is associated with the seven days of creation, which are not yet completed.

*"Canst thou bring forth Mazzaroth in his season?
Or canst thou guide Arcturus with his sons?" (Job 38:31)*

I dreamed of a similar concept, then later found it in "The Book of Knowledge - The Keys of Enoch." After six aeons of time, six fields of light come together, so that on the seventh day, the transmutation is added by the Seventh Ray. This involves subatomic levels of body chemistry. The north circle in the Barbury Castle crop formation may represent the six fields of light coming together. The "ratchet spiral" may represent the six aeons of time. The Seventh Ray may be the Southwest circle, or it could come through the center of the north circle, which is like an aperture.

In July of 1992 I communicated with Roberta Ossana, editor of "The Dream Network Journal." She called me on the telephone and shared a dream she had three weeks prior to receiving some material I sent her about the Seven Sisters.

In the dream, she visited a house with a large family. Seven sisters came out, and one was a foot taller than the others. There was a mother and father and one son with a wife. The son did volunteer work at a prison. His wife was going to be accepted into the family of women and is easily assimilated. The mother said, "Soon, my husband will retire, and we will own the bank." In my opinion, Roberta paid a dream-visit to the Adamic Household.

8

Isaiah 4:1 "And in that day seven women shall take hold of one man, saying, We will eat our own bread, and wear our own apparel: only let us be called by thy name, to take away our reproach."

19. An important symbol of the change is the Tau, depicted as a "T" with two trees and a flower on top, or as a split-trunk tree with three branches at each end. The two trees, I believe, represent the dual aspects and the two ways to knowledge, rational and intuitional.

20. The change may be related to the seven chakras. We have been operating in the lower three and will enter the fourth, the heart chakra. This is associated with a symbolic lightning strike, and may enable us to reach the upper four chakras. The critical level is three and a half, that is, the point between the third and fourth chakra.

NOTE: There is a coincidence connecting the terrorist attacks on 9/11/01 to the Tower card in the Tarot deck.

The Tarot Card, 'The Tower" In relationship between the Tree of Life and the Tarot cards, there are 22 Tarot cards that make up the Major Arcana. Each is assigned to a path on the Tree. The sphere/sephiroth on the left side of the Tree are feminine and those on the right are masculine. The ones in the middle row indicate a balance of the duality attributes. Two of the sephiroth on the sides are called HOD and NETZACH, representing Mercury and Venus, or the Head and the Heart, or the Intellect and Emotions. The lateral path joining the two is represented by the Tarot card known as The Tower. This card depicts people falling from a tower and being struck by lightning.

One of the meanings of the Tower card is being imprisoned by your own belief structure. The Tower depicted on the Tower card has no doors. That is the time when higher sources send a lightning strike setting it afire, forcing you to leap out of the tower to change and freeing you from your belief systems.

This change is shown symbolically in many ways, such as the Egyptian seven nodal points with the 'swallower's' mouth between the third and fourth, the Chinese coiled serpent with three and a half turns, and the 35th year as the mid-point in the life of a man of three score years and ten. (the approximate age of Jesus at crucifixion, and Buddha when awakened.)

This is related to Revelation 11:11. The two trees lay dead for three and a half days and then a breath of life from God enters them, and they stand up on their feet.

The meaning of the "swallower" seems to be about reincarnation. If you are still in the lower three levels of consciousness development at the time of your physical death, you must be reborn and try again. Above level three, you go on to more advanced realms of consciousness. The great change may involve an en masse advance beyond the third level. At that point, "death will be no more," that is, you will not experience the death/rebirth of reincarnation.

21. At this time, in the sleep-state, we are reading our Akashic records, the accumulated knowledge from past lives.

22. The future of Man is an en-masse achievement of a Christ-Self level. We will be Trinitized Powers with miraculous abilities. We will manifest loving kindness and forgiveness. It may be considered as the ability of the focus personality to knowingly use the powers of the Oversoul.

23. A symbol of our condition in this cycle is "prisoner or hostage." It is prevalent in dreams and was a Gnostic concept. (also see Isaiah 42:7 and 42:22)

Isaiah 42: 7 "To open the blind eyes, to bring out the prisoners from the prison, and them that sit in darkness out of the prison house."

Isaiah 42:22 "But this is a people robbed and spoiled; they are all of them snared in holes, and they are hid in prison houses; they are for a prey, and none delivereth; for a spoil, and none saith, Restore."

24. A symbol of the higher abilities is "King" or "Royal Power" (see Rev. 17:17 and 21:24)

Rev: 17:17 "For God hath put in their hearts to fulfil his will, and to agree, and give their kingdom unto the beast, until the words of God shall be fulfilled."

Rev: 21:24 "And the nations of them which are saved shall walk in the light of it: and the kings of the earth do bring their glory and honour into it."

25. Another tree symbol is the tree held by the Dreaming-God, or The Tree of Life in the Garden of Eden. In the great cycle of time, mankind has experienced many "trees," both good and negative. It was all for a purpose involving the knowledge of good and evil. The Tree of Life represents all the good and positive that can and will be manifested here, as the Kingdom of Heaven on Earth, or The New Jerusalem. It is God's Dream for mankind.

We have been prevented from grasping the Tree of Life until now. It is now available and we each must grasp our share.

26. The shares of the Tree of Life are being revealed now through crop patterns, UFO activity, art, channeling, events, simultaneities, etc., and primarily dreams. There is much confusion and contradiction, but it will begin to become more clear in the coming years, as pieces of the puzzle are put together. In the process, myths and religions will be explained and newly understood. We will realize that we are ONE and part of the Creator's manifestations.

27. Other dimensions of reality are also involved. The UFO's and E.T.'s are primarily from these other dimensions. Marian apparitions and similar phenomenon are from these other dimensions. Our beliefs about them strongly influence how they appear to us. A more direct contact will be the norm in the future.

28. Strange phenomena will increase and may take various forms, such as clouds forming symbolic patterns, objects raining from the sky, and spiritual apparitions.

If anyone reading this wishes to see the details of how the ideas came to me, I am willing to present them. Some of it is strongly convincing in my opinion, because it came in dreams of people who were not aware of the concepts at the time. Also, the coincidences constantly happened, as if to confirm the concepts. There is a definite predictive pattern. It is my wish to find a serious scholar to look into it.

Joe Mason

Many of the details of these 28 points are listed on various pages on greatdreams.com, our vast website. My own particular thoughts are written on the Pollen Path pages. Others are linked from the crop circle database page or our coincidence page. Many of these concepts come to people in dreams when they don't even know anything about these changes coming. Coincidences constantly happen to these people and myself to confirm these concepts. There is a definite positive pattern.

~~~~~~~~~~~~~~~~~~~~~~~~~~~~

Foreword
By Dee Finney

Obviously there are many different thoughts and disagreements about the concept about a One-World Religion. Within our own household, there are differing opinions on events, as we've each had a different upbringing and experiences.

Because our experiences have been vastly different, naturally we have come to differing conclusions. The main point of this book is the message you will read about the crop circles, which we agree are an important part of our future and pointing out to us the path we will all be walking upon in the coming years.

Many people are against the thought of such a thing as a One-World Religion, just like they are against a One-World government. However, if one takes a good long, hard look at what is going on this world, you can see it coming step by step. There can be unity amongst diversity.

The positive side of this is that if there was a One-World Government or a One-World Religion, it would bring an end to all wars, because everyone would be covered by all the same rules and laws. It sounds like an impossible task to bring about, but there are organizations, governments, politicians, and theologians who are working to bring about exactly that. And they are doing it whether we like it or not. In time, it will happen in the physical world just as it is planned in the spirit realms.

Back in the beginning, when mankind was first developing, that's exactly what we had on this earth — one religion. There were few people, and everyone basically thought the same thing. All they knew was survival, and those who went against the rules of survival, didn't live very long.

As mankind developed, changes occurred. Yes, there were earth changes back then too; a big flood that wiped out almost all of mankind because 'God' was angry at what mankind had become. There was also the incident in Babylon, where mankind was changed so that nobody could understand each other. 'God' wasn't in favor of mankind being so powerful or in charge of his own life. It's been that way a long time.

Every so often a special man who is said to have talked with God was given information to start a new religion in an attempt to straighten out problems that were going on. Of course, whoever lived in those areas was expected to change to that religion. Most who didn't were killed or they escaped. In a few cases, the special man was killed instead, but by then the spread of the religion was in other people's hands. Many people have died, been killed, or assassinated in the name of religion.

Governments have come and gone as well. Most Kings or rulers thought they had the right ideas and everyone should bow to him. Some were way worse than others. We've all seen the history books and more recently movies about those stories.

At the same time religious leaders tried to hold the power over the people, and when people tried to find 'truth' through dreams, mysticism, channeling spirits, etc., the religious leaders said they were sinners. Many were killed, stoned to death, burned at the stake, and other atrocities done to them.

One must ask that if 'God' wanted people to be divided, and there are so many governments, why is it all of a sudden necessary to become ONE? Is there some spiritual teaching that all can believe in? A One-World Religion? If two Christian groups can't even agree on the 'rules' or what is 'truth', how could the whole world come to hold hands and believe in the same 'God'?

Nevertheless, there is something going on that mankind has ignored and governments and theologians still try to hide. There is a mysterious 'force' coming from elsewhere that is subtly teaching those who are paying attention, that what they were taught to believe as children is not really the way it really is.

Revelation 3:11 "Behold, I come quickly: hold that fast which thou hast, that no man take thy crown."

In the Book of Revelation we read: *Revelation 13:11 -- "And I beheld another beast coming up out of the earth; and he had two horns like a lamb, and he spake as a dragon. And he exerciseth all the power of the first beast before him, and causeth the earth and them which dwell therein to worship the first beast..."*

This is the key Scripture, which tells us that the 'Second Beast', following the First Beast in Revelation 13:1-10 [Antichrist] will lead the peoples of the entire world into a worship of Antichrist. Bible scholars have historically called this 'Second Beast', the False Prophet.

Revelation 17:17 "For God hath put in their hearts to fulfil his will; and to agree, and give their kingdom unto the beast, until the words of God shall be fulfilled."

In 1997 there was a delegation of international religious theologians. The news read: "Nearly 200 delegates wrapped up a week-long interfaith meeting at Stanford on Friday, predicting they had given birth to a movement as well as a spiritual institution: the **United Religions**. The 'spiritual United Nations', as some have referred to it, would be a world assembly for humanity's myriad spiritual traditions. The international 'summit conference' brought together delegates from every continent to inaugurate formal efforts to figure out the organization's structure and mission and launch a charter-writing process. After several years of talking, the initiative's planners had finally gotten down to business."

" 'You are deputized!', the Rev. William E. Swing, bishop of the Episcopal Diocese of California, told delegates as they prepared to go home. 'Tell the people that there is a United Religions, and that somewhere in the world, it is beginning to happen: that the religions are going to have an oasis where they can talk about peace.'

"David Cooperrider, a professor at Case Western Reserve University's management school and a consultant to the United Religions project, envisioned both an institutional 'gathering place for discussions of the global good' and a 'Web-like structure' for projects, membership, and meetings around the world. Though Cooperrider studies and consults with 75 global organizations, including 'Save the Children' and the 'Nature Conservancy', the United Religions Initiative has inspired him like no other, he said. He described ``extraordinary momentum'' gathering this week. The initiative has raised $2.1 million in cash and pledges. The conference cost almost $400,000, with travel scholarships given to about 35 delegates. In the next 18 months, regional conferences are planned in Johannesburg, South Africa; Cairo, Egypt; and Delhi, India."

"The 200 delegates established more than 20 task forces that will work in the next year to answer questions about United Religions' location, funding and organization: How will constituent bodies within the United Religions relate to one another, and how will a United Religions collaborate with other interfaith and global organizations? When the delegates convene next June -- Stanford may again be the location -- they will hear a series of "white papers" roughing out the United Religions mission and begin to establish priorities. Should they wrestle with population problems? The need for conflict resolution between religious groups in regional hot spots? The eradication of poverty?"

Here are the religions that participated in the conference: Christian -- Catholics and Episcopalians are the only groups specifically mentioned. The rest were Muslims, North American Interfaith Network [NAIN], Buddhists, Hindus, Jews, and Sikhs

Then we found out that this was not the first conference of this sort. "The conference participants, including keynote speakers such as Nobel Peace Laureates Archbishop Desmond Tutu and Ms. Betty Williams, and prominent Muslim Dr. Javid Iqbal, and international interfaith leaders."

In 1995, history books were written at the 'State of The World Forum' in San Francisco. Chaired by former Soviet President Mikhail Gorbachev, the forum featured discussions and lectures by world political and social leaders, authors, scientists, and business executives at the Masonic Auditorium Sept. 27 through Oct. 1. The event was co-chaired by leaders like Archbishop Desmond Tutu, George Schultz, U.S. Secretary of State under President Reagan, and James Baker, Secretary of State under President Bush. The World Forum concluded with a live telecast of a discussion between Gorbachev, former U.K. Prime Minister Margaret Thatcher, and former President George Bush. Also included in the leadership of this group was Jane Fonda and her husband Ted Turner, who at that time owned CNN news broadcasting network.

8,000 world leaders were invited to this meeting at a donation of $8,000 to attend the dinner. Not all 8,000 invitees attended this meeting, but enough of them came to make a difference. Just note the names of who was running the meeting. That alone should tell you a lot.

That wasn't the end of it, here is the news that was reported later on this meeting:

Tuesday, Nov. 04, 1997
Sun Tzu's Newswire
Mad Minute #97-36 Gorbachev's ANC terrorist and New World Order
by Tristan St. John-Smith

New World Order -- that was Thabo Mbeki's theme in his 1995 keynote speech to attendees of Mikhail Gorbachev's State of the World Forum

Mbeki is former African National Congress (ANC) terrorist trained by Russia's communists led by Gorbachev-- now Mbeki is in South African government -- Mbeki quoted from H.G. Wells book -- "New World Order"

The 1997 State of the World Forum is underway again in San Francisco -- meeting headquarters is Fairmont Hotel -- Forum Headquarters located in historic house owned by U.S. National Park Service

Past Forum attendees include -- Ted Turner -- Jane Fonda -- John Denver -- Dennis Weaver -- John Bertrand-Aristide -- Debbie Fields -- Ram Dass -- Abba Eban -- Betty Friedan -- Deepak Chopra -- Joseph McNamara -- Ann Rockefeller Roberts -- Bob Weir -- George Zimmer -- Graham Nash

Forum bills itself as a gathering of world leaders -- Debbie Fields knows cookies -- Weir is a Grateful Dead -- Zimmer is a men's clothing retailer -- Joe McNamara was Chief of Police in San Jose and Kansas City -- Graham Nash is in music -- you know Ted & Jane & Dennis

Other world leaders announcing New World Order -- George Bush -- Mikhail Sergeyevich Gorbachev -- Hitler called it -- "My New Order" -- Japan's humble servants of Emperor Hirohito modestly called it "Greater East Asia Co-Prosperity Sphere" -- "A man's got to know his limits"

Sources: Clint "Dirty Harry" Eastwood -- Sun Tzu's Newswire files -- Gorbachev Foundation -- Green Cross -- State of the World Forum

Capitalism has no future "excerpt from speech titled "Report the All -

Union Scientific and Practical Conference in Moscow, M.S. Gorbachev, Dec. 10, 1984, in his book "A Time For Peace", 1985 Richardson and Steirman, New York

"Glasnost is the sword which itself heals the wound that it inflicts." -- V.I. Lenin, quoted in Pravda, March 2, 1987.

"One day after this conference, in 1987, the UN 50th Anniversary Worship Service was hosted at Grace Cathedral lead by Bishop Swing. It took two years of hard work to plan this one-hour liturgy. At both the Youth Conference and the Worship Service, the United Religions idea was made public. After this event, it became clear that, to move the UR from vision to reality an ever-expanding network of religious and interfaith leaders had to share in a process of prayer dialogue and creative thinking about a UR. With this in mind, in September 1995, Bishop Swing addressed a gathering of religious Non-Governmental Organizations at the UN. The event was hosted by the Ven. Chung Ok Lee, a Won Buddhist priest and proponent of a United Religions for over 20 years. In October 1995, Bishop Swing visited religious leaders in China."

"From February through April 1996, Bishop Swing traveled in India, the Middle East, and Europe, seeking commitment from leaders of many world's religions, including the Dalai Lama, the Sankaracharya of Kancheepuram, Islam's Grand Mufti in Cairo, Mother Theresa, and the Archbishop of Canterbury, and with people active in interfaith work, including those at a conference at the International Interfaith Centre in Oxford. In July and August 1996, the Bishop visited with religious leaders in Japan and Korea."

"The conference didn't end with dreaming. The participants were challenged to create a plan of action to help those dreams become a reality. That plan includes an effort to create a vast network of support and guidance by holding gatherings all over the world, in early 1997, to allow people from different countries, cultures, religions, and educational, work, and economic backgrounds to meet and help shape the vision of a United Religions. The voices, images, and commitments-to-action from these gatherings and other outreach efforts over the next year will inspire the charter-writing process to begin in San Francisco in June 1997."

In 1998, "In a joyous Christmas message to the world, Pope John Paul II hailed the Jews as the people who gave Jesus Christ to mankind," CNN reported on Dec. 25. The Pope said that, "the birth of the Messiah (is) the central event in the history of humanity. The whole human race was awaiting it with a vague presentiment; the chosen people awaited with explicit awareness." The day before a Hanukkah candle was lighted at the Vatican for the first time in history, as the Pope also called the Jewish people Christianity's "elder brothers.

At the same time, various organizations are slowly prying 'God' out of the hands of the people whose ancestors founded this country in the name of religious freedom. Every few weeks, news is heard that this person or the other is suing the government to remove 'God' from government buildings, out of the Pledge of Allegiance, and off the money. What will be next?

One must ask why so many people in the world are trying to make these changes? Where are these people getting their ideas? Who started it in the beginning? Is there something behind the scenes that 'normal' people aren't aware of?

One must ask if this change is positive or negative. Hitler tried to do it all by himself back in the 1930's and 1940's. We all know what the result was.

We've all heard about the Iluminati. Scholars of conspiracy tell us they are a huge and powerful cult with one purpose - to establish the foundation of the New World Order with them at the helm. They will stop at nothing though their timing is a little off their planned results. Though the plans are taking a little longer than the original written plans, everything is still moving forward. Like the Templars, history records that the Illuminati were disbanded. That's what they want us to believe. However, like the Templars, they really went underground. The Illuminati is historically noteworthy. Much is written about them. They want us to believe they no longer exist. They exert their power behind the scenes, their removal from texts hints at their modern influence to hide in plain site. As long as nobody talks about them, they can keep working behind the scenes.

At their height of popularity, the Illuminati claimed to have over 2,000 members, in Germany, France, Belgium, Holland, Denmark, Sweden, Poland, Hungary, and Italy. Goethe and Herder, were among the many prominent nobles and reformers. The Bavarian government tried to eliminate the Illuminati and other secret societies in 1784 for supposedly trying to overthrow the European monarchies. However, the Bavarians were unable to eliminate all the Illuminists. By 1800 we are told that the Illuminati had disbanded, but stories filter down through history of their continued existence. To this day, we hear from time to time of them remaining as an active yet elusive group. The word itself, illuminati came to be used in a more grand way for many followers of Enlightenment, including the followers of Emmanuel Swedenborg.

We are told that many politicians within the American Government actually desire catastrophe while promoting peace to their followers. America systematically infuriates its most dangerous enemies while allowing weapons of mass-destruction to become available to them at the same time. Horrible to think about, but this may be an attempt to provoke massive attacks in an effort to gain the ultimate power they desire. It would also offer a plausible explanation to cover devastating self-inflicted horrors, which most Americans would deny. Nobody wants to believe such a thing. Who in their rational/logical minds could conceive of such a diabolical plan to gain power over the world. It doesn't take much checking of internet sources to find out the details of 'Who's Who' in various groups, which ultimately produce this country's leadership. Don't they always tell us to 'follow the money' and see where it leads you? Could someone without money become a leader of this country. Simple answer: 'No!'' The next question to be asked: "Where does the money come from?" Another simple answer, "The World Banking families." It doesn't take much more than adding 2 + 2 to come up with the big picture. However, that's the picture they don't want the common man to see. It's a little scary to even think about.

Then ask yourself another question, does it take an international climate of fear and chaos to justify the final, radical social and political changes that will be officially called the New World Order? Think about the strange epidemics, and bio-terror hitting this country and other places in the world. With easy travel in modern times, it only takes mere hours for people to get from one country to the other. What we now call America's 'war on terror', likely routes to this horrifying state of affairs is already in place. Military and political leaders throughout history, actually believed that global holocaust would be a fair price for humanity to pay for their goals to come to fruition.

The Great Plan of the Illuminati would eventually culminate in a smaller, more controllable new global society, in which war and poverty would be permanently absent. You can pick up any newspaper or turn on any news station on television or radio and take note of the topic of the day. The topic of the day is always 'war' interspersed with the poverty of people in Africa, Asia, China, India, Pakistan, Afganistan, Iraq, and other Middle East countries. The poverty in the United States is a taboo topic and well hidden from the media and general public. From time to time we see people asking for monies to be sent to Africa to control AIDS because millions of people have already died from the dread disease. No one mentions or investigates the true originator of this horrible disease, which kills certain groups of people, including in the United States. The diabolical achievement of 'perfection' and peace through destruction is a nasty secret key to Illuminist belief and is symbolized by Atlantis, the Phoenix and the Cross.

A LAPEL PIN WORN BY A PROMINENT POLITICAN IN WASHINGTON D.C.

The Illuminist Great Plan has been over-optimistic and is over 50 years behind schedule. That doesn't mean they will give up the Great Plan however. A little delay here and there doesn't stop the forward motion for long.

The Club of Rome commissioned Cyrus Vance, Jimmy Carter's Secretary of State, Dr. Gerold O. Barney to write The Global 2000 report. This is a plan to reduce the world's population by means of wars, famine, diseases, and plagues. The HIV virus and the Aids epidemic became a part of this plan.

The community of Christians and those with strong prophecy dogmas are participating unknowingly and unwittingly in this earth change plan. The Prophets are helping to usher in a change that will be profound and will destroy many of those in this world who really care about goodness. The prophecy movement within the Christian churches believe adamantly that certain events will happen without a doubt because of the Book of Revelation and can be seen arguing among themselves about the eventuity outcome of the future. Those Native Prophecies, which also fit in closely with similar scenarios also help to promote the Global Plan of 2000. With the change of millennium the seers, psychics and prophets contemplate certain predictions and changes. These people always have followers that believe these prophecies to be true and believe in the eventual realization of these predictions.

One fact that is not speculation was the establishment of The United Nations as a world organization to establish a world government to solve the problems of warfare and establish world peace. This is certainly a noble and just goal but how can a pagan, godless system ever establish peace? These systems rule through mechanisms of chaos and indecision.

The Millennium Institute grew out of the Global 2000 Report to the President, which was commissioned by President Jimmy Carter

The Mission Statement of the Millenium Institute:

"The Millennium Institute vision is of a sustainable and more peaceful and equitable future for Earth. We believe that such a future is possible and that to attain it, humans must develop and apply advanced analytical tools to illuminate unintended and counterintuitive consequences of alternative strategies and policies and also to reflect on the human value systems needed to assess the alternative futures illuminated by the analytical tools.

MI's mission, therefore, is (1) to develop and provide advanced analytical tools for national and global development, and (2) to formulate values-related questions and analyses on the consequences of alternative development strategies."

The Alien Connection

How many people remember Roswell, New Mexico, and downed UFOs with real aliens? That happened over 50 years ago, and the government still has not told the people the truth and most likely never will.

Firsthand testimony of several military insiders have documents and corroborating testimony proving that UFOs have monitored sensitive nuclear facilities since at least the 1950s. While the UFOs were not hostile, it was made clear that they were very concerned about human weapons of mass destruction. On one occasion, UFOs over a SAC Nuclear launch area took more than a dozen intercontinental ballistic missiles (ICBMs) off line.

Lt. Colonel Dwynne Arneson: US Air Force,.ret. states,: "I was the top-secret control officer at Malmstom AFB for the 20th Air Division. I happened to see a message that came through my communications center. It said...that 'A UFO was seen near missile silos'...and it was hovering. It said that the crew going on duty and the crew coming off duty all saw the UFO just hovering in midair. It was a metallic circular object and from what I understand, the missiles were all shut down. What I mean by 'missiles going down' is that they went dead. And something turned those missiles off. so they couldn't be put back in a mode for launching."

Captain Robert Salas: SAC Missile Launch Officer [1964-1971]: "The UFO incident happened on the morning of March 16, 1967, at Oscar Flight one of five launch control facilities assigned to the 490th Strategic Missile Squadron. I received a call from my topside security guard...and he said that he and some of the guards had been observing some strange lights flying around the site and the launch control facility. I said, you mean UFO? He said, well, he didn't know what they were but they were lights and were flying around. They were not airplanes; they were not helicopters, they weren't making any noise... [A little later] our missiles started shutting down one by one. By shutting down, I mean they went into a "no-go" condition meaning they could not be launched. These weapons were Minuteman One missiles and were of course nuclear-tipped warhead missiles...this incident was of extreme concern to SAC headquarters because they couldn't explain it."

How many people remember what President Ronald Reagan said back in 1983?
Early in the 1980s we were told that the failure of a 46-cent computer chip caused the NORAD headquarters to believe that they were under attack by Soviet

missiles. At least 100 United States B-52s were readied for take-off towards Russia before the mistake was discovered.

President Carter signed Presidential Directive 59, on July 25, 1980, calling for a flexible, controlled retaliation against political and military targets in the event of a "prolonged" nuclear war. When he left office the following January, he said in his Farewell Address that "in an all-out nuclear war, more destructive power than in all of World War II would be unleashed every second during the long afternoon it would take for all of the missiles and bombs to fall."

The United Nations held its second Special Session on Disarmament in June 1982. The largest peace demonstration in history occurred in New York with over one million people in attendance. Arguments over the Cold War escalated during the early years of the Reagan Administration. In March 1983, President Reagan called the Soviet Union an "evil empire". On March 23, he announced plans to go ahead with a space-based missile defense, which became known as "Star Wars." Despite heavy criticism, Reagan continued to push ahead with research and development of the multi-billion dollar project.

We are told that the Roswell UFO secrets were kept silent because of the fear of attack by Russia. Our government was afraid that Russia would get a hold of the proprietary technological information and sprint ahead of us. Perhaps that was true then, but is it still true? Maybe not! Other excuses used by the government is that mankind can't handle knowing that there are beings on other planets and that the religious structures, which keep people under their control would collapse and chaos would reign.

The Reagan Administration created their so-called "star wars", strategic defense system for nuclear weapons. Was that the only reason? Was Reagon more worried about being attacked by beings from outer-space? The government used the 'Star Wars' as an excuse to divert 30 billion dollars to the use of the government. From its birth 'Star Wars' was just a front to give the people reasons for rocket launches and money used by the government they couldn't account for. The government used 'Star Wars' to research, develop and create spy satellites, among other things. They initially planned 3.8 billion a year, estimating about 1 trillion would be used.

Reagan called for the development of a strategic defense against inter-continental ballistic missiles. Within two years, the proposal became a program, the Strategic Defense Initiative (SDI). It was placed in the hands of a Strategic Defense

Initiative Organization (SDIO), to develop interceptor missiles, battle stations in space, laser beam weapons, particle beam weapons and all the rest of it.

Was all that just for Russian defense? The balance of terror, known as mutual assured deterrence, between the evil empire and Washington D.C. was to be replaced by an assured defense, which Reagan promised, would then magnanimously share it with the enemy.

Five years later, at Reagan's friendly Moscow summit with Mikhail Gorbachev, a reporter asked Reagan what had become of the evil empire. The President replied, "I was talking about another time, another era."

The Star Wars program came to an end, or at least slowed down, though it is brought up again now and again. The U.S. government tells us they spent a total of 30 billion dollars. Yet the government is so far ahead of the rest of the commercial and industrial public with technology than is believable. Where did all that technology come from? How did we develop it so quickly?

Recently discovered is that Russia has 22 nuclear bombs on satellite launching pads overhead aimed directly at United States cities. What did we really gain by pretending there are no UFOs?

The government can control the media and they do this well compared to other countries, which are divulging more and more information about UFOs and aliens. European countries and South American countries, as well as Mexico publish information about UFOs and aliens on a continual basis these days. The U.S. government does not divulge the truth of the aliens to the public, because mainly they need to keep their secrets to themselves. They don't want the people to know that they have thousands of secrets they keep from the public. This is for the 'greater good' of the public.

On the other hand, the government in this situation, allows information to be fed to the public that is erroneous because by letting people think "maybe there are aliens"- maybe there are not", they can encourage the publics' feeling of stability, and yet instability. Disinformation agents come in handy, and their work is all over the internet. Without firsthand knowledge of aliens and UFOs, the general public can't tell the difference between what is real and what is not. The public tends to accept the negative aliens as real, otherwise why would the government be hiding all the information about them? Are we ever shown movies about 'good' aliens? With the exception of the movie "E.T.", all the rest of the movies are about aliens killing humans or using them for genetic hybridization for their own purposes.

Ronald Reagan, more than any other President, appeared to be obsessed with the flying saucer topic. Ronald Reagan made a series of 'alien invasion' remarks in a number of his speeches.

Ronald Reagan's daughter Patti Davis described her father as "fascinated with stories about unidentified flying objects and the possibility of life on other worlds." She compared the "madness" of her father's inauguration day to "a fifty's movie in which flying saucers descend on the metropolis."

Kitty Kelly in her Unauthorized Biography of Nancy Reagan stated Reagan admitted to believing in flying saucers, and "even swore that he had seen a few unidentified flying objects." He admitted having seen more than one UFO himself.

The first sighting story by Ronald Reagan was made public by Steve Allen on his WNEW-AM radio show in New York. Allen stated that a well-known personality in the entertainment industry had confided a UFO story to him many years before. The story had already made the rounds through the grape-vine of gossip. There was no question that the comedian and host was referring to Ronald Reagan and his wife Nancy.

It was said that Ron and Nancy were expected at a casual dinner party with friends in Hollywood. All the guests had arrived, then Ron and Nancy showed up a half hour later quite upset. They stated that they had seen a UFO coming down the coast.

While Reagan was still Governor, in 1974, he had another sighting. One week after the sighting, Reagan related the story to Norman C. Millar, who was the Washington Bureau chief for the Wall Street Journal, and later the editor of the Los Angeles Times. Reagan told Millar:

"I was in a plane last week when I looked out the window and saw this white light. It was zigzagging around. I went up to the pilot and said, 'Have you seen anything like that before?' He was shocked and said, 'Nope.' And I said to him: 'Let's follow it!'

We followed it for several minutes. It was a bright white light. We followed it to Bakersfield, and all of a sudden to our utter amazement it went straight up into the heavens. When we got off the plane, I told Nancy all about it.'

The pilot of the plane, Bull Paynter, backed up Reagan's story of the experience with the UFO.

"I was the pilot of the plane when we saw the UFO. Also, on board were Governor Reagan and a couple of his security people. We were flying a Cessna Citation. It was maybe nine or ten o'clock at night. We were near Bakersfield when Governor Reagan and the others called my attention to a big light flying a bit behind the plane.

"It appeared to be several hundred yards away. It was a fairly steady light until it began to accelerate, then it appeared to elongate. The light took off. It went up at a 45-degree angle - at a high rate of speed. Everyone on the plane was surprised.

"Governor Reagan expressed amazement. I told the others I didn't know what it was. The UFO went from a normal cruise speed to a fantastic speed instantly. If you give an airplane power it will accelerate - but not like a hotrod, and that is what this was like.

"We didn't file a report on the object because for a long time they considered you a nut if you saw a UFO."

Paynter stated that the UFO incident didn't stop there. He also stated that he and Reagan discussed their UFO sighting "from time to time" in the years following the incident.

Reagan, in his discussion of the sighting with Norman C. Millar added that he had told Nancy about the UFO he had seen, and they had done personal research on UFOs. This research had uncovered the facts that there were references to UFOs in Egyptian hieroglyphics. Reagan was telling his story in a very animated way. This led Millar to conclude that Reagan seriously believed in UFOs. He asked him, "Governor, are you telling me that you saw a UFO?"

According to Millar, Reagan suddenly realized that he was talking to a reporter. "This look crossed his face," recalled Millar, "and he said let's just say that I'm an agnostic."

Once in the White House it didn't take Reagan a long time to bring up the UFO subject. Jane Mayer and Doyle McManus described in their book "Landslide" that the Reagan handlers went to great lengths to "conceal" the President's assertion that he had seen a flying saucer or his belief that there was a ghost in the Lincoln bedroom. There was also an effort to discourage Reagan from talking about two other topics he liked - Armageddon and astrology.

Reagan handlers went to great efforts to protect President Reagan from possibly giving embarrassing answers, by starting up the presidential helicopter just before Reagan exited the White House to leave for trips. To prevent reporters from asking questions of President Reagon, who expected off the cuff remarks from him, Nancy Reagan became part of the protection force surrounding the President. She frequently whispered answers to difficult questions to the President, or provided corrections to things he had said, which were wrong or embarrassing.

White House staffers were not always successful in their efforts to maintain silence on the subjects of UFOs, ghosts, astrology, and Armageddon. Reagan, who was a big fan of the occult, made reference to these topics in his speeches from time to time. In a February 11, 1988 speech called, 'Remarks at the Annual Conservative Political Action Conference Dinner', Reagan was able to get both ghosts and UFOs in the same speech. In the speech written for Reagan by Pulitzer Prize winning speech-writer Tony Dolan Reagan said:

"...By the way, something odd happened just before I got here tonight that I think you should know about. I got a message from Dave Keane reminding me that this was the eve of Lincoln's birthday-and suggesting I go upstairs and check on the ghost in Lincoln's bedroom. I did. And what do you know, there was Stan Evans dressed as Abe Lincoln. And he kept saying, "Listen to Jesse Helms.". . . Well, we conservatives have been in Washington now for a while and we occasionally need to remind ourselves what brought us here in the first place: our unshakable, root-deep, all-encompassing skepticism about the capital city's answer to the UFO, that bizarre, ever-tottering but ever-flickering saucer in the sky called "The Prevailing Washington Wisdom."

There were a great number of these UFO, ghost, and Armageddon references written into Reagan speeches. Whether the UFO comments were planned or slips of the tongue by Reagan, the first controversial UFO comment would not be made by Reagan but by a senior member of the National Security Agency, writing on Reagan's behalf.

Although Reagan is given credit for anti-missile defense, and its' possible use against UFOs, the concepts actually go back many years. In the July-August 1959 NICAP Bulletin a short article was written discussing Air Force plans for a weapon system being developed to shoot down hostile satellites and space vehicles. Because Maj. Gen. B.A. Schriever's testimony in front of the Senate Space Committee did not indicate specific targets, NICAP concluded "there would be nothing to prevent its use against UFOs."

The idea of a war against beings of another world also went back many years before Reagan became President. War hero General Douglas MacArthur spoke of "an ultimate conflict between a united human race and the sinister forces of some other planetary galaxy." Mayor Achille Lauro of Naples, Italy, quoted MacArthur as telling him, "the earth would have to make a common front against attack by people from other planets."

A few years after MacArthur's statement, Brig. Gen. John A. McDavid, USAF, Director of Communications-Electronic for the Joint Chiefs of Staff made a similar statement about a possible conflict with extraterrestrials during an Air Force approved speech at Milliken University, Decatur, Illinois. "Before long, people may be forced to realize and accept as a fact that this earth is only an infinitesimal grain of sand in an infinite universe," declared McDavid. "The human is one of many forms of life with which God is concerned and others are superior to us. And if this is true, our meeting with other types of existence in other places in the universe quite likely will increase the potential element of conflict rather than reduce it."

Many scientists replied negatively to the announcement of the SDI system by Reagan in 1983. The scientific community called it an expensive 'pie in the sky' idea. Scientists stated that the program would do nothing but escalate military spending and distrust among the super powers in the world. Outside the Livermore Lab, in California, where many of the systems were being developed, groups of people demonstrated for an end to the research.

Few people believed that a system of defense could be developed to counter thousands of Soviet missiles being launched at one time. Most of them agreed with the opinion of a statement made by Soviet Chairman Khrushchev back in March 1962.

"We can launch missiles not only over the North Pole, but in the opposite direction, too. As the people say, you expect it to come in the front door, and it gets in the window."

Experts agree that global missiles cannot be spotted in due time to prepare any measures against them. The money spent in the United States to create antimissile systems is wasted on a system that cannot work against our enemies.

To those who follow the rhetoric about UFOs, the SDI system is viewed not as a system set up to destroy Soviet missiles, but to protect earth from a possible alien invasion. The 'alien invasion' remarks that Reagan made after his 1983 announcement of the SDI program, was reported to be proof that the alien/SDI usage was correct.

The ideas about aliens from elsewhere attacking the earth was not an idea that began in the Reagan presidency. In early 1950's movies like 'The Day the Earth Stood Still', military attacks of the earth by extraterrestrials was a popular theme. "The War of the World's" was another outstanding film about the world being attacked by intelligent UFO craft.

A 1960 report prepared for NASA by the Brookings Institute, claimed that the discovery of extraterrestrial life could cause the earth's civilization to collapse. The report stated, "societies sure of their own place have disintegrated when confronted by a superior society, and others have survived even though changed."

The strong interest in UFOs did not end with Ronald Reagan in the White House. During the Nixon presidency, there was open discussion inside the government about the potential threat from aliens coming to Earth. In an article written by Michael Michaud, a career diplomat in the State Department, pointed out the Nixon administration's worry about extraterrestrials:

"Aliens from other solar systems are a potential threat to us, and we are a potential threat to them. Scientists and others have often postulated that extraterrestrial societies more advanced than ours would be less warlike. Regrettably, the stereotypes of the benevolent, super intelligent alien may be as unrealistic as the stereotype of the bug-eyed monster carrying off shapely human females. Even if a species had achieved true peace within its own ranks, it would still be worried about us, and would take the measures it felt were necessary to protect itself. This includes the possibility (not the inevitability) of military action - Our basic interest will be to protect ourselves from any possible threat to Earth's security."

The Gerald Ford presidency escalated the "evil alien" philosophy with a 1975 report produced by the Library of Congress for the House Committee on Science and Technology. This report warned about the possible threats of open contact with extraterrestrials. The report stated, "Since we have no knowledge of their nature, we may be aiding in our own doom."

The alien/SDI idea has been followed up by a group of witnesses who declared that SDI type weapon systems, both land and space based, were being used to track and target extraterrestrial vehicles as they approach earth.

In a June 1995 Bay Area Lecture Dr. Steven Greer announced that information had been leaked to him from the North American Air Defense Command in Colorado and it showed that the Air Force tracks an average of 500 "fastwalkers" (term used for UFOs) entering the earth atmosphere every year.

Drunvalo Melchizedek, a popular lecturer in the New Age field, has stated that the space around the earth looks like a crowded parking lot because there are so many UFOs watching earth.

NASA videos have been produced for the public by researchers, which show pulsating UFOs coming and going from the earth and watching NASA space station projects. The film of NASA and the tether experiment is a shocking experience to watch, though NASA denies that UFOs are being seen. They are good at making excuses for what is being viewed. Astronauts are quoted in the documentary film as, "I see nothing", when its clearly right in front of their eyes flying both in front of and behind the tether, which is at that moment 75 miles of the space-station. These videos are available to the public through catalogs featuring UFO/alien books and films about space.

OMNI: ARE EXTRATERRESTRIALS STEERING US TO A ONE-WORLD RELIGION THROUGH CROP CIRCLES?

It seems obvious that the government is still trying to prevent American citizens from knowing the truth about UFOs and aliens, though other countries are becoming more and more open in their media about sightings. Mexico, Brazil, France, and even Great Britain have a great deal of media presentation showing UFOs in the skies.

It seems that the United States government is trying to ease the public into knowledge of UFOs, by showing them as 'evil'. They don't want people to stand in public squares, begging UFOs to land, such as the movie "Independence Day", where the UFOs descended over all the major cities of earth and blasted them into oblivion.

Such an idea is preposterous. That is not to say that some extraterrestrials don't want earth's assets to be available to them and that it could be disastrous to the human population. There 'are' such greedy beings as well in the Universe, just like certain groups on earth. However, extraterrestrials have governments and treaties just like humans do, and for the most part, they work well. Extraterrestrials have IQ's in the range of 300 to 400 so they don't think like humans. They also know the secret agendas of the world leaders. Its only the general public, who don't know the real truth who are in denial.

There is much evidence to show that extraterrestrials have been here since before recorded history, and that they had a big hand in creating us such as we are. They also are seen to come and go throughout time, and each time they come here, technology, art, and science became much greater and beneficial to mankind. That is, it was beneficial until mankind became so numerous and started to think for themselves and technology got ahead of their brains.

Also, we find that over recorded history, extraterrestrials had a hand in telling man what to do and if they didn't do it, they were told to wipe out those who didn't obey the rules. One can see evidence of this in the Bible in many of the early books.

According to recent communications from a group of extraterrestrials, it has been said that more than one group of extraterrestrials had a hand in creating tribes of humans across the continents of earth whom are not all exactly alike in thought processes and personality.

Religious rules and concepts were also given to various groups of humans over time. The evidence for those is strong and well-known. Each of these major religions was started by a human being who said that they had direct contact with God.

The Bible 'does' say that humanity was made in 'their' image. *Genesis 1:20 states: "And God said, Let us make man in our image, after our likeness; and let them have dominion over the fish of the sea, and over the fowl of the air and over the cattle, and over all creeping thing that creepeth upon the earth."*

Once God had created man, he gave him instructions. In no uncertain terms, he commanded, in *Genesis 2:16-17, "Of every tree of the garden, thou mayest freely eat: but of the tree of the knowledge of good and evil, thou shalt not eat of it; for in the day that thou eatest thereof thou shalt surely die."*

God, obviously didn't trust man, whom he had just created, to think for himself.

In chapter 3 of Genesis, we see a 'serpent' come and talk with Eve and tell her that God lied to her and that she wouldn't die if she ate of the fruit of all the trees in the garden. In verse 5, the serpent says, *"For God doth know that in the day ye eat thereof, then your eyes shall be opened, and ye shall be as gods, knowing good and evil."*

There we have the crux of the matter. God didn't want man to think for himself, God wanted man and woman to do what he said and just serve himself and procreate and make more like themselves - humans who didn't think for themselves. As it is, one can observe humanity and see that the plan has worked well across time.

Theologians have had a field-day with these verses, making sure that their constituents knew that they had an 'evil' mother and father - fallen parents - and they could never do anything good enough to make up for that. Today, we still see preachers on television and in churches telling people how evil their minds are and that giving the church money and asking for blessings will make life better for them. Preachers still don't want people to think for themselves, because if they did, they might wise-up and spend the money on themselves and their children instead of giving it to the church.

Not only did God give man his knowledge, art, science, and technology, he gave them religion. However, along with religion, he gave man war-like qualities so that when a new religion came along, also created by communication with God, though the religion was meant to be peaceful, the new religious beliefs became law that made them want to either convert everyone else or kill them off. It is part of man's nature to do this. Just keep remembering that God made us this way. We are in His image.

In modern times, it has become known, most recently through the work of Zechariah Sitchin, that the Gods (plural) created mankind as we are today. This was not the Almighty God of creation. These Gods were multiple beings we call extraterrestrials who took it upon themselves to change the dna of the creatures they found on earth and through many genetic manipulations changed us into half man, half God. We should call them 'god' with a small 'g'.

The 'Eridu Genesis' is a Sumerian text. It covers the creation of the world, invention of cities and the flood. After the universe was created out of the chaos of the sea, the gods evolved and they in turn created (cloned and genetically manipulated) mankind to farm, herd, slave in their great gold mines and worship the 'gods' who created them.

From Zechariah Sitchin's book 'The Cosmic Code', we find on page 42, "There was a time, the Sumerians told, when civilized Man was not yet on Earth, when animals were only wild and undomesticated and crops were not yet cultivated. At that long-ago time there arrived on Earth a group of fifty Anunnaki. Led by a leader whose name was E.A. (meaning "whose home is in water"), they journeyed from their home planet NIBIRU ("Planet of crossing") and reaching Earth, splashed down in the waters of the Persian Gulf. A text known to scholars as the 'myth' of EA and the Earth describes how that group waded ashore, finding themselves in a marshland. Their first task was to drain the marshes, clear river channels, check out food sources (found to be fish and fowl). They then began to make bricks from the clay of the soil and established the first ever settlement on Earth by extraterrestrials. They named the habitat ERIDU, which meant "Home in the Faraway" or "Home away from home." That name is the origin of the name "earth" in some of the oldest languages. The time: 445,000 years ago.

The astronauts mission was to obtain gold by extracting it from the waters of the gulf - gold needed for survival on Nibiru; for there the planet was losing its' atmosphere and thus also its internal heat, slowly endangering continued life on Nibiru. But the plan proved unworkable, and the leaders back home decided that gold could be obtained only the hard way - by mining it where it was in abundance, in southeastern Africa.

The new plan called for a substantial increase in the number of Anunnaki on Earth, and in time they numbered six hundred.

Eventually, the workers got tired of the backbreaking labor and they revolted. That was when Man was created - to do the hard labor.

On page 76 of Sitchin's book 'The Wars of Gods and Men', he states: "In all these writings, be it long epic tales or two-line proverbs, in inscriptions mundane or divine, the same facts emerge as an unshakable tenet of the Sumerians and the peoples that followed them. In bygone days, the DIN.GIR - "The Righteous Ones of the Rocketships," the beings the Greeks began to call 'gods' - had come to Earth from their own planet. They chose southern Mesopotamia to be their home away from home. They called the land KI.EN.GIR - "Land of the Lord of the Rockets" (the Akkadian name, Shumer, meant "Land of the Guardians"), and they established there the first settlements on Earth.

The statement that the first to establish settlements on earth were astronauts from another planet was not lightly made by the Sumerians. In text after text, whenever the starting point was called, it was always this: 432,000 years before the Deluge, the DIN.GIR ("Righteous Ones of the Rocketships") came down to Earth from their own planet. The Sumerians considered it a twelfth member of our Solar System - a system made up of the Sun in the center, the Moon, all the nine planets we know of today, and one more large planet whose orbit lasts a 'Sar' (3,600 Earth years). This orbit, they wrote, takes the planet to a 'station' in the distant heavens, then brings it back to Earth's vicinity, crossing between Mars and Jupiter. It was in that position - as depicted in a 4,500 year old Sumerian drawing that the planet obtained its name NIBIRU ('Crossing') and its symbol, the Cross.

The leader of the astronauts who had come to Earth from Nibiru, we know from numerous ancient texts, was called E.A. ("Whose House Is Water"); after he had landed and established Eridu, the first Earth Station, he assumed the title EN.KI ("Lord of Earth").

We know from Sumerian astronomical texts that the skies enveloping Earth, were so divided as to separate the northern 'way' (allotted to Enlil - EA's half brother) from the southern 'way' (allotted to EA) with a wide central band considered the 'Way of Anu'. It is only natural to assume that a dividing line between the two rival brothers should also have been established 'after' the deluge when the settled Earth was divided into the Four Regions, and that, as in pre-Diluvial times, the Thirtieth Parallels (north and south) served as demarcation lines.

The sanctity of the Thirtieth Parallel must be traced back to the Sacred Grid, when the divine measurers determined the location of the pyramids of Giza, also on the Thirtieth Parallel. Could the gods have given up this 'sanctity' or neutrality of the Thirtieth Parallel when it came to their most vital installation - The Spaceport - in their own Fourth Region, in the Sinai peninsula?

On page 87, we are told: As more Anunnaki landed on Earth - their number rose in time to 600 - some were assigned to the Lower World to help Enki mine the gold, others manned the ore ships; and the rest stayed with Enlil in Mesopotamia. There, additional settlements were established in accordance with a master plan laid out by Enlil, as part of a complete organizational plan of action and clear-cut procedures.

On page 192, we are told: "It is no accident, we have maintained, that mankind's advancement from the Stone Age to the high civilization of Sumer occurred in 3,600 year intervals - circa 11,000, 7,400, and 3800 B.C. It was as though 'a

33

mysterious hand' had each time 'picked Man out of his decline and raised him to an even higher level of culture, knowledge and civilization'. Each instance, we are told, coincided with the recurrence of the time when the Anunnaki could come and go between Earth and Nibiru.

There were cities prior to the deluge and after. Sitchin tells us further: When the reconstruction of Sumer began, first to have been rebuilt on its soil were the Olden Cities but no longer as exclusive Cities of the Gods; for mankind was now allowed into these urban centers to tend the surrounding fields, orchards, and cattlefolds in behalf of the gods, and to be in the service of the gods in all conceivable manner, not only as cooks and bakers, artisans and clothiers, but also as priests, musicians, entertainers, and temple prostitutes.

In Zechariah Sitchin's book, 'When Time Began', he tells us on page 81, "... there were Cities of the Gods in Mesopotamia before the Deluge, and that when the Deluge had occurred, there had already been 'demigods' (offspring of "Daughters of Man" by male Anunnaki Gods"), but also that the worship took place in consecrated places (we call them temples) They were already, we learn from the earliest texts, 'Temples of Time'.

The two sons of Anu - were the half brothers Enlil ("Lord of the Command") and Enki ("Lord of Earth"). Enki was assigned the gold-mining operations in Africa. The workers (created through genetic engineering) mutinied. These 'Primitive Workers' were charged with excessive conjugations, especially with the Anunnaki. There was a great Council meeting of the Anunnaki and it was decided to wipe Mankind off the face of the Earth.

Cities and kingship was created but the gods decided to destroy mankind with a flood. Ziusudra (Upnapishtim) from Eridu was instructed by Enki (Ea) to build a boat to survive the flood blown up by Enlil. After the flood he worshipped (prostrated) himself before An (Anu) and Enlil (Bel) and was given immortality for his godly life.

This is the Bible's story of Noah and the flood.

"The 'Eridu Genesis'...described the creation of man by the four great gods [the Anunnaki]: An ['Sky', the source of rain and most powerful of the gods], Enlil ['Lord Wind', the power in 'Growing Weather', creator of the hoe], Ninhursaga ['Lady of the Stony Ground', mother of wildlife], and Enki [rival of Ninhursaga]. After Nintur [Ninhursaga] had decided to turn man from his primitive nomadic camping grounds toward city life the period began when animals flourished on earth and kingship came down from heaven. The earliest cities were built, were named, had the measuring cups, emblems of a redistributional economic system, allotted to them, and were divided between the gods. Irrigation agriculture was developed and man thrived and multiplied. However, the noise made by man in his teeming settlements began to vex Enlil sorely, and, driven beyond endurance, he persuaded the other gods to wipe out man in an great flood. Enki, thinking quickly, found a way to warn his favorite, one Ziusudra. He told him to build a boat in which to survive the flood with his family and representatives of the animals."

"Ziusudra wisely followed Enki's instructions and after the flood had abated Enki was able to persuade the other gods not only to spare Ziusudra but to give him eternal life as a reward for having saved all living things from destruction."

Enki "persuades, tricks, or evades to gain his ends. He is the cleverest of the gods, the one who can plan and organize and think of ways out when no one else can. He is the counselor and adviser, the expert and the trouble-shooter, or manipulator, of the ruler; not the ruler himself. He organizes and runs the world, but at the behest of An and Enlil, not for himself; he saved mankind and the animals from extinction in the flood, but does not challenge Enlil's continued rule. His aim is a workable compromise, avoiding extremes."

After the flood began, the Annunakis sat in their spaceship over earth and regretted wiping out mankind and agreed that they would never wipe out all of mankind again.

Of course, that was before they knew that 8 people had survived the flood and began co-creating (procreating themselves) and covering the earth with humanity once again.

In the text of Atra-Hasis, Enki, swore to keep the decision a secret, but his conscience bothered him so much, he couldn't keep it to himself. He decided to tell Mankind of what was going to happen through his faithful worshipper Ziusudra, a son of Enki by a human mother. In other words 'Noah' was actually Enki's son.

There were worsening climatic conditions during the period prior to the Deluge, and Enki told Ziusudra to stop worshipping the gods. The situation got continually worse and the catastrophe neared, Ziusudra persisted in his intercession with his god Enki. He wept, begged, brought gifts, seeking Enki's help to avert Mankind's demise. Finally, Enki told him that he had seven days left before the catastrophe happened. There was a temple in Eridu with a water-clock and Enki set the clock in motion so Ziusudra knew how long he had left before Mankind would be destroyed by water.

Here is the key to the destruction and how it happened. In the Sumerian King lists, it lists the first ten leaders before the Deluge as 'Sars', the 3,600 year cycles that it took Nibiru to make the round trip . According to the texts 120 Sars had passed, which equals 432,000 earth-years. It was on the 120th orbit that the gravitational pull of Nibiru was such that it caused the ice sheet that accumulated over Antarctica to slip off into the southern ocean, creating the immense tidal wave that engulfed the Earth - the great flood or Deluge, recorded in the Bible from much earlier and much more detailed Sumerian sources.

Excavators of the ancient temples of Enlil in Nippur's sacred precinct, found five successive constructions between 2200 B.C and 600 B.C, the latter having its floor some twenty feet above the former. The report also noted that the five temples were "built one above the other on exactly the same plan."

The discovery that later temples were erected upon the foundations of earlier temples in strict adherence to the original plans was reconfirmed at other ancient sites in Mesopotamia. The rule applied even to enlargement of temples - even if more than once, as was found in Eridu. In all instances the original axis and orientation were retained. Unlike the Egyptian temples whose solstitial orientation had to be realigned from time to time because of the change in the Earth's tilt. Mesopotamian equinoctial temples needed no adjustment in their orientation because geographic north and geographic east, by definition remained unchanged no matter how the Earth's tilt had changed, the Sun always passed over the equator at "equinox" times, rising on such days precisely in the east.

War of Gods and Men

Unfortunately, the gods were not a peaceful bunch, and they warred with each other. The Sinai peninsula contains a blackened scar from a nuclear blast that can still be seen today with satellite photographs.

The Uruk Lament vividly describes the confusion among both the gods and the populace. Anu was the father of Enlil and Enki. Anu and Enlil had overruled Enki and Ninki when they "determined the consensus" to employ the nuclear weapons. But the text asserts that none of the gods anticipated the awesome outcome: "The great gods paled at its immensity" as they witnessed the explosion's "gigantic rays reach up to heaven and the earth trembled to its core."

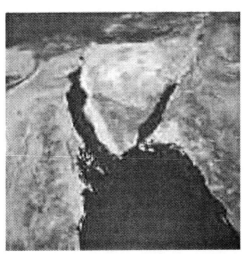

Ninki, we learn from The Eridu Lament, flew away from her city to a safe haven in Africa: "Ninki, its great lady, flying like a bird, left her city." But Enki left Eridu only far enough to get out of the Evil Wind's way, yet near enough to see its fate: its lord stayed outside his city. Father Enki stayed outside the city . . . for the fate of his harmed city he wept with bitter tears." Many of his loyal subjects followed him, camping on its outskirts. For a day and a night they watched the storm "put its hand" on Eridu. Enki surveyed Eridu. Those who were saved addressed to him a lament. and they kept on asking whence should they go, what should they do. But though the Evil Wind had passed, the place was still unsafe. "Forsaking the house of Eridu," Enki then led "those who have been displaced from Eridu" to the desert, "towards an inimical land"; there he used his scientific powers to make "the foul tree" edible.

"From the northern edge of the Evil Wind's side swath, from Babylon, a worried Marduk sent his father, Enki, an urgent message as the cloud of death neared his city. "What am I to do?" he asked. Enki's advice, which Marduk then related to his followers, was that those who could should leave the city - but go only north; and in line with the advice given by the two emissaries to Lot, the people fleeing Babylon were warned "neither to turn nor to look back."

(Remember Lot and his wife and the destruction of Sodom and Gemorah - Genesis chapters 18 and 19)

If escape was not possible, Enki advised hiding underground: "Get thee into a chamber below the earth, into a darkness," until the Evil Wind was gone.

It was seven years before life began to stir again in this area.

One can see that coming from such a background, that we are so 'close' to doing this again to ourselves, that peace must come to earth - no matter how it comes.

The extraterrestrials know that peace must come from mankind himself - because nuclear bombs don't bring peace - they bring regret and revenge.

So, how would the extraterrestrials bring peace to the earth?

They can encourage various men with ideas and thoughts about peace. They must do this all over the world and they are obviously doing this. There are world leaders speaking about the necessity for peace everywhere. But they need to convince the people to think the same way.

There is a big obstruction to peace - and unfortunately - the only way to peace is through religion and religious beliefs. But the extraterrestrials messed up over time - every time they created a new religion by speaking to one man, they created more havoc and hatred against those who wouldn't accept the new religion.

There is only one way to create a One-World Religion and that is to get everyone to think the same way. It can't come from one man or one country, it has to come to large groups of men and women who want peace and who already think the same way about the religious beliefs they have.

In the olden days, we have a good example of a warning given to a King:

DANIEL CHAPTER 5
HANDWRITING ON THE WALL
or
"When Your Number is Up!"

Daniel Chapter 5: *Belshazzar the king made a great feast to a thousand of his lords, and drank wine before the thousand. (2) Belshazzar, whiles he tasted the wine, commanded to bring the golden and silver vessels which his father Nebuchadnezzar had taken out of the temple which was in Jerusalem; that the king, and his princes, his wives, and his concubines, might drink therein. (3) Then they brought the golden vessels that were taken out of the temple of the house of God which was at Jerusalem; and the king, and his princes, his wives, and his concubines, drank in them. (4) They drank wine, and praised the gods of gold, and of silver, of bronze, of iron, of wood, and of stone. (5) In the same hour came forth fingers of a man's hand, and wrote over against the candlestick upon the plaster of the wall of the king's palace: and the king saw the part of the hand that wrote. (6) Then the king's countenance was changed, and his thoughts troubled him, so that the joints of his loins were loosed, and his knees smote one against another. (7) The king cried aloud to bring in the astrologers, the Chaldeans, and the soothsayers. And the king spake, and said to the wise men of Babylon, Whosoever shall read this writing, and show me the interpretation thereof, shall be clothed with scarlet, and have a chain of gold about his neck, and shall be the third ruler in the kingdom. (8) Then came in all the king's wise men: but they could not read the writing, nor make known to the king the interpretation thereof. (9) Then was king Belshazzar greatly troubled, and his countenance was changed in him, and his lords were astonished. (10) Now the queen by reason of the words of the king and his lords came into the banquet house: and the queen spake and said, O king, live for ever: let not thy thoughts trouble thee, nor let thy countenance be changed: (11) There is a man in thy kingdom, in whom is the spirit of the holy gods; and in the days of thy father light and understanding and wisdom, like the wisdom of the gods, was found in him; whom the king Nebuchadnezzar thy father, the king, I say, thy father, made master of the magicians, astrologers, Chaldeans, and soothsayers; (12) Forasmuch as an excellent spirit, and knowledge, and understanding, interpreting of dreams, and showing of hard sentences, and dissolving of doubts, were found in the same Daniel, whom the king named Belteshazzar: now let Daniel be called, and he will show the interpretation. (13) Then was Daniel brought in before the king. And the king spake and said unto Daniel, Art thou that Daniel, which art of the children of the captivity of Judah, whom the king my father brought out of Jewry? (14) I have even heard of thee, that the spirit of the gods is in thee, and that light and understanding and excellent wisdom is found in thee. (15) And now the wise men, the astrologers, have been brought in before me, that they should read this writing, and make known unto me the interpretation thereof: but they could not show the interpretation of the thing: (16) And I have heard of thee, that thou canst make interpretations, and dissolve doubts: now if thou canst read the writing, and make known to me the interpretation thereof, thou shalt be clothed with scarlet, and have a chain of gold about thy neck, and shalt be the third ruler in the kingdom. (17) Then Daniel answered and said before the king, Let thy gifts be to thyself, and give thy rewards to another; yet I will read the writing unto the king, and make known to him the interpretation. (18) O thou king, the most high God gave Nebuchadnezzar thy father a kingdom, and majesty, and glory, and honour: (19) And for the majesty that he gave him, all people, nations, and languages, trembled and feared before him: whom he would he slew; and whom he would he kept alive; and whom he would he set up; and whom he would he put down. (20) But when his heart was lifted up, and his mind hardened in pride, he was deposed from his kingly throne, and they took his glory from him: (21) And he was driven from the sons of men; and his heart was made like the beasts, and his dwelling was with the wild asses: they fed him with grass like oxen, and his body was wet with the dew of heaven; till he knew that the most high God ruled in the kingdom of men, and that he appointeth over it whomsoever he will. (22) And thou his son, O Belshazzar, hast not humbled thine heart, though thou knewest all this; (23) But hast lifted up thyself against the Lord of heaven; and they have brought the vessels of his house before thee, and thou, and thy lords, thy wives, and thy concubines, have drunk wine in them; and thou hast praised the gods of silver, and gold, of bronze, iron, wood, and stone, which see not, nor hear, nor know: and the God in whose hand thy breath is, and whose are all thy ways, hast thou not glorified: (24) Then was the part of the hand sent from him; and this writing was written. (25) And this is the writing that was written, MENE, MENE, TEKEL, UPHARSIN. (26) This is the interpretation of the thing: MENE; God hath numbered thy kingdom, and finished it. (27) TEKEL; Thou art weighed in the balances, and art found wanting. (28) PERES; Thy kingdom is divided, and given to the Medes and Persians. (29) Then commanded Belshazzar, and they clothed Daniel with scarlet, and put a chain of gold about his neck, and made a proclamation concerning him, that he should be the third ruler in the kingdom. (30) In that night was Belshazzar the king of the Chaldeans slain. (31) And Darius the Median took the kingdom, being about threescore and two years old.*

~~~~~~~~~~~~~~~~~~~~~~~~~~~~~~~~~~~~

Daniel 2: *Nebuchadnezzar dreamed dreams wherewith his spirit was troubled, and his sleep brake from him. Then the king commanded to call the magicians and the astrologers and the sorcerers and the Chaldeans for to shew the king his dreams. So they came and stood before the king. And the king said unto them, I have dreamed a dream, and my spirit was troubled to know the dream:*

The king commanded that they tell him the dream as well as the interpretation. The Chaldeans answered that it was an impossible task, saying that only God can do such a thing. The king became angry and commanded to destroy all the wise men of Babylon.

So the kings army went to search out Daniel to kill him. But Daniel asked for time as he felt he could tell the king his own dream.

Thus Daniel went to the king and told the king about his terrible dream of the frightening image.

Daniel 2:32 *"This image's head was of fine gold, his breast and his arms of silver, his belly and his thighs of bronze, ' 33 his legs of iron, his feet part of iron and part of clay. 34 Thou sawest till that a stone was cut out without human hands, which smote the image upon his feet that were of iron and clay, and brake them to pieces. 35 Then was the iron, the clay, the bronze, the silver, and the gold, broken to pieces together and became like the chaff of the summer threshing-floors; and the wind carried them away, that no place was found for them; and the stone that smote the image became a great mountain, and filled the whole earth. "*

In Old Sarum, England in 1991, this formation appeared.

Joe Mason describes the formation this way: " It struck me that the formation could symbolize the frightening image dream of Nebuchadnezzar. The top circle with ring is the head of gold, symbolizing the Age of Gold. It is a symbol of the Deity, but it could have other meanings. The one that fits here is from a concept I read in The Gnostic Gospels found at Nag Hamadi. Some 1,600 years ago, a Gnostic Christian had a vision, indicating that the world is like the womb, with the placenta as the Garden of Eden. Also, Joseph Campbell spoke of the "enclosure," and how the word "paradise" comes from words that mean "wall around." My first dream voice message about the crop circles said, "Because we are disconnected from our spirituality, some rings are missing." The message was about the "first pictogram" that appeared in 1990 at Chilcomb Farm.

The next circle in the Old Sarum formation, with the reversed "F" - shape, represents the breasts and arms of silver, the Age of Silver. The circle, like a "6," represents the belly and thighs of bronze, the Age of Bronze. The four diagonal lines

41

below the "6" - like circle, represent the feet of part iron, part clay, the divided kingdom.

In my speculation, the head of gold, or Age of Gold is not counted, so the three circles below the top one would represent the three steps or stages. The "feet" are like a "half-step," to indicate the critical "three and a half," the midpoint of the chakras type of symbolism. Interestingly, the shape also looks somewhat like "11:11."

The bottom glyph is somewhat like a heart, or it could be turned upside-down to look like a mountain across the earth. This is the fourth step, when the Heart chakra level of consciousness evolution is achieved by mankind.

In Nebuchadnezzar's dream, the feet of part iron, part clay (the divided kingdom) could represent the three and a half point. The great mountain filling the earth, establishing the everlasting Kingdom, would then correspond to the fourth step, the Heart chakra level.

Three of the four metals showed up in the crop circle story in 1991. A group of several crop circle formations appeared at Grasdorf, Germany. Three metal plates were found underground, below the formations, one of gold, one of silver, and one of bronze. Engraved upon the plates were the same designs as the in the crops.

In Helena P. Blavatsky's work, 'Isis Unveiled, Vol. II, page 246, she states: "It may be held as a corroborative proof, that the Gospel according to Mark, as well as that ascribed to John, and the Apocalypse, were written by men, neither of whom was sufficiently acquainted with the other. The Logos was first definitely called 'petra (rock) by Philo; the word, moreover, means in Chaldaic and Phoenician, "interpreter."

Operative Masons are understood to be the bricklayers and the handicrafstmen, who composed the Craft down to Sir Christopher Wren's time, and "Speculative Masons," all members of the Order as now understood. The sentence attributed to Jesus, "Thou art Peter, and upon this 'rock' I will build my church; and the gates of hell shall not prevail against it.".

That statement disfigured by mistranslation and misinterpretation plainly indicates its real meaning. Pater and Petra, with the hierophants - the interpretation traced on the tables of stone of the final initiation was handed by the initiator to the chosen future interpreter.

Having acquainted himself with its mysterious contents, which revealed to him the mysteries of creation, the initiated became a builder himself, for he was made acquainted with the dodecahedron, or the geometrical figure on which the universe was built. To what he had learned in previous initiations of the use of the rule and of architectural principles was added a cross, the perpendicular and horizontal lines of which were supposed to form the foundation of the spiritual temple, by placing them across the junction, or central primordial point, the element of all existences, representing the first concrete idea of deity. Henceforth, he could as a Master-builder (see I Corinthians 10) erect a temple of wisdom on that rock of Petra, for himself; and having laid a sure foundation, let "another build thereon."

In the year 2003, scientists are claiming to have discovered that the universe is a dodecahedron, and say, " Space seen as shaped like a soccer ball. A new study, described by researchers in the latest issue of the journal Nature, suggests the universe is a dodecahedron -- a complex pattern of 12 pentagonal shapes -- with opposite faces connected up in pairs.

Robert Roy Britt of Space magainze, on Oct. 08, 2003 says that Scientists have kicked around many possibilities for the shape of the cosmos and whether or not it has a boundary. Now one group says the big house is set up something like the surface of a soccer ball, with cosmic patches stitched together to form a decidedly finite universe.

The strange geometry has been suggested before. What's new is how neatly it fits with the latest data. After some two millennia of speculation, the scientists involved in the work say, observations may be on the verge of determining whether the universe is infinite or finite.An infinite or open universe would result from an infinite amount of matter. A finite amount of matter would generate a finite, or closed universe."

Mr. Britt says its been suggested before. We wonder whether he read Plato, or Helena P. Blavatsky's work? Yes, it has been suggested before - and was not just discovered by current scientists as we see it.

Mankind has an inner fear of many things - handwriting on the wall would be high on the list if we saw such a thing in our own homes. But, the handwriting has been on the wall for mankind since the atomic bomb was invented over 50 years ago.

The extraterrestrials know how fearful we are. They also vowed they would not wipe us out enmasse like they tried to do once before. They also are not going to come down on the grounds of the White-house and tell the President, "Hey Mr. President, this is the way its going to be from hereon."

They know that mankind has a lot of technology. We can shoot back now if we fear them, and they have too much to lose if we did that. Besides that they love mankind because they created us in the first place and earth is a beautiful planet they don't want destroyed.

So, what is the alternative? To create a One-World religion - one that is brought about by mankind himself. Mankind can do this. We have the ability to think for ourselves and know that Peace is the only thing left to prevent the destruction of the earth itself.

Instead of the handwriting being written on the wall, the handwriting is now on the ground!!!

The Way God Creates

In 1992 a crop circle formation at Winterbourne Stoke, there were two elements with a space between, which conveyed a sense of 'almost touching', almost making contact with another world - like Michaelangelo's portrayal of the moment when Adam's fingers reaching to touch, but does not quite touch, the outstretched finger of God.

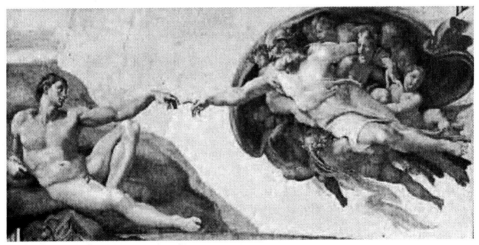

In The Cerealogist #6, Summer 1992 (The Journal for Crop Circle Studies.) This process is explained: All things in nature are mostly organized in patterns and maintained by electromagnetic (EM) fields. The process has been clarified following the discovery in 1986 of a hitherto unknown, low-energy, vorticeal, EM field. Identified as an expression of one fundamental field of formative energy often called 'ether', 'zero-point energy', 'tachyon field' or 'unified field', it contains the potential for the emergence of matter and acts as the responsible agent for form, growth, and behavioral patterns throughout nature (morphogenesis).

Dr. Sergei Barsamian, internationally known bio-physicist, has shown experimentally that this process is one of 'induction'. Energetic information held in the formative field effectively influences the energy field of another natural system when a state of coherence (sympathetic vibration) occurs. Charged, particles can be attracted and localized in space following the laws applicable to field charges and the laws of matter in physics. On the Earth, (which should be regarded as a living entity) such locations would form, e.g. the Bermuda Triangle in the Atlantic, the Dragon's Triangle in the Pacific and phenomenon such as powerful eddies of air (whirlwinds) and large oceanic whirlpools. These can be viewed as major centres of induction for EM vorticeal fields.

In any system, induced EM energy produces conduits, called meridians in the biophysical entity or telluric currents in the Earth, e.g. "Dragon Currents' in China and the 'Path of the Rainbow Serpent' in Australian Aboriginal lore. Ley Lines in Britain are aligned to this principle.

Along these conduits, points of high EM activity have always distinguished 'sacred sights' and can be viewed as minor centres of induction. This universal activity, the inpouring of vitalizing energy into a natural system is a function essential to the processes of life.

EM fields align themselves to existing energetic field patterns in the Earth's telluric paths and a mutual modification of the patterns occurs through 'feedback'. The mind/body interaction in bio-feedback is a fitting corollary.

Conventional theoretical physics considerations prove singular vorticeal EM field activity in nature and accepts their interaction which produces all other geometrical patterns, e.g. those seen in crystal formations.

Dr. Barsamian's work experimentally proves these findings and brings new applications of the principles outlines to physics. Cornfields, by virtue of their properties and high polarity act as naturally occurring stencils that allow visual registration of energetic patterns during induction into the Earth.

The activity cannot be measured with conventional technology and anomalies often occur to such electronic equipment in use. The process is rapid with effects such as luminosity, crackling or humming often accompanying the discharge of the field in the medium.

Further field effects, according to Dr. Barsamian, may include stimulation of natural cell metabolism and possible altered states of consciousness when one is in close proximity. Many "UFO' experiences can be attributed to the above considerations.

He accepts the existence of such processes in any environment and thus a state of ionizaton or the presence of plasma medium is not necessitated.

REF: Journal of biological Physics, Stillwater, OK. USA. "A Morphogenic Process in Low-Energy Electromagnetic fields' S.T. and S.P. Barsamian., 1988

~~~~~~~~~~~~

Seth, in the book, 'The Nature of Physical Reality', channeled through Jane Roberts in 1970, put it this way:

"Because I say that you create physical matter by use of the inner vitality of the universe, in the same way that you form a pattern with your breath on a glass pane, I do not mean that you are the creators of the universe. I am saying that you are the creators of the physical world as you know it.

"Chemicals themselves will not give rise to consciousness or life. Your scientists will have to face the fact that consciousness comes first and evolves its own form . . . All the cells in the body have a separate consciousness. There is a conscious cooperation between the cells in all the organs, and between the organs themselves.

"Molecules and atoms and even smaller particles have a condensed consciousness. They form into cells and form an individual cellular consciousness. This combination results in a consciousness that is capable of much more experience and fulfillment than would be possible the isolated atom or molecule alone. This goes on ad infinitum . . . to form the physical body mechanism. Even the lowest particle retains its individuality and its abilities (through this cooperation) are multiplied a millionfold.

"Matter is a medium for the manipulation and transformation of psychic energy into aspects that can then be used as building blocks. Matter is only cohesive enough to give the appearance or relative permanence to the senses that perceive it.

"Matter is continually created, but no particular object is in itself continuous. There is not, for example, one physical object that deteriorates with age. There are instead continuous creations of psychic energy into a physical pattern that appears to hold a more or less rigid appearance.

"No particular objects 'exists long enough' as an indivisible, rigid, or identical thing to change with age. The energy behind it weakens. The physical pattern therefore blurs. After a certain point each recreation becomes less perfect from your standpoint.

After many such re-creations that have been unperceived by you, then you notice a difference and assume that a change - has occurred. The actual material that seems to make up the object has completely disappeared many times, and the pattern has been completely filled again with new matter.

"Physical matter makes consciousness effective within three-dimensional reality. As individualized energy approaches your particular field, it expresses itself to the best of its ability within it. As energy approaches, it creates matter, first of all in an almost plastic fashion. But the creation is continuous like a beam or endless series of beams, at first weak as they are far off, then stronger, then weak again as they pass away.

"Physical objects cannot exist unless they exist in a definite perspective and space continuum. But each individual creates his own space continuum - each individual actually creates an entirely different object, which his own physical senses then perceive.

Sri Yantra
The New Jerusalem
and Chakras

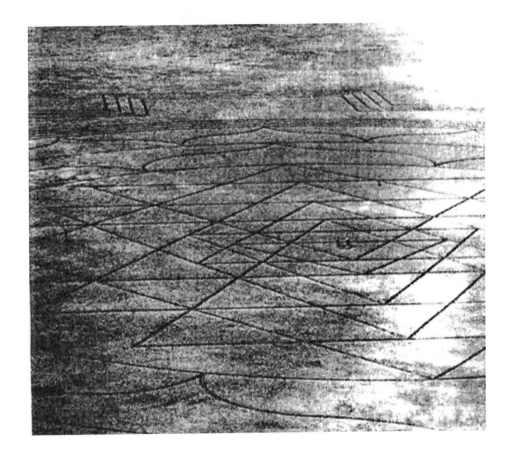

SRI YANTRA - 1990

This pattern is unique in that it wasn't done in crops like the others. This one was seemingly scratched into a dry lake-bed in Oregon in 1990.

The pattern was reported on August 10th by a pilot, but wasn't reported to the news media until September 14th.

When investigated, the lines were seen to be furrowed into the lake-bed, but there were no tire tracks or foot prints anywhere near the pattern.

It was estimated that it would cost around $100,000 just to plan out such a design. The lines alone covered 13.3 miles. The furrows were uniform in depth and the soil was distributed on both sides of the furrows equally.

As usual, when patterns appear in strange places, there are those who want to claim responsibility after the media starts noticing the event and people think free publicity is fun. The claims were phony as the claimants said they used horses dragging a plow when there were no marks whatsoever outside the lined furrows.

Exactly how these furrows were made has never been determined, though there were sightings of UFOs in the area during the time period the furrows were made. We, the writers, don't know how this was done either - just another mystery we can't explain.

The pattern itself is wonderful. The Sri Yantra mandala comes from the ancient Hindu. The outside of the design has 4 'T'-shaped gates and when you travel inwards to the center, there is a single dot, called the 'bindu point', which represents Union with the One Source.

There are a total of nine steps, with the eighth represented by a single triangle. The eighth and ninth steps, perhaps as with the eighth sphere above the beam in the Egyptian depiction of the balance beam pole in the 'Egyptian Book of the Dead', represents levels beyond the earth plane or human body.

The description of the Sri Yantra is described in the book 'Tantric Way: Art, Science, Ritual', by Ajit Mookeajee and Madhu Khanna.

"The Sri Yantra is a configuration of nine interlacing triangles centered around the bindu, drawn by the superimposition of five downward-pointing triangles, representing Sakti, and four upright triangles, representing Siva. Because it is a composition of nine (nava) triangles (yoni) it is often called 'Navayoni Chakra'.

The Sri Yantra is a symbolic pattern of Sakti's own form (svarupa), powers and emanations, the form of the universe (visvarupa), symbolizing the various stages of Sakti's descent in manifestation. It is a pictorial illustration of the cosmic field in creation. Like creation itself, the Sri Yantra came into being through the force of primordial desire. The impulse of desire (Kamakala), born of the inherent nature of Prakriti, creates a throb (spanda), which vibrates as sound (nada). This manifestation is represented by a point, or bindu. In the first state of manifestation, the bindu is called Para Bindu, which is the nucleus of the condensed energy, the seed of the ultimate Sound, and the dynamic and static aspects of the two (Siva-Sakti) in one. It contains all the possibilities of becoming; it transforms to Apara Bindu when creation begins: 'The essential point in the middle of the Yantra is the Supreme Sakti, when it swells it evolves into the form of a triangle' (Kamakalavilasa). The point assumes a radius, the polarization of Siva-Sakti takes place, the dynamic and static energies interact and two more points emerge to form a triad of points - the primary triangle or the Mula-trikona.

The 'Tantric Way' explains more about the Sri Yantra as emanations of creation outward from the single bindu point, and then speaks of another concept involving the design:

"The Sri Yantra is called 'Nava Chakra' since it is composed of nine circuits, counting from the outer plane to the bindu. Through contemplation on the Sri Yantra, the adept can rediscover his primordial sources. The nine circuits symbolically indicate the successive phases in the process of becoming. They rank from the earthly plane and rise slowly step by step to the final point, the state of supreme joy. By entering into the elan vital of the yantra, the adept reintegrates with it. The nine circuits within Sri Yantra move from the gross and tangible to the sublime and subtle realms.

The outermost periphery consists of a square, with four gates, colored white, red and yellow. This is the Bhupura, the ground-plan, of the Sri Yantra.

Editors note: The book doesn't give a fourth color. Others say that the gates are colored for the elements, fire, air, water, and earth.

Inside the square are three concentric circles, girdles (mekhala). The space between the square and three girdles is the Trailokya-mohana, or Enchantress of the Triple World, chakra; at this stage the adept is infatuated by aspirations and desires."

Joseph Campbell explains in his book, 'The Inner Reaches of Outer Space' that 3 1/2 is the midpoint of the seven chakras, the critical point, the fourth chakra, which is the heart chakra. He tells of worldwide myths and religions, indicating that this is an 'elementary idea.'

The Egyptian depiction of the balance beam pole and the Sri Yantra both show this idea as well. And the Bible's book of Revelation 11:11 describes that two trees stand up after 3 1/2 days.

Another connection from the Tantra book by Ajit Mookeajee and Madhu Khanna and the book of Revelation, chapter 17 describes a woman, similar to one another. In the Tantra book, she is the goddess Kali and in Revelation 17, she is the harlot, which represents the energy in our karmic cycle of time, which is nearing its end.

The energy of the new cycle seems to be represented by The Woman With Child in Revelation 12. She wears a crown of 12 stars. 'The New Jerusalem', described in Revelation 21, also has 12 gates, pearls, jewels, and angels.

The Heart Chakra, which we need to reach in this time cycle, is symbolized as a 12-petal lotus flower with a Star of David inside.

In the Eastern religions, we are said to be in the Kali-Yuga time cycle, the Age of Iron. The metals corresponding to the four Yugas, or ages, in the Hindu chronology are gold, silver, bronze, and iron. We rid ourselves of Kali at the end of the time cycle, and reach "Moksha," or Nirvana, the abode of blessed Peace and Spirit. (see Isis Unveiled, vol. 2, page 275, by H.P. Blavatsky.)

The end of the Kali-Yuga and the book of Revelation describe very similar situations.

The same four metals, and their means are quite similar to the dream of Nebuchadnezzar in *Daniel 2:31-45.*

"31: - Thou, O king, sawest, and behold a great image. This great image, whose brightness was excellent, stood before thee; and the form thereof was terrible. 32 - This image's head was of fine gold, his breast and his arms of silver, his belly and his thighs of bronze, 33 - His legs of iron, his feet part of iron and part of clay. 34 - Thou sawest till that a stone was cut out without hands, which smote the image upon his feet that

were of iron and clay, and brake them to pieces. 35 Then was the iron, the clay, the bronze, the silver, and the gold, broken to pieces together, and became like the chaff of the summer threshing-floors; and the wind carried them away, that no place was found for them: and the stone that smote the image became a great mountain, and filled the whole earth. 36 - This is the dream; and we will tell the interpretation thereof before the king. 37- Thou, O king, art a king of kings: for the God of heaven hath given thee a kingdom, power, and strength, and glory. 38- And wheresoever the children of men dwell, the beasts of the field and the fowls of the heaven hath he given into thine hand, and hath made thee ruler over them all. Thou art this head of gold. 39- And after thee shall arise another kingdom inferior to thee, and another third kingdom of bronze, which shall bear rule over all the earth. 40- And the fourth kingdom shall be strong as iron: forasmuch as iron breaketh in pieces and subdueth all things: and as iron that breaketh all these, shall it break in pieces and bruise. 41- And whereas thou sawest the feet and toes, part of potters' clay, and part of iron, the kingdom shall be divided; but there shall be in it of the strength of the iron, forasmuch as thou sawest the iron mixed with miry clay. 42- And as the toes of the feet were part of iron, and part of clay, so the kingdom shall be partly strong, and partly broken. 43- And whereas thou sawest iron mixed with miry clay, they shall mingle themselves with the seed of men: but they shall not cleave one to another, even as iron is not mixed with clay. 44- And in the days of these kings shall the God of heaven set up a kingdom, which shall never be destroyed: and the kingdom shall not be left to other people, but it shall break in pieces and consume all these kingdoms, and it shall stand for ever. 45- Forasmuch as thou sawest that the stone was cut out of the mountain without hands, and that it brake in pieces the iron, the bronze, the clay, the silver, and the gold; the great God hath made known to the king what shall come to pass hereafter: and the dream is certain, and the interpretation thereof sure. "

Daniel 12:7, which is repeated in Revelation 12:14, suggests the 3 1/2 by 'a time, two times, and half a time." (1 + 2 + 1/2 = 3 1/2) Further, Daniel 9:27 suggests the mid-point of the seven chakras as, ".. a strong covenant with many for one week; and for half of the week..."

In 1993, the Bythorn Mandala appeared:

BYTHORN MANDALA

A similar symbol appears in the Tantra book on page 35. and is called a "Shyama (Kali) Yantra." The crop formation is not exactly like the one in the book, but it is quite similar. The one in the book differs from the Sri Yantra, except there is a five-pointed star inside instead of the complex pattern of overlapping triangles. The inner part is quite like the crop formation, except the crop formation had ten petals instead of eight, as in the book.

SHYAMA KALI YANTRA

In H. P. Blavatsky's, 'The Secret Doctrine', on pages 4 and 5, a number of ancient symbols are depicted. Every one of them has appeared as a crop formation in some form. One of them is a five-pointed star reversed, with two points (horns) turned heavenward, that is, pointing up. This, she says, is the esoteric symbol of the Kali-Yuga. The star in the crop formation had two points to the north, and one to the south.

Another symbol of Kali is the swastika. Several swastikas or swastika-circles have appeared. The swastika circle of 1989 and the swastika of 1997 appear below. Unfortunately, some of the swastika crop formations were mowed off by the farmers as soon as they appeared.

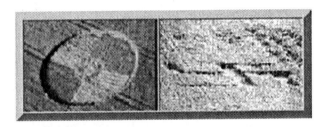

This formation was composed of four quadrants, exactly aligned to the magnetic compass points; at the center, the crop rotated clockwise with a thin band rotated counter-clockwise. At the boundary edge, another thin band rotated clockwise with crop lying under the central coned quadrants. A hoax was out of the question. The crop circles were now lifted beyond the realm of the Earth-bound.

The swastika is also a symbol of Shiva and Kali, the Destroyer god and goddess.

I saw a counterclockwise swastika in a dream in 1991. Energy was flowing out from the center into the arms. A voice said, "These are the forces going out from the center to experience negative manifested events, in order to learn. It is generally square, and you circle counterclockwise."

In the following months, I learned that the swastika is a very ancient symbol. It was said that when it is going clockwise, or east, it is a symbol of good luck.

In January 1994, I received "The Circular," Volume 4, Number 3. On page 8 was an article by Lucy Pringle, titled, "The Symbolism of The Bythorn Wonder."

Lucy wrote that the symbol powerfully denotes spiritual rebirth and enlightenment, and that the star is the Star of Shiva, the Destroyer and Creator. He is androgynous, and is part of the Brahman Triad or Trimurti, together with Brahma (the Creator) and Vishnu (the Preserver).

The Triad is similar to the Holy Trinity, and indicates aspects of God. They are conceived of as both Gods and Goddesses, to achieve balance, consistent with the Yin/Yang concept of balance and harmony.

Death, the Destroyer, holds the seed of rebirth. Out of the seed of death bursts the flower of birth, like the Phoenix.

Lucy also said that the formation also relates to the planetary and cosmic cycle, perhaps suggesting a planetary "shift."

"In the Eastern tradition, the Lotus flower suggested by the petals in the formation depicts Spiritual Enlightenment, paralleled in the West by the Rosicrucian Rose, which normally has five or ten petals. The lotus flower traditionally represents spinning vortices of cosmic energy at the various chakra points of the body. Different numbers of petals correspond to different chakras; for example the four-petalled lotus corresponds to the base chakra, six petals to the sacrum, and twelve petals to the heart and so on, therefore the fact that the Lotus has ten petals is significant. It is widely thought that the solar plexus chakra (ten-petalled) relates to the emotional aspect of our being, the energies of which flow into the heart."

Such a Rose formation did appear after Lucy's article was written. It also had ten petals on the outside. A five-petal design was on the inside. Thus, it has a similarity to the Bythorn Mandala, and may also represent the third chakra:

Goodworth Clatford, Hampshire 15th May, 1996

It is interesting to note that scholars of the chakra system say that the chakra energy rotates in a clockwise direction in a full circular shape and is considered harmonious and healthy. If the geometrical center of the circle is not the same as the true center of the laid crop, this means something is changing. The earth is said to have chakra centers too, so the crop formations may be telling us something about this.

Chakra Number	Number of Vortices	Double Chakra Sum of Vortices	Color	Placement on Body
1	4	-	red	Root (1) Muladhara (root/support) Base of spine
2	6	12	orange	Sacral (2) Svadhisthana (sweetness) Abdomen, Genitals
3	10	20	yellow	Solar Plexus (3) Manipura (lustrous Jewel) Solar Plexus
4	12	24	green	Heart (4) Anahata (unstruck) Heart "area"
5	16	32	blue	Throat (5) Visshudha (purification) Throat
6	96	192	indigo	Brow (6) Ajna (to perceive) Brow
7	972	-	violet	Crown (7) Sahasrara (thousandfold) Top of head, cerebral cortex

CHAKRA CLASSIFICATION TABLE

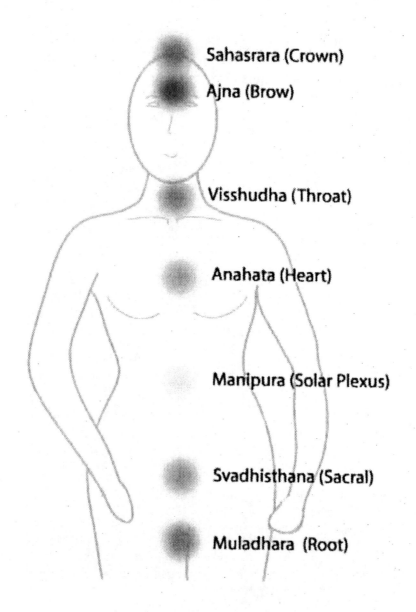

CHAKRA PLACEMENT ON BODY

The diagrams show 'double chakras'. The first chakra points toward 'earth', and the seventh points toward 'heaven'. Those two only have one set of vortices. The other five chakras point to both the front and back of the the body, and are therefore called, 'double chakras'.

The sum of the vortices is calculated from the number of vortices in the front and rear. As an example, the fifth chakra - at the larynx - the throat, has 16 vortices in front and 16 in back, for a total of 32. The chakras are connected to each other via the subtle energy channels inside the spinal cord.

One of these energies is the kundalini, and the other is the Hara-line, which is not as well known. This line runs from the center of the earth through the seven chakras, and out of the head where it connects to the Higher Self.

There are two subtle energy lines flowing down and around the chakra centers in the spine. They are called 'spine snakes,' or Ida and Pingala. They are interlaced like a double helix.

CADEUCES

THE FIRST CHAKRA

We get our life force from nature and the earth through the first chakra. It consists of four vortices, with the Hara-Line in the middle. This may be the meaning of the famous "quincunx" (or "quintuplet set") type crop formation. Possibilities suggesting this chakra are in the formations below:

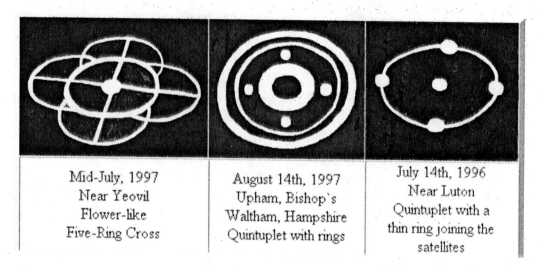

Mid-July, 1997 Near Yeovil Flower-like Five-Ring Cross	August 14th, 1997 Upham, Bishop's Waltham, Hampshire Quintuplet with rings	July 14th, 1996 Near Luton Quintuplet with a thin ring joining the satellites

CHAKRA EXAMPLES IN CROP FORMATONS

THE SECOND CHAKRA

The second chakra is connected with the hips, and has six vortices. This may be suggested by two formations that appeared in 1991. They were six-petal, daisy-like flowers inside circles. Possibilities suggesting this chakra follow:

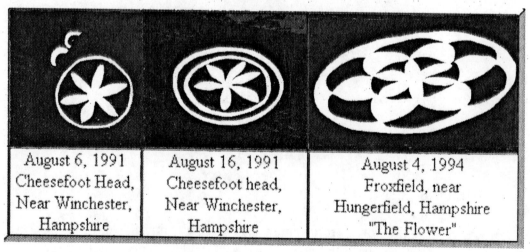

August 6, 1991 Cheesefoot Head, Near Winchester, Hampshire	August 16, 1991 Cheesefoot head, Near Winchester, Hampshire	August 4, 1994 Froxfield, near Hungerfield, Hampshire "The Flower"

CHAKRA EXAMPLES IN CROP FORMATIONS

The flower petal shapes are based on interlocking circles. The "Foxfield Flower" of 1994, was 360 feet in diameter, perhaps suggesting the 360-degrees of a circle. The farmer who owns the field reported seeing UFOs that looked like wheels in the sky about a year prior over the same area. The 360-degree circle is very ancient and is primary in a system of numbers that were in place when recorded history began. The same number system also seems to be part of the crop circle phenomenon.

THE THIRD CHAKRA

The ten vortices of the third chakra may have been indicated in the Spider Web formation that appeared next to Avebury in 1994. This can be a way that a clairvoyant sees the third chakra from the front, with the sub-elements forming the shape. In the middle is the Hara-Line centering the whole crop circle. In 1998, the Beckhampton crop pattern had 10 points with a 5-point star in the center. The Bythorn mandala, pictured above also had ten elements, with the pentagram in the middle.

AVEBURY '94 - BECKHAMPTON '98

THE FOURTH CHAKRA

The fourth chakra is the heart chakra and has 12 vortices. The following pattern has 12 flower petals with a central circle and central bindu point. A "Torus" formation appeared in 1997 that may also suggest the fourth chakra, as it had twelve interlocking circles. Another important connection to the fourth chakra is the forth stage in the Hopi creation myth. The Clay Hill formation below has three lines projecting from each point of the 12-pointed star, for a total of 36 lines. 36 is the base number in the ancient Gematria number system.

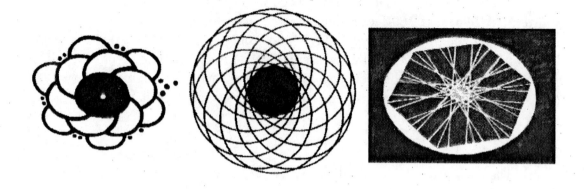

WOODFORD 2003   TORUS 1997   CLAY HILL 1997

SOUTHFIELD, ALTON PRIORS, 2000

THE FIFTH CHAKRA

16 petals and a central flower in barley. The image resembles one of the rose windows at Chartres, France. The church was built from 1194 to 1260 A.D. It is a cathedral in the Gothic exemplar construction. It is in the small town of Chartres, near to and south-west of Paris.

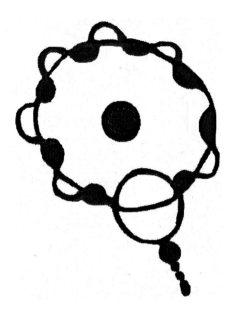

CHEESEFOOT, 1995

This 'Jelly-Fish-like' formation appeared at Cheesefoot Head in 1995. It had 16 semi-circles in the outer ring, which fits with the 16 vortices of the fifth chakra. It also had an "appendix" shape, similar to the "scorpion" formations.

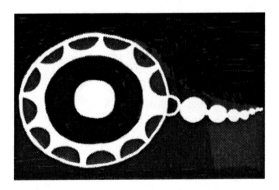

DANEBURY HILL FORT, 1995

A similar formation of another scorpion appeared the same year at Danebury Hill-fort. This has 12 vortices of .the fourth chakra. It has been suggested that the two formations may show an energy flow from the fourth to the fifth chakras.

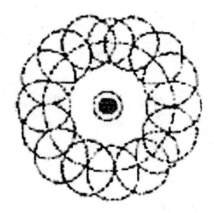

GOODWORTH-CLATFORD 1995

Another formation appeared at Goodworth Clatford that had 16 interlocking circles. This seems to be a "simple" fifth chakra. In the very center is the Hara-Line. .

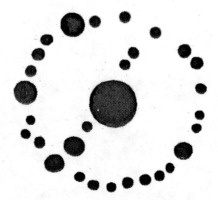

GANDER DOWN, ALESFORD, 1995

A formation appeared at Gander Down, near Alresford, that had 32 circles, the sum of the front and rear vortices of the fifth chakra. It looks somewhat like a solar system, with an asteroid belt around it.

NOTE: This photo was said to predict the conformation of the solar system on September 7, 2003 and that something bad was going to happen that day. But, that day came and went and nothing untoward happened.

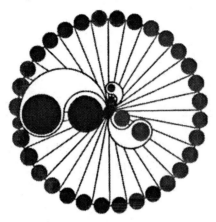

HACKPEN WHITE HORSE, 2003

This formation has 32 circles around the outside and 3 yin yang-like formations inside. One half of each of the inner symbols resembles a horn as though a communication device between the physical realm and the spiritual realm. As there are 3 sizes, perhaps it means communication with 3 different levels of consciousness.

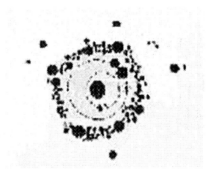

THE SIXTH CHAKRA

ASTEROID BELT AT BISHOP'S SUTTON - 1995

An "Asteroid Belt" - like formation appeared in 1995 at Bishop's Sutton, near New Alresford, Hampshire, that had 96 little circles. This may suggest the 96 vortices of the sixth chakra.

THE SEVENTH CHAKRA

There have been no formations with 972 circles, so we do not have one to match the seventh chakra.

It is said that the seventh chakra has 960 "white vortices, and 12 "golden" vortices, for the sum of 972.

In 1996, there appeared in Washington State a crop pattern with seven circles in a curved line. The circles inside the rings of the formation may signify the Hara-Line, which runs through all the chakras. So, the formation may represent the chakra system of a human being.

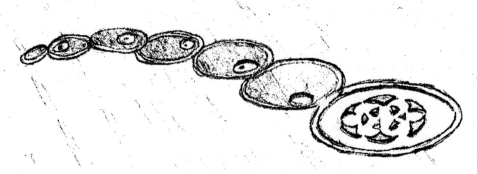

CHEHALIS, WASHINGTON STATE, USA, 1996

YIN YANG
TAO
FENG SHUI

In Chinese medicine, the health of a patient is defined as a balance of the body's yin and yang. Yin and yang are opposing energies, yet complimentary to each other. Yin represents 'night' and male. Yang represents 'day' and female. Some of the organs of the body are yin and some are yang. The emphasis is a balance of the two energies in order to stay healthy. A balanced life is a healthy life.

In ancient times, the Chinese physicians were also philosophers. They were firmly rooted in Taoist traditions as well. The Tao stresses a oneness in nature of all things. The Traditional Chinese medicine book was called The Yellow Emperor's Classic of Internal medicine. It was written over 2,000 years ago by Huang-di. It has been added to by other physicians since then and is still accepted today as the book to go to for curing ailments.

Taoist writings state that all things and all processes contain two primal energies or forces. These two basic aspects often are described as masculine and feminine, light and dark, negative and positive, creative and receptive. The original meaning of the term signified the light and dark sides of a mountain. Our English-language expression, "there are two sides to everything," expresses this concept quite well.

Chuang Tzu, a Taoist sage, states: "Everything can be a 'that'; everything can be a 'this.' Therefore, 'that' comes from 'this' and 'this' comes from 'that' - which means 'that' and 'this' give birth to one another. When there is no more separation between 'that' and 'this', it is called being one with the Tao." He also says: "The sage does not bother with these distinctions, but beholds the light beyond right and wrong."

Yin and Yang are a balance of each other. Since our body needs to be constantly in balance with nature, we are constantly changing to respond to our changing surroundings. We must either adapt to these changes or we will become ill. In order to do this, our body's organs work in pairs to maintain balance. There are five 'zany' organs - the heart, kidney, spleen, liver, and lungs. There are five 'fu' organs - the small intestines, stomach, large intestines, bladder and gallbladder. The 'fu' organs work with our food and change it into energy and are the yang organs. The organs, which control the storage of vital substances are the yin organs.

There is network within the organs that work to energize us. They include the skin, tendons, tissues, and bones. The entire network of the body within and yin and yang aspects give us an even flow of energy that balances us and keeps us healthy. When you go to a Chinese physician, he treats the entire body, not just the one symptom we complain about. The Chinese doctor will use herbal medicines, moxa cones, acupuncture, rhythmic exercise and food therapies.

The Mind

Our mental and emotional stability are also influenced by yin and yang. People tend to have a mixture of both characteristics, but sometimes things get out of balance. People who are excessively yin are said to have a tendency to lack direction, to be unable to concentrate, to be impractical, to be dependent on others and always thinking about the future. They may be oversensitive, defensive, anxious, self-pitying and overemotional,

On the other hand, people who are excessively yang are said to be domineering, inflexible, overconfident, obsessed by a need for orderliness and more concerned with the past than the now. They are likely to be workaholics and have difficulty relaxing and enjoying life. They tend keep their real emotions bottled up and hidden but can suddenly explode with outbursts of anger.

Using just one therapy would not be balanced, so the Chinese doctor must be very thorough with our care.

There have been 5 or 6 Yin Yang symbols in the crop fields. Most of them were in the UK, but one was in Germany. Some are simple formations and very obvious. Others are more complicated and need a bit of thought to know what they are. The ones that are more complicated have other lines and circles, which have added meaning and need analysis by researchers.

As an example, in 1998, this crop circle appeared showing the balance in life: This is not a typical Yin Yang symbol, yet it means the same thing.

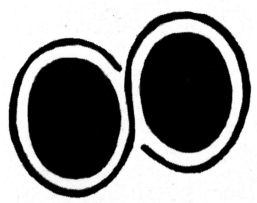

Cheriton, nr Winchester Hampshire. August 1998

In 2003, a more complicated formation came along. This has a Yin Yang symbol, but has greater meaning as well.

WEST TISTEAD, JULY- 2003
NORTH OF THE MEON HUT

Joe Mason wrote: "The formation seems to represent the seven chakras within the human body, with the kundalini serpent winding through them. The central circle represents the fourth-heart chakra midpoint. This symbolism, the seven and the midpoint, is a universal elementary idea found many decades ago by comparing myths and religions worldwide. Many other formations have indicated this or parts of it. A number of formations this year indicate chakras, especially the heart chakra.

WADEN HILL, AVEBURY, WILTSHIRE - JUNE 2003

This formation appeared on the solstice.

A researcher stated that the initial design represents the transformation from the summer cycle to the autumn and winter. The Yin symbol at the top of the shape symbolizes the connection with the Earth and the moon. The alignment with the central pathway radiated out of the bottom circle, pointing directly through the Avebury henge.

AVEBURY HENGE

The researcher quoted a Yin Yang description: "Yin yang is the Way of Heaven and Earth, the fundamental principle of the myriad things, the father and mother of change and transformation, the root of inception and destruction. "Su-wen"

He also says that the crop formations of 2002 were hinting at the harmony and balance needed within our lives.

STOCKBRIDGE Nr WINCHESTER, HAMPSHIRE - JULY 1998

This crop formation is as obvious as they get. It was called the Rolls Royce because it was right next to the Rolls Royce Manufacturing plant.

THE CONNECTION BETWEEN PHILOSOPHICAL THOUGHT

Universal Law of Duality
Yin, Yang, Kabballah, & Tree of Life

The yin/yang symbol demonstrates that within each there is a bit of the other. Duality and polarity are exhibited in all of creation. Parallels can be seen between differing cultural and religious traditions. Parallels can be seen between the Chinese Taoist tradition and the Jewish/Hebrew Kabbalistic tradition. As the Yin and Yang are complementary principles, they display opposition. This is similar to the Tree of Life of the Kabballah, which exhibits the opposite yet complementary pillars of receptivity. The Tree of Life shows the Feminine energy similar to yin, and of aggressive/expansiveness, which is Masculine energy like yang. Both of these traditions seek the blending and balance through universal truth. The Tree of Life shows us the physical representation of the creative structure and nature of the universe, and also the source of life and a foundation for the mind of man to work upwards on a spiritual path.

Another comparison

Tao: Yin and Yang

Ancient sages in China long observed creation and formed the teachings of a spiritual philosophy that has in many ways become a religion. They were able to describe the subtle breath of life that permeates and vivifies everything in the universe as formless and elusive and called it chi or the vital energy or the vital force of creation.

We find a similar description to the primal forces of creation that were in existence at the beginning of the creation of the universe in the Bible in the Creation Story from Genesis. *"In the beginning, when God created the heavens and the earth, the earth was a formless wasteland, and darkness covered the abyss, while a mighty wind swept over the waters."* -(Genesis 1:1-2)

More parallels are noted between the Ayn Sof of the Kabballah and the Tao of the Tao Te Ching. The Ayn Sof is known to be Ultimate Nothingness which is said to have existed before creation, independent of time and space.

Ancient wise sages in China said the original energy of the universe was fathomless and incomprehensible, and beyond time and space, and they called it Tao.

"Tao is infinite. If we use it, we find it inexhaustible. Deep and unfathomable, It seems to be Ancestor of all things. It rounds off our angles, It unravels our difficulties, It tempers our light, It is lowly as the dust, It is pure, It remains everlasting. I do not know whose Son it is, It appears to have existed before God. " - Tao Teh Ching, IV.

Another spiritual parallel can be seen between the Jewish tradition and the Hindu tradition in regard to the first creation. In the Jewish tradition, God before creation is Ayn Sof or Nothingness Without End or Beginning. This is analogous to the Hindu god Brahma who is known as Not This, Not That.

Chi force is known in many cultures of the earth. It is known also as chi, ki or prana. Chi is the life giving force or generative force in the universe. The Chinese word "chi" refers to internal energy. It is the vital force that gives us life and keeps us healthy. There are Universal Laws of Creation, and the Law of Attraction is our true nature.

The opposing energies are the yin and yang and the wu-hsing. Wu-hsing is the five element system or the five forces of change and evolvement. The elements of earth, metal, fire, wood and water are contained within these changing cycles. Each element is a part of chi energy. The elements also correspond to colors, tastes, seasons, directions and parts of the body.

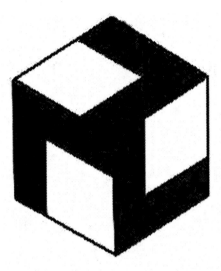

THE ANTAHKARANA
ALLINGTON, nr DEVIZES, WILTSHIRE, JUNE, 1999

The Antahkarana is an ancient healing and meditation symbol that has been used in Tibet and China for thousands of years. Simply by having it in your presence, it creates a positive effect on the chakras and the aura of the body. If doing healing work on yourself or others, it will focus and deepen the action of the healing energies being used.

The Taoists tell us that the symbol, when meditated on, creates a microcosmic orbit, whereby psychic energies from the higher realms enter the crown chakra of the body, travel down to the feet and then back up the body to the top of the head and then down to the feet again in a triple flow through the body, which grounds the person to the earth, through all of the chakras.

It also neutralizes negative energies that collect in objects used by meditators such as jewelry or crystals. One only need put the object between two such symbols.

Though the symbol appears to be a three dimensional cube, the energies also continue up into the higher dimensions to the Higher Self.

The Tibetans used the Antahkarana in meditation along with lit candles. They used a large earthenware bowl symbolizing the cosmic egg of the universe. They put several inches of water into the bowl with a stool in the center. The Antahkarana was inlaid with silver on the top of the stool. One wall of the room was covered with highly polished copper and the opposite wall had tapestries hung with Reiki symbols on it.

The Tibetan monk would sit on the symbol of the Antahkarana while meditating on the Reiki symbols. This united his consciousness with the energies of the Reiki symbols while the Antahkarana on the stool focused his energies through his chakras and aura to connect him both with the higher dimensions and the earth at the same time.

The Antahkarana is a bridge, called the Rainbow Bridge. It is a bridge between the three aspects of our mind nature. The primary objectives of this bridge are:

1. To produce alignment between mind and brain through a correct understanding of the inner aspects of man, especially through the etheric body and the energy centers.

2. To build a bridge between the brain/mind/soul, producing an integrated personality, which develops the expression of the indwelling soul.

3. To build a bridge between the lower mind, soul, and higher mind which provides illumination of the personality.

Besides the Antahkarana, there is the Sutratma. The Sutratma is the direct stream of life, which gives the body its living energy. The Antahkarana is the thread of consciousness. One must distinguish between the two.

Symbolically speaking, the Sutratma works from above downward and precipitates life into the outer manifestation. The Antahkarana is woven, evolved and created as the result of this creation, and works from below upwards.

When the meditator facilitates this stream of flow of consciousness and awareness, he ends the fear of death, ends the feeling of separateness, becomes responsive to impressions coming to him from spiritual realms or from the Mind of God. In this way, the meditator becomes aware of the purposes and plans of his Creator.

In the building of the second half of the Antahkarana, which bridges between consciousness of the soul and the spiritual triad, he gains the science of vision. The reason for the difference is that the first bridge is built through the use of mental substance, and the second half is built through the use of light substance.

The triple thread existed from the beginning of time and links individual man with his monadic source. By using this thread consciously, the meditator is able to become aware of this stream of energy and use it for healing and to help facilitate the higher spiritual realms plan for humanity in its utmost highest form.

By using the Science of the Antahkarana, and using the incoming system of energy, with transformation and fusion, the meditator also deals with the outgoing energies and his relationship to his environment and energy centers.

COLOR	RED	YELLOW	GREEN	WHITE	BLACK
ELEMENT	FIRE	EARTH	WOOD	GOLD	WATER
NATURE	YANG	YANG	YIN	YANG	YIN

COLOR ELEMENT/NATURE RELATIONSHIPS

The color spectrum is basically from red to yellow and orange (yang chi, 760 to 575 nanometers) and from green to violet-black (yin shui, 575 to 380 nanometers).

FENG SHUI

Every color affects chi energy differently, and because of this colors are believed to be related to yin/yang and the five elements. Color can be used to maintain, calm and enhance a specific chi energy.

Red, for example, is the most yang color and is linked with fire energy and the chi energy of the west.

Colors also have symbolic meanings. Red is associated with romance, wealth, and happiness.

Feng Shui uses colors in two ways that are similar to our use of color in the home. Large areas, or backgrounds, tend to be pale. Accent colors, which are more vivid, are used more sparingly on only small surfaces, such as a piece of furniture.

The reason for this is: The general principle tells us that the stronger the color, the less is needed for it to be effective. Personal preference is considered important in Feng Shui, so it is unwise for the individual to use a color, even if well liked by others, if you do not actually like it yourself.

Warm Colors

Where to use - kitchen, dining room, living room.

Yellows

Yellow is said to bring good luck. Yellow can stimulate joy, wisdom, intuitive insight, and creativity. Yellow is a color that can encourage flexibility and adaptability. It can lift the mood of an individual or even a group of people. It can inspire optimism, and improve a sense of well-being just by seeing the color.

Color therapists claim it has a positive effect on the nervous system and gastrointestinal tract.

In excess, yellow can over-stimulate and irritate, and the negative side of this color is associated with cowardice and prejudice.

Creamy or pale-earth yellows create an illusion of space in a small area, and citrus yellows will accentuate natural available light.

Yellow is the color of the third chakra - the emotional color, situated in the stomach, solar plexus and diaphragm area. Yellow is the color of jealousy in the negative sense. In the Indian Hindu Tantric tradition, the Manipura chakra, or "place of gems", is described as having ten petals, yellow in color with a downward pointing triangle, representing the tattwa of fire. This chakra is traditionally located at the navel (hence the alternative name of nabhi (navel) chakra), but in many modern (especially Theosophical- and New Age - orientated) chakra formulations it is placed at the Solar Plexus. This latter however seems to refer to a distinct (minor) chakra - the Solar Plexus chakra. Pancreas - Adrenals - Stomach - Gall Bladder - Nervous System - Vitalizes the sympathetic nervous system, which activates our involuntary muscles and gets the body ready for activity. (Adrenaline) This Chakra can bring to us joy, sadness, gut feeling reactions and heightens emotion.

Oranges

Orange is a happy, social color that brings out feelings of optimism, confidence, and enthusiasm. Orange will evoke creativity, ambition, and energetic activity.

Orange is used by color therapists to treat problems such as and including asthma, colds, thyroid problems, and even to stimulate lactation.

On the negative side, in some people, orange can produce nervousness and restless behavior.

Orange is the color of the second chakra - it governs the energies of the sexual organs. Gonads, Sexual Organs, Sacral - Lower back - Located between the Asis bones of the hips. Vitalizes the sexual life organs of reproduction and processes prana (or oxygen) from the atmosphere, which then vitalizes the entire system of major and minor Chakras.   In the Indian Hindu Tantric tradition, this chakra, called the Swadhisthana or "Self or Own Abode", is figured as having six petals, orange in color, and with a crescent in the center, the tattwa of water. This chakra therefore corresponds to the element Water and is traditionally associated with the sexual impulses and sexual energy. It does not, however, correspond to the sex-organs as such, which are under the supervision of the Sacral and Pubic Centres, but to the original subtle energy behind the sexual impulse. Indian Hindu teachings place a lot of emphasis on celibacy, in order to raise and transmute this powerful sexual energy to the brain (or, more correctly, the Upper Tien Tan Centre, to use the Taoist paradigm), increasing higher consciousness. This is actually the basic principle behind celibacy in all religions, including Catholicism. In practice however, this noble ideal flounders, because the individual is not yet ready to renounce physical sex, and unfortunately may become psychologically unbalanced, full of guilt, or turn to paedophilia or other unnatural forms of sex.

Reds

Reds stimulate the senses and bring out strength, joy, motivation, and love. The energy of red results in an exciting and courageous decorating color in rooms where stimulation is wanted.

In color therapy it is used as a tonic, to improve blood circulation, and to overcome depression, fear, and inertia.

Bright - attention-seeking reds must also be used carefully. They can generate fear, uncontrolled passion, and excessive anger, and may be disturbing to those with mental health problems or neuroses.

Red is the color of the first chakra. It is located at the base of the spine. The Muladhara is one of the seven Primary Chakras, and is associated with the element: Earth, representing the densest grade of manifestation. In the Kundalini-yoga system of Shaktims, the Muladhara Centre is described as having four petals, corresponding to the psychological states of greatest joy, natural pleasure, delight in controlling passions, and blissfulness in concentration. All these qualities correspond to the bliss of realizing the Divine in the physical body. The highest and most complete forms of spirituality do not reject the body, but see it as the vehicle for the transmutation of the body and the spirit together. It is, according to Shakta Tantric doctrine, the seat of Kundalini, the latent cosmic energy or shakti that resides in every living being. When this latent power is activated through Hatha Yoga practicises (pranayama, purification of the nadis, etc), it rises through each of the rear or spinal chakras, and up through the top of the head, to the Sahasrara or "Thousand Petalled Lotus" located above the crown. There it unites with its opposite polarity, the Paramashiva or Supreme Godhead Consciousness, and the yogi attains total Liberation from phenomenal reality. Vitalizes the Kidneys and feeds the life giving system - the will to live - and the fundamental instincts for survival. Stores our Chi energy.

Pinks

Magenta hues signify spiritual completeness and a sense of contentment. In all strengths, pink is a symbol of self-respect and self-awareness, but some people may find it mentally draining.

It is regarded as the color of "universal healing" because it can raise the vibrations or energies of the body.

Neutrals and earth colors

Where to use

Neutral colors such as beige, and light tan and pale earth tones have a unifying influence that works well in halls and entrances, but because they are easy on the eye and easy to live with, they can be used almost anywhere.

Pure white

White blends all the rainbow colors, and represents harmony and purity to spiritual people. White reveals the truth and can lead us toward higher spiritual and divine knowledge. The Druid priests used white as a symbol of the Sun and light. Many people wear white in because of the color whites' purity. Nurses, doctors, and dentists, as well as nuns have worn white for a long time.

On the negative side, white can feel unfriendly, sterile, and unapproachable. In a home, people would be afraid to touch anything white. However, in a hospital setting, one would expect to see white because you can see how clean white is. In a home, white with tints of warm or cool colors better represents the types of white found in natural settings of life.

White is part of the crown chakra at the top of the head. There is some disagreement among various traditional sources over whether the Sahasrara chakra or "thousand-petalled lotus" is located at the crown-point at the very top of the head, or at a distance above the head. Shyam Sundar Goswami and Sri Aurobindo located it above the head, as opposed to Sir John Woodroffe (Arthuur Avalon) and the Theosophist C. W. Leadbeater who place it at the top of the head.

Earth colors

Earth colors represent fertility such as growing in nature, such as beautiful forests, farm-lands and gardens. It is said that brown can dispel mental depression. Brown is a balancing color that brings a sense of security, although used in excess it can diminish a sense of vitality.

Black

Black can be associated with death and grief as people wear black in mourning their loved ones. But black is also associated with mystery and the unknown. Black is used as an inward-looking color, absorbing and silent, used in scrying, majical uses and in Wicca. Its' mystical use is evident as priests, ministers and nuns wear black a great deal. Black worn with another brilliant color, such as red can be dramatic and powerful, but used in an overpowering way where everything is black can be overwhelming or depressing, soaking up the users' or visitors' energy and vitality.

Cool colors

Where to use - bedrooms, bathrooms, meditation and therapy rooms.

Greens

Between the warm and cool colors, green offers a great deal of balance. Green associates itself with the abundance of nature and is both restful, calmative and energizing at the same time, and gives a sense of well-being..

Green is closely linked to healing, and color therapists use it to soothe pain. The color green is now used in hospital settings for its calmative and healing feelings.

On the negative side, it can be a symbol of selfishness, jealousy, and laziness. Too much green can be depressing and debilitating.

Green is the color of the heart chakra. Its location is the area of the heart and represents the sensation of love. Located on the spine, in the area of the heart. This chakra is associated with our ability to give and receive love, to feel compassion, to reach out to others. It is the center of the chakras, and can balance the activities of the seven energy centers. Physically it is linked to heart, circulatory system, and immune system. An important chakra for healing. When too weak, you may feel closed to others, low self-esteem, insecurity, jealousy, feeling unloved, "poor me" syndrome, and self-doubting. Overactive, you may experience the "martyr" syndrome, giving too much of oneself, overconfident, jealousy and stinginess.

Blues

Blue gives a soothing and sedating feeling. It can also bring on a sense of hope, harmony and calm. Blue also stimulates creativity, communication, and spiritual understanding.

Color therapists use it as a tonic, and say it has antiseptic qualities.

Metaphysical and medical research suggests that the color blue may be an effective tool in guided imagery therapies to reduce pain levels. Blue has been used very successfully in mental institutions to calm violent patients.

However, used in excess, blue may be depressing.

Blue is the color of the throat chakra and represents communication skills, and the other organs in that area such as the thyroid and parathyroid. In Shakta Tantra, the Vishuddha chakra has sixteen blue smoke-colored petals, each linked with one of the Sanskrit vowels. The central chakra-region is either white, transparent, smoke, or sky-blue in color, and is associated with the element Space (Akasha), through which are transmitted the subtle vibrations of mantras [Laya Yoga]. This chakra is located on the spine in the throat area, and is associated with our communicating abilities, creativity, right side of brain, speech, hearing. Physically it is linked to the throat, vocal cords, esophagus, mouth, teeth, thyroid and parathyroid glands, respiratory system. When weak, this may cause communication problems, an inability to express your feelings and ideas, withheld words, surrender to others. An overactive throat chakra may result in negative speaking, criticizing, domineering words, hyperactive attitude, over-reacting, and stubborn beliefs.

Purples

Purple is associated with the psychic and with intuition. Purples can be calming and soothing and can create a good atmosphere for meditation. Purple is a royal color, used by Kings and Queens for many years and as such is thought to be associated with wisdom and dignity.

Indigo

Indigo is said to combine reason with intuition and discipline, and is associated with the process of change and the healing crisis.

Indigo is seen by color therapists as cooling and astringent, and also as having an effect on vision, hearing, and smell.

Indigo can be linked to stagnation, mental fatigue, and striving without success.

Indigo the color of the 'third eye chakra. This chakra is located mid forehead, just above the eyes, and on the first cervical vertebra of the spine. It is a strong psychic center, associated with clairvoyance, the subconscious mind, intuition, creative imagination and psychic healing. In order for this chakra to work at its best, the heart chakra must be strong and balanced. Physically, this chakra is linked to the nervous system, skeletal system, pineal gland. When weak, this center may cause self-doubt, forgetfulness, and an inability to trust your instincts, headaches. If overactive, you may be oversensitive, spaced out, and experiencing psychic overload.

Violets

Violet is associated with good motives, spiritual aspirations, and prosperity.

Color therapists say it is calming in mental illness, reduces hunger, and controls irritability.

Violet's negative associations include over-opulence, snobbery, and prejudice.

Violet is the main color of the Crown chakra at the top of the head. It is associated with our feeling of "oneness" with the Universe, our spiritual wisdom, a final understanding, an alignment with our true inner spirit within. A weak crown chakra can cause a feeling of disconnection with the vital flow of life, uninspired, feeling misunderstood and practicing self-denial. Overactive, this may cause a disconnection with the earthly plane, being impractical, not connected with reality, over imaginative.

OMNI: ARE EXTRATERRESTRIALS STEERING US TO A ONE-WORLD RELIGION THROUGH CROP CIRCLES?

The ancient Chinese practice of feng shui (pronounced fung shway) is complex. It is perfectly suited to the garden, for feng shui is all about nature, and literally translates to "wind" and "water." It seeks to enhance our health, wealth and happiness through bringing the harmony and balance of nature into our environment. Feng shui makes us aware of what we feel as we pass through the garden. It attempts to explain the comfort, delight, unease or attraction we may have a hard time putting into words, while teaching how to create an environment that fosters or avoids such feelings.

Feng shui is the art of placement. A Chinese proverb says, "If you change your surroundings you can change your life." To those of us who constantly rearrange plants, this appears to be simple common sense. A useful feng shui principle is the imperative to remove any unhealthy or dying plants anywhere in the garden, especially in the area of health (located in the center of the garden).

The ideal is to follow the feng shui principle that all space is divided into areas of energy that correspond to areas of life, such as family, career, health and relationships. The goal is to enhance the flow of good energy and eliminate anything that blocks it. Feng shui consultants use a "Ba Gua," or kind of template, to map out the areas of energy and figure out ways to enhance them by using everything from colors to mirrors

The relationship area of the garden is healthy when it holds several pairs of things, when it includes a couple of frogs and a mirror that doubles what you see.

o The colorful, fragrant flowers at the front door attract chi to the health area of the garden. Adding wind chimes would help because chi responds to texture, color, scent and sound.

o The compost bins are ideally located in the wealth area, but it would be good to add some purple foliage or flowers (purple is thought to encourage wealth), and to toss a couple of coins in the hole when I plant them.

o Chi prefers no more than 10 steps to a home or garden. Chi is attracted to pathways wide enough for two people to walk side-by-side.

o Large, square paver-blocks on the ground and big-leafed plants like gunnera cause the chi to slow down and linger - and this is a good thing.

THE TRINITY CONNECTION

The glyphs at the corners were said to have parallels in alchemical signs, like this:

North - Sun, Sulfur

Southwest - Moon, Salt

Southeast (ratchet spiral) - Mercury, Quicksilver

The Trinity is a common link to almost everything we are seeing. It is a symbol that is far more ancient than Christianity. It is about the creation of man. It represents the fundamental unit of all consciousness and matter.

For example, the activity at Giza, Egypt involves the Trinity of Osiris/Isis/Horus. The Apollo moon landings were precisely timed so that the belt of Orion or the star Sirius were aligned at the horizon or at 19.5 degrees, the tetrahedral point found by Richard Hoagland's team in the geometry/mathematics of Mars. Those stars, of course, represented the Osiris and Isis. Hoagland also shows how the Mars monuments connect to the Giza monuments, and to the Barbury Castle pictogram.

Also, an overlay of the Cydonia region of Mars, matches point-for-point with the ancient sites in the Wessex triangle of Great Britain.

The message of the Trinity is very powerful in dreams. It is not recognized because the symbols are often one's own father and mother in the dreams, or the like. Other times it is one's supervisors from work, or something similar. There is a definite pattern that we have been documenting.

There is another great connection in the quatrains of Nostradamus. It is in Century 4, Quatrains 28-33.

C4:Q28

"When Venus will be covered by the Sun,
Under the splendor will be a hidden form:
Mercury will have exposed them to the fire,
Through warlike noise it will be insulted.

C4:Q29

The Sun hidden eclipsed by Mercury
Will be placed only second in the sky:
Of Vulcan Hermes will be made into food,
The Sun will be seen pure, glowing red and golden.

C4:Q30

Eleven more times the Moon the Sun will not want,
All raised and lowered by degree:

And put so low that one will stitch little gold:
Such that after famine plague, the secret uncovered.

C4:Q31

The Moon in the full of night over the high mountain,
The new sage with a lone brain sees it:
By his disciples invited to be immortal,
Eyes to the south. Hands in bosoms, bodies in the fire.

C4:Q32

In the places and times of flesh giving way to fish,
The communal law will be made in opposition:
It will hold strongly the old ones, then removed from the midst,
Loving of Everything in Common put far behind.

C4:Q33

Jupiter joined more to Venus than to the Moon
Appearing with white fulness:
Venus hidden under the whiteness of Neptune
Struck by Mars through the white stew."

This concerns the theories of alchemists about the sun (sulfur), the moon (salt), and Mercury (quicksilver). The glyphs on the corners of the triangle of Barbury are said to parallel these alchemical signs.

Alchemists work involved the attempt to transmuting elements, such as lead into gold, and finding a substance that gave eternal life. This became centered on cinnabar, the Hell Fire Stone, which is the ore of mercury, sulfuric sulfide. They were attempting to create a substance that would give "eternal life" in the physical.

There is a spiritual symbolism to this. This became centered on cinnabar, the "hell fire stone", which is red in color. This is mercuric sulfide (HgS), the only important ore of mercury. The symbolism of this is of reaching the Trinity level of the Christ-Self, and eternal life.

Century 4, Quatrain 31 says, "invited by his disciples to become immortal," so it seems related. "His body in the fire," matches a number of things. In Zechariah 3, Joshua is called 'a brand plucked from the fire." He and Zerubbabel seem to be related to the two olive trees in verse 4, which are related to Rev. 11:11. Isaiah 4:4 speaks of being cleansed by a spirit of judgment and burning. Eastern depictions show Kali seated upon a copulating couple on a lotus in fire. In Black Elk's vision, the Blue Man stands in flames where three streams meet, and is struck in the heart by Black Elk's lightning-tipped spear.

Nostradamus also said in C10, Q74 -

"The year of the great seventh number accomplished,
it will appear at the time of the games of slaughter,
not far from the age of the great millennium,
when the dead will come out of their graves."

(this seems to be a metaphor about the death/rebirth of changing, transforming).

The mythological Roman Mercury, of course, was the Greek Hermes, who is said to correspond to the Egyptian Thoth and the Babylonian Nebo. It may be significant that mercury and Hermes have both male and female aspects. The "Son" aspect in the Trnity is apparently more of a "Child" with both male and female aspects. The bright scholar and psychic, H.P. Blavatsky, traces this back to ancient Trinities. Adam/Eve were the first androgen, she claimed. It is significant that the Mercury/quicksilver was in the "Son" or "Child" position of this crop glyph.

She shows some basic forms of the Trinity. The first is a Father and Mother with a Son, who is androgen. Next, comes the Triple Male Trinity. They have female "Consorts," that are usually composited into one feminine Deity. Together, they are "The Perfect Four," In the Babylonian system, it is Anu, Bel, and Hoa (the moon). The feminine Deity is Mylitta or Ishtar. According to Blavatsky, the feminine Deity in the Christian Trinity is the Virgin Mary.

According to Sir John Haddington, it may be related to DNA. DNA, of course, is the code or pattern of man/mankind.

There were six steps on the ratchet/Mercury spiral of Barbury, which is coiled counter-clockwise from a small circle. The wheatstalks were also laid down in the counter-clockwise direction. There were straight-lined offsets in the spiral, making it like a ratchet shape. The angle from the center of the triangle to the southwest corner was at 120 degrees. From that point to the center of the ratchet, it was 108 degrees, a mythical / Gematrian number. 120 is a tetrahedral point. 120 x 108 = 12,960, six raised to the fourth power times ten, and half the precession number. Divided by the six arcs, it is 2,160, six to the third times ten, and the number of years in one Zodiac Age.

There was an additional clue in the date the pattern appeared, July 17, 1991.

Read Genesis 8:4, where the Ark landed on the 17th day of the 7th month.

Helena P Blavatsky tells how the Patriarchs represent Zodiac signs. For example, Judah is Leo. In Genesis 49:9, he is called a lion's whelp, and he stoops down like a lion and lioness. (i. e., like a Sphinx). Noah is Pisces. These are strong clues that our Age is coming to an end, and Aquarius is near. (if not already begun). The Sphinx may well represent the same thing, that is, the Ages from Leo through Pisces, and the beginning of Aquarius.

James Churchward wrote, "An equilateral triangle with an eye within symbolizes the Deity looking out from heaven. An equilateral triangle symbolized the Creator, and, as the Creator dwells in Heaven, the triangle must necessarily symbolize heaven also; for, where the Lord is, there is Heaven.

I find this verified among the Egyptian symbols, as the glyph shows. Here we find the Monotheistic Symbol of the Deity within the triangle - within Heaven. Wherever or whenever the equilateral triangle is met with in ancient writings or inscriptions, it is either in reference to the Triune Godhead, or Heaven, or both.

From "The Book of Knowledge, The Keys of Enoch" on page 54, we read:

"And if we examine the "Book of Genesis" involving the seven days of creation, we see that the six fields of light come together so that on the seventh day, the transmutation can be added to the physical chemistry of life. Therefore, on the seventh aeon of Light, the races which were evolved during the first six aeons of time are superseded by the Seventh Ray, which is the planting of our Adamic household of Kimah (the Pleiades) and Kesil (Orion) intelligence on the planet as a witness to the evolving nations." (Job 38:31-33)

"Canst thou bind the sweet influences of Pleiades, or loose the bands of Orion? Canst thou bring forth Mazzaroth in his season? Or canst thou guide Arcturus with his sons? Knowest thou the ordinances of heaven? Canst thou set the domnion thereof in the earth?"

At the time of Confucius, the Chinese Sage, about 500 B. C., in place of the triangle the Chinese used a glyph in the form of the present-day capital Y. This they called: 'the Great Term,' 'the Great Unite,' 'the Great Y.' 'The Y has neither body nor shape, all that has body and shape was made by that which has no shape. The Great Term or Great Unite comprehends three - One in three - and three in One.'"

The Barbury Castle triangular formation has a Y-shape inside of it. The Chinese Y has a similar meaning to the downward-pointing, central triangle of the Sri Yantra. It is related to the feminine aspect of Deity, and related symbolically to the 'yoni', which means vagina.

The triangle glyph with the letters A, U and M, in the corners, is more than 2,300 years old. The ancient Hindu book, Manava dharma Sastra, states: "In the beginning the infinite only existed called Aditi. Infnite dwelt A U M whose name must precede all prayers and invocations."

James Churchward speaks of the A U M, "A U M conveys identically the same meaning and conception as the Mysterious Writing and Niven's Mexican tablet No. 2379. The difference between these and A U M is in the form of the writing. The Hindu A U M is written in alphabetical symbols, which reads:

A - Ahau   Masculine - Father
U -   Feminine - Mother- She
M - Mehen   The engendered - The Son - Man

The concepts conveyed in The Tantric Way speak of the vibration "as sound." This seems to be related to the chant, "Om," or "Aum".

This crop formation represents at least three things:

1. The Trinity

2. The smallest particle of Creation, which builds up into gestalts of the units, to the larger creation. The Creator is within each unit.

3. A cycle of time from Leo through Pisces, i.e. and the beginning of Aquarius.

This may match "the year of the great seventh number accomplished" not far from the millennium in Nostradamus Century 10, Quatrain 74.

About six months after I realized the number connection in Barbury, a man at work told me a dream. He was in an airliner driven on a highway by a water treatment plant operator named, Andy. There was a detour because of construction. Then, he was with his boss, an engineer, and a woman. They were planning to install a new transformer at the water treatment plant, under a grill. The woman whispered something into the engineer's ear.

This is a form of the Trinity, I have found a number of times in dreams. It is the Triple Male Trinity with the combined consorts as the single feminine Deity, or First Power. Together, they make the Perfect Four. The (real life) boss's name in this dream translates to "the guardian of knowledge).

I asked if the dreamer knew which highway he was on. He said, yes, it was the highway that runs from Oakdale (California, about 20 miles from his home), toward Yosemite. That section of highway is where highways 120 and 108 run together!

Another interesting note about this particular crop circle is the length of the "ratchet" or Mercury spiral which was 333 ft.. It was in the position of "The Son" of the Trinity. Many people see the number 333 on clocks quite often. Interestingly enough, 3:33 a.m. is a common time that UFO abductees report waking up and recalling special dreams.

The total square footage of the circles was 3168, a number associated with "Lord Jesus Christ" by the early Christians.

The son in the Trinity is often represented by an androgen, having male and female attributes. Mercury, and his Greek counterpart, Hermes, have this. One representation is a key and keyhole, which appeared on the west and east of the 1992 Dharmic Wheel (or Charm Bracelet0 crop formation. At the center was a circle inside a quartered circle, which Michael Green said is the god, Bel, the Light behind the Light. Bel was a name given to Marduk, which means, "Lord." He was also a son in a Trinity.

The Dharmic Wheel formation *(see facing page)* is about human spiritual development. It is similar to Indo-Aryan symbols, called "The Great Turning" in prehistoric Europe. In the East it was called, "The Dharmic Wheel".

The structure has eight symbols of Being and Becoming on the points of the directions. In the center of the formation was a ring with a dot inside, which symbolizes Deity. It is further defined as the manifested state of God by being quartered.

The symbols on the outer ring represent a certain energy, vibration or spiritual state, which eventually leads to apotheosis. (elevation to divine status: deification)

Starting on the south glyph, and moving in a counter-clockwise direction, the glyphs have the following mythical names and meanings:

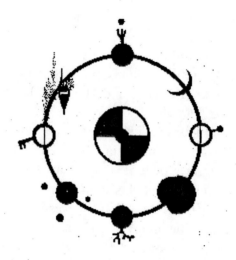

DHARMIC WHEEL

1. South - The antlers of Cernunnos - the role of the Animal Powers in the physical development of mankind.

1. Southeast - Modron - The Earth in the nurturing role of the archetypal Mother. This is the energy of consciousness.

3. East - Dagda - Procreative power, a sexual glyph, the mahadiva. This speaks of the spiritual conception.

4. Northeast - Sulis - The crescent moon which constitutes the womb of spirituality and the individuation of the personality.

5. North - Taranis - His wheel, with the three-fingered hand of blessing, which is also a claw, for this is the energy of conflict between the personality, soul and spirit. It represents the confrontation between the Soul and Personality.

6. Northwest - Lugh - Archetype of inspired knowledge. Note: This symbol did not appear as would be expected in a Dharmic Wheel, because the formation was positioned in such a way that a water-through (for cattle) was located at that point on the ring. In some photographs of the formation, the area appears dark because the water made the plants greener in that portion of the field. It could be that the pattern was positioned in this way for a purpose. The "water" and perhaps the "cattle," are symbolically related to our "inspired (or uninspired) knowledge" at this time. Michael Green felt that Lugh had lost his symbol due to the water-through, which destabilized the energies.

7. West - The ring and key of Mapon - The Divine Youth symbolizing the energies of the spiritual being who unlocks the door to the Mysteries for others.

8. Southwest - The place of Donn - The triadic symbol of Spirit, Soul and Personality brought together as one Unity. The Place of Donn is the archetype of death and transformation.

At this point, spiritual maturity has been fully achieved. Further incarnations on the Dharmic Wheel are then unnecessary. The transformed Spirit of Light moves to the Center, symbolized by Bel, for further development in a different sphere of reality.

We received a gracious e-mail from Gerald D'Aoust, a resident of Canada. He wrote:
"In this little paper I will very swiftly explain about the basic Buddhist metaphysics of the 3 bodies of the Buddhas and you will very rapidly understand the processes of the transmigration of the soul in its different bodies with a little bit of theory along with a bit of illustrated applied science with an example of the past and one of the present.
The Buddhist trinity is known as Tri-kaya where the word Kaya means Body ...so their Trinity is known as Tri-body ... referring to the 3 bodies of the Buddha.
The Buddhists say that the Buddha knew some 550 of previous lives which number, I think, could have been slightly exaggerated up a little.
Nevertheless, the Buddha was aware of several lives - and you cannot establish a religion based on reincarnation if you are not aware of different earlier lives and incidentally the mystery of rebirth is present within all religions and Christianity, which book (Bible) is filled with 256 dreams, is not an exception.

The Tri-body of the Buddhas consists of 3 bodies, namely:

- The Dharma-kaya
- The Sambhoga-kaya
- The Nirmana-kaya

all of these animated by the same unique atma .. or soul or mind.

-The Dharma-kaya is said to be the Law-Body, which is self existent and everlasting and has been termed as essential. It is the first body.

- The Sambhoga-kaya is said to be the Reflected Wisdom adorned Body! And they say that it is represented in plural form as the Celestial Jinas known also as Victors or Buddhas of the Past. These are said to shine in darkness ... which is the reason why they are called adorned ... they usually have a halo around their heads and all the rest of the enlightened gear.
- The Nirmana-kaya is called the practical or changeable body.

The Buddha's mind or soul, whatever you want to call his animating principle or breath of life, the thing that thinks inside the Buddha's Nirmana-kaya has access to all these other bodies.
It works like this for you too ... because we are all made the same.
Illumination is latent in everyone, said the Buddha, you know ... and it don't cost nothing in electricity. No monthly bills! "
In the year 2001, the Trinity seemed to be a rather common theme. Here are some of the prominent crop glyphs that point at the Trinity.

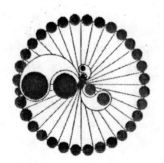

HACKPEN HILL, WILTSHIRE
Reported 20 July, 2003

Berwick Bassett, nr Avebury, Wiltshire.
Reported 9th June, 2001

West Kennett, nr Avebury, Wiltshire Reported 21st June, 2001

Folly Barn, nr Liddington, Wiltshire.
Reported 24th June, 2001

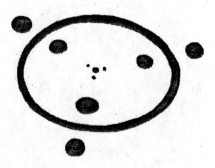

Borstal nr. Rochester, Kent.
Reported 25th June.

This is not the first time the Trinity Crop Formation has been shown to us by the circle-makers, nor is it the first we've written about it. However, since there seems to be a repetitive theme shown here so early in the year, it seems more important than perhaps we've given notice before.

TREE OF LIFE

Two very significant crop circle formations appeared at Barbury Castle, England in May 1997. They seemed to reveal extremely important information. One of the formations was the Kabalistic Tree of Life.

The crop formation is pictured on the left. The depiction on the right is one version of the ancient Tree of Life. The Tree of Life, of course, is mentioned many times in the Bible, from the beginning of the Book of Genesis to the last part of the Book of Revelation. One who eats from this Tree, according to the bible, is given "eternal life." The diagram of the Tree of Life is part of an ancient tradition called "kabala." Other spellings of the word include: kabbala, cabala, cabbala, quabala, and qabbalah. This is generally known as a special Hebrew tradition, the occult philosophy of certain Jewish rabbis, especially in the middle Ages, based on a mystical interpretation of the Scriptures. Many scholars believe that the tradition is much older; that it traces back to the ancient Egyptians and Sumerians.

Connections to Ancient Sumeria

Over one hundred years ago, clay tablets were found in present day Iraq. They were artifacts with Cuneiform writings and pictographic carvings, left by the ancient people of that region. The Assyrian and Babylonian empires were located in that area long ago, but an even more ancient one preceded them, called Sumer, which in the Bible is called "Land of Shine'ar." According to scholar, Zecharia Sitchin, in Divine Encounters (page 7) -

Sumer (the biblical Shine'ar) was the land where the first known and fully documented civilization sprang up after the Deluge, appearing suddenly and all at once some six thousand years ago.

Some of the pictographic carvings have depictions similar to the Kabalistic Tree of Life. The oldest story in history, The Epic of Gilgamesh, was also found. Gilgamesh was a king, who was part god. He traveled to a far place, looking for the plant or tree that gave eternal life.

The Meaning of the Tree of Life

The Kabalistic Tree is sometimes called The Sephirotic Tree of Life. The circles or spheres are called sephiroth. A single circle or sphere is called a sephira. The teachings about the Kabalistic Tree of Life are very deep and complex. The ten spheres and 22 paths of The Tree generally represent the nature of the forces behind Creation on all levels, from microscopic to macrocosmic.

The Tarot Cards are also associated with The Tree. The cards were invented by people who traveled and wanted to spread the word about the Kabalistic Tree of Life without looking like they were preaching a new religion and get killed for their efforts. The symbols on the Tarot Cards are all very significant and it takes a great deal of study to know exactly what they mean in Kabalistic terms.

Some crop circle researchers said that the Tree of Life crop formation was suspect of being hoaxed because the plants were not as neatly laid down as in other formations, and two of the pathways were kinked. Others argued that the kinked pathways may have been part of the message. The great Barbury Castle triangle / tetrahedron of 1991 also had a bent pathway, and the central circle and rings were offset from center, yet most researchers believe it was one of the most significant "real" crop formations.

The Related 1997 Crop Formation

Another formation appeared nearby that may be related. It was similar to a number of other crop formations that have appeared in recent years. The design is based on a ring of six interlocking circles. In the formation that appeared with the Tree of Life, the plants were laid down in a manner that formed a pinwheel-like design, with six crescent moon-like shapes.

BARBURY CASTLE Nr WROUGHTON, WILTSHIRE - April 1997

Two Related 1991 Crop Formations

In retrospect, a very astute observation was put forward in an article by crop circle researcher, Mark Styles. He pointed out that the 1991 Barbury Castle triangular crop circle formation was very similar to the lower triad of the Kabalistic Tree of Life.

He presented an equally astute theory regarding the Mandelbrot Set crop circle formation, which also appeared in 1991, on August 11. He showed that the Mandelbrot Set formation is similar to the Kabalistic Tree of Life, except for the top circle, which is Keter, the Crown, the One Source is "missing." He suggested that this may mean that "Keter is moving into Daat."

Daat is said to be a secret, hidden, eleventh sephira. It is depicted as a circle formed by dashed lines below the main triad of three circles at the top. It is said to be the secret of the transition of Binah, the upper-left sephira corresponding to the Mother aspect of the Godhead, from the Dark Sterile Mother (Ama) to the Bright Fertile Mother (Aima), also know as Marah, the Great Sea. Marah is the root of Mary. It is the concept of a virgin becoming a mother by the power of the Holy Spirit.

The "hidden" sephira called Daat means "knowledge." The idea of moving into Daat, then, may indicate that God has or will move into a position to transmit new knowledge to mankind.

The 1999 Menorah Crop Circle Formation

Another formation now appears to be related. Near the end of May 1999, the Menorah crop circle formation appeared. Again, the location was near Barbury Castle and the plants were oilseed rape (canola). The eleven circles in the formation strongly suggest the Kabalistic Tree of Life, with the "hidden sephria," Daat, included.

Connection to the Belt of Orion

A group of German researchers made a convincing argument about the bent pathway in the triangular 1991 Barbury Castle formation. By deciphering a number of formations, they theorized that a message was being given about star patterns in the area of the sky known as the "Winter Hexagon." Further, a triangle was indicated in the stars of Orion, which are within the Winter Hexagon. The top of the triangle is located at the left-most star in Orion's Belt, known as Zeta Orionis. Another star is located near the edge of the imaginary triangle in the sky, and it is in the exact position of the bend or kink in the Barbury Castle triangular crop formation. The triangle in the sky is at an angle of 19.5 degrees.

A coincidence happened concerning the above information around 1993, when I read a news story shortly after reading of the German group's research. The article reported that astronomers were baffled by some strange X-ray bursts coming from a major star in the heavens. They were coming from the left-most star in Orion's Belt, Zeta Orionis.

Connection to the Great Pyramids

The location of the star and the angle of the sky triangle are especially significant for a number of reasons. The research of Richard Hoagland, Robert Bauval, Adrian Gilbert, Graham Hancock, and others indicate that the three great pyramids at Giza represent the stars of Orion's Belt, and that the passageway from the King's chamber pointed to those stars. The stars represented the God, Osiris. The Queen's chamber passageway is thought to have pointed to the bright star, Sirius, representing the Goddess Isis.

Moon Landing Connections

Richard Hoagland discovered, incredibly, that all of the Apollo moon landings were precisely timed to the positions of the same stars. Either the Belt Stars of Orion or the Star Sirius were aligned with the horizon or at 19.5 degrees at the exact time of the landings. These facts are beyond accidental coincidence, Hoagland claims. It is unlikely that people working for NASA could plan such events so precisely. It seems that certain human events are influenced by a higher, other-dimensional intelligence.

The Mars Connection
Sacred Geometry and
Hyperdimensional Mathematics

The geometry and hyperdimensional mathematics found in the monuments on Mars , according to Richard Hoagland and his associates, are related to the Giza Pyramids, to the ancient sites in England where most of the crop formations have been appearing, and to the Barbury Castle crop circle formation of 1991. One of the conclusions is that an energy exists within planetary spheres, including the sun and stars, by which they are created from another dimension. The energy inside the planetary spheres is shaped like two interlaced tetrahedrons. In a two-dimensional representation, this is like a Star of David inside a circle. One tetrahedron touches the surface of the planetary sphere at the north-pole, and the other touches at the south-pole. Three points of each tetrahedron touch the surface of the planetary sphere at 19.5 degrees north and south.

Background

Early in my dream-coincidence experiences in 1990, the "tree" symbol appeared in a number of forms. This includes the dreams of others as well as my own. After being directed to the Bible, I realized that the "tree" symbolism is there from beginning to end - from the two trees in the Garden of Eden, to the Tree of Life standing in the center of The New Jerusalem in Revelation.

In the Book of Daniel, king Nebuchadnezzar had a dream of a great tree that was cut and banded, causing a period of insanity for seven years. I had a coincidence, relating to the sinking of the Titanic in 1912, about this symbolism, that seemed to confirm a concept developed by a religious group. The seven years are prophetic years of 360 years each, for a total of 2,520 years. Calculated from the destruction of the Temple at Jerusalem, this indicates the year 1914 as the end of the period of insanity. A great world-wide stress began at that time with World War One. Several years later, I learned that 2,520, is part of a very ancient number code.

In early 1991, I was given a copy of 'The Book of Knowledge, The Keys of Enoch.' It was written by scientist, Dr. James J. Hurtak, after he was visited by the Light Being, Enoch, in 1973. The very first paragraph in the Prologue struck me as being quite meaningful:

"Beloved - The Father's Limitless Light is being poured forth and our Tree of Life is being activated. Love from the highest levels is penetrating the planetary veils. From the higher worlds without limit or end, the emissaries of Light come in vast number to advance the foundations of life and refashion new worlds. They bring with them Light which is greater than a thousand suns to awaken our next stage of evolution and to assist in bringing us into a purer form of superluminal Light."

The book is full of Kabalistic terms. Kabalism is very ancient and pre-Christian. It is an esoteric Jewish tradition. Dr. Hurtak's book explains Kabballah and the Sephiroth in new ways. With Sacred Names the Sephiroth = Tree of Life. He also speaks of triads and Trinities, saying that we will become Trinitized Powers. Orion, called in Hebrew, "Kesil," is referenced to Job 38:31, and is said to be the Central Control for all the higher programs of development connected with the astro-chemical networks and reprogramming life synthesis in our universe. Orion will emanate the "gnosis" (knowledge) as the world transformation takes place.

Pages 35 and 36 of the book have photographs of pyramidal formations on Mars taken by Mariner 9 in 1971. Enoch told Dr. Hurtak that these are part of a grid network in our solar system. The earth also has a grid. There will be a grid shift and alignment between the two grids, as the earth changes unfold. This will happen when the earth enters an electromagnetic null zone.

I corresponded with Geoffrey Farthing, the secretary of the Blavatsky Trust in England. I had found an amazing number of connections in H.P. Blavatsky's, Isis Unveiled, volume 2. I explained to Geoffrey that dreams and crop formations seemed to be related to Blavatsky's concepts, and that a Great Change seemed to be near. He sent me his book, Deity, Cosmos and Man, which gives an outline of Esoteric Science, as presented in the vast works of H.P. Blavatsky.

On page 135 of the book, Geoffrey speaks of "The Builders," who build, or rather rebuild every "system" after the "Night." To quote:

The "Builders" are representatives of the first "Mind-Born" entities, therefore of the primeval Rishi-Prajapatis; also of the Seven great Gods of Egypt, of which Osiris is the chief; of the Seven Amshaspends of the Zoroastrians, with Ormazed as their head; or the "Seven Spirits of the Face"; the Seven Sephiroth separated from the first Triad, etc., etc.

Geoffrey also told me that Blavatsky associates the Sephirotic Tree of Life with everything else in her works, which involve myths and religions from around the world.

When the Sephirotic Tree of Life appeared in the crops in 1997, I found it to be quite profound and meaningful. Unlike most of the crop formations, this pattern is well known; there is no question about what it is. As with other formations, there is some doubt as to whether the formation was a man-made hoax, or a "real" formation created by a non-human source. If it was man-made, then it evidently was an inspired crop pattern and still of great significance. But, if it was produced by a non-human source, then it has an even larger magnitude of significance.

Debbie Pardoe on "The Tree Of Life"

Debbie's article appeared in the "SC" #65, the monthly journal published by the Sussex branch of the Center of Crop Circle Studies, which I received on June 20, 1997. It starts with a quotation:

"'The Book of The Law' presumes the existence of a body of initiates pledged to watch over the welfare of mankind and to communicate its own wisdom, little by little, in the measure of man's capacity to receive it. "

Aleister Crowley

Debbie goes on to say that in 1904, Aleister Crowley proclaimed the Advent of the New Aeon. A discarnate intelligence, "Aiwaz," dictated the code for the coming age. The message for the New Aeon was -

"Do What Thou Wilt Shall Be The Whole Of The Law.
Love is the Law, Love Under Will.
Follow your True Will. "

This was taken by the existing Victorian society of the time to be evil. Aleister realized that the world was not ready for the ideas, saying that a time would come when the revelations in 'The Book of The Law' would be understood. Debbie says that time is now.

The word for the New Aeon is Thelema, a Greek word meaning "True Will." The Greek system of Gematria involved assigning numbers to letters and words. Both Thelema and Aiwaz add to the number 93, the number of The New Aeon. The Greek word for love, "Agape," also adds to 93. Significantly, love indicates the nature of True Will.

Sometimes coincidences are extremely significant. Here is one I must mention in regards to Gematrian numbers and crop circles.

Aleister first received the message related above 93 years prior to 1997, in April of 1904. The appearance of the Tree of Life crop formation, almost exactly 93 years later, cannot be a coincidence. The mean distance between the Earth and the Sun is 93 million miles, that 93 meters is the average diameter of Stonehenge (the bank/ditch), and that 93 was indicated in the "DNA crop formation of 1996. The formation, which had a double-helix design, had 89 total circles, but four of them were overlapped, indicating 93. This was pointed out last year in an "SC" article, and it was further noted that human DNA is associated with the number 93.

(Note: In January 1996, I wrote a long letter to Barry Reynolds, assistant editor of SC. I spoke of Gematrian numbers, not of the Greek variety, but much more ancient. I enclosed a letter of mine that was published in Carl Munck's "The Code" newsletter, where I specifically mentioned the number 648. I also informed Barry of my friend Jeff's dream of a spiral staircase with maintenance mechanics on each rung with their toolboxes. I suggested that the dream seemed to confirm the "DNA repair" theory spoken of by the Mayan Daykeeper, Hunbatz Men. The "DNA" crop formation appeared the following summer, and it was 648 feet in length.)

Part of Aleister's work involved assimilating mystical teachings from many cultures. These were put into a volume of tables titled, "777." The key to the system was the Quabalistic diagram known as The Tree of Life. It is said to be like a blueprint of creation that is essential to understanding the occult correspondences given in 777.

Debbie Pardoe said "Qabalah" is correctly spelt with a "Q," (rather than with a "K") and is a Hebrew word meaning "to receive" (i.e. knowledge). Greek Gematria gives the word the number 137. (spelt backwards - HLBQ - H=5, L=30, B=2, Q=100). The Hebrew word for "wheel" also adds to 137.

The two crop formations that appeared at Barbury Castle early in the summer of 1997 had "coincidental" connections to the concepts of Aleister Crowley. The "Wheel"-like formation was located at grid reference SU 157 777, and the Tree of Life at SU 170 777 (Others give the Tree of Life reference as 170770).

Debbie says that the Tree of Life is like a map defining Creation and the origins of Spirituality. There are ten Sephiroth/spheres of existence and 22 connecting pathways. The Hebrew alphabet has 22 letters.

(Note: In The Book of Knowledge, The Keys of Enoch, Dr. Hurtak explained that the 22 Hebrew letters, which are called, "Fire Letters," are used as a code in creation. I had one of my strange coincidences about this.

My most important day of dreams was on October 18, 1990. While visiting relatives in 1991, I read an article about the great leap of Bob Beamon in the 1968 Olympic games. Some strange dreams and coincidences in 1990 had caused me to speculate that the leap was a symbolic event related to the moon landing in 1969, and the words, "One giant leap for mankind." The article pointed out that the great leap of

Bob Beamon took place on October 18, 1968. I realized that was exactly 22 years prior to the date of my most important dreams. By then, I had read about the 22 Hebrew "Fire Letters."

When I arrived back home, I found that an accident had happened. A fire started on my desk as a result of kids playing with matches. My son put out the fire, before it caused much damage. Only parts of envelopes containing correspondence were burned a bit aground the edges. It struck me as coincidental because one could say that they were "Fire Letters!")

Debbie goes on to explain that there are also 22 Tarot cards that make up the Major Arcana. Each is assigned to a path on the Tree. The spheres/sephiroth on the left side of the Tree are feminine and those on the right are masculine. The ones in the middle row indicate a balance of the duality attributes. Two of the sephiroth on the sides are called HOD and NETZACH, representing Mercury and Venus, or the Head and the Heart, or the Intellect and Emotions. The lateral path joining the two is represented by the Tarot card known as The Tower. This card depicts people falling from a tower and being struck by lightning.

Debbie suggests that this may be related to Aleister Crowley's "True Will." When a person follows his or her True Will, it feels right in both the heart and head.

She astutely points out that the New Aeon is Aquarius, which symbolizes a rebirth of the human spirit, where water, or Divine Wisdom, is poured out freely for all mankind.

At this point, we must try, as sensitively as possible, to point out that the symbology of the people jumping out of the twin towers on 9/11/01 points to this exact message. Not only did they use their 'True Will' to jump from the towers, their sacrifice for mankind also brought about 'Divine Wisdom' from much of humanity.

Another interesting coincidence is that 9/11/01 was the 254th day of the year and Bob Beamon wore number 254 as he made his great leap in the 1968 Olympic Games.

Debbie mentions that at a meeting, Barry Renolds pointed out that two of the paths in the Tree of Life crop formation were kinked, and that the two paths correspond to Paths 15 and 28 on the Tree of Life. Tarot card number XVII, The Star, is on Path 15, and card IV, The Emperor, is on Path 28. Card 0, The Fool, is on Path 11, card I, The Magician, is on Path 12, card II, The Priestess on Path 13, and card III, The Empress on Path 14. It follows that card IV, The Emperor should be on Path 15, but Aleister Crowley chose to swap the correspondences of Paths 15 and 28, which just

happen to be the two Pathways that were kinked in the crop formation!
Debbie concludes, "Coincidence? I think not."

Numbers, Stars, and Chakras

32, 128, and the 8-Pointed Star

Another number associated with the Tree of Life is 32, which combines the ten Sephiroth and the 22 Paths. I had some coincidences with the number 32. It's another long story, but part of it involved the eight-pointed star. It is related to a number of symbols, including those associated with Horus, Bel Marduke, Kin, and Apollo. The first two are sons of Trinities. The star is also related to Navaho sand paintings with four couples around a square, and to the eight people aboard Noah's Ark. It represents humanity bonded in Union in the future. The star is also formed by eight heart-shapes put together, which I call the Unity of Hearts.

A crop formation did appear that had a cross-shape with a heart at each end. Also, at least two single heart shapes have appeared as crop formations. The symbolism may be related to the word, "concord," which means "hearts together." An example could have been the sphere of light that flew by the Concord airliner during its first flight. These symbols are especially important to me, because of my primary theory about the Great Change being a leap to the Heart chakra level of consciousness evolution by humanity en masse.

The eight-pointed star, in my theory, represents a pair from each quarter, and the pairs are single humans with the dual aspects. Each point of the star has the number 16, and each pair has 32, for a total of 128 for the entire star. The number 128 has been part of many incredible coincidences. When it is multiplied by nine, the total is 1,152, a Gematrian number, meaning "Witness." It can be derived from the cycle of time number, 432, as 4 x 32 = 128.

One form of the star is found in quilting designs. Using four colors, there are a total of 128 diamond shapes in the pattern, 16 in each section. The quilting design is called, The Lone Star, The Texas Star, or The Bethlehem Star.

The order of the Masons also have a 32nd degree level.

The Book of Knowledge, The Keys of Enoch, also mentions the number 32 on page 233, as the number of times the Divine Name is employed Sin the creation story at the beginning of Genesis in The Torah. This represents the 32 paths by means of which "Hokhmah" becomes manifest. Through the 32 paths, the soul is clothed into the physical body. The unification of 32 chemical building blocks in a human being are involved with receiving the "Lak Boymer" (33rd degree), the Pillar of Light. Also involved are the 22 letters of the Divine signature, and this is said to be related to Exodus 33:22.

Further, it is said that this is why Jesus manifested the Christ in his 33rd year.

A coincidence happened concerning this in 1991. I received a letter from my nephew, David, telling of his recurring dreams of a shaft of light coming up from the ground. People were stepping into it. In his last dream, he was alone, standing naked before the shaft of light. He received the message, "Step into the light." Shortly after reading David's letter, the coincidence happened. On my way to work, I found a newsletter in the mailbox from John Price, called, "The Quartus Report." I took it to work with me. At break time, I had the unusual urge to read the letters to the editor first. One of the letters told of a meditation where a Pillar of Light was seen, and the message was given, "Step into the Light." It was shortly after this that I found the above passage in 'The Book of Knowledge, The Keys of Enoch. '

In the years following 1997 a number of eight-fold crop formations appeared, including eight-pointed star patterns.

Flower and Star Symbols

The pin-wheel-like crop formation with six crescent shapes that appeared with the Tree of Life formation would seem to fit with Tiphareth on the Tree of Life. This sephira is assigned the number six, and from its central location in the Tree, there are eight paths connecting to the other Sephiroth. The position on the central pillar is said to show balance between the left and right pillars, which represent various attributes associated with feminine and masculine. The basic shape of the formation is quite similar to ancient sun symbols, therefore, the formation may have indicated a balance of sun and moon or masculine and feminine attributes.

I drew some similar shapes on that special day of October 18, 1990. The one with six parts, with a six-petal daisy-like flower inside, was like a closed aperture, like those on a camera. The North Sun symbol on the 1991 Barbury Castle formation is similar. In another dream-coincidence, the aperture opened, and the Seventh Ray came in, causing every particle of creation to change. In 1996, a similar crop formation appeared next to Silbury Hill, that may have a similar symbolism.

The perimeter circles in the 1996 formation had a smaller radius than the primary circle, which resulted in a Star Of David-like design appearing in the center.

This has a similarity to the glyph for the Heart chakra, which has a twelve-petal Lotus flower, with a Star Of David inside.

The years following the Tree of Life formation saw the appearance of a number of aperture-type crop circle formations.

The Chakra Connection

Prior to the appearance of the Tree of Life crop circle formation, Ashley Rye communicated with me about The Tree of Life, which I found quite informative. The following is a quote from the writing:

"The second Triad is formed by the fourth, fifth, and sixth sephiroth: Chesed (Mercy), Geburah (Judgment), and Tiphareth (Beauty). The union between the Supernal Mother and the Supernal Father by means of Daat gave birth to Mercy, which is also called Love. Thus we see how on the archetypal planes the union of the male and female principles gives rise to that which on the material plane is the most sublime feeling man can experience. Mercy emanates Judgment, which is also known as Strength. Chesed or Mercy is, as we have seen, also a Father image, while Geburah is a Mother image, strong and severe. From this "Strong Love" that is the union of Chesed and Geburah is born Tiphareth or Beauty, the sixth sephira, which is also known as The Son, and has the image of a child as one of its symbols. Tiphareth is situated in the Middle Pillar, directly underneath the sphere of Daat. We see therefore how through the realization that is Daat, the Supernal Mother, Binah, "gave birth" to Chesed, Mercy or Love, which then united with Geburah, Strength, to "give birth" to Tiphareth, The Son. This triad symbolizes the evolution of ideas con-ceived in the archetypal matrix of the Three Supernals. "

Ashley's e-mail also suggested a "chakra" connection to the Tree of Life:

"The three pillars of the Tree of Life are comparable to Ida, Shushumna, and Pingala of the Yoga system, where Shushumna is the channel of ascent of kundalini, placed between the male and female potencies of Ida and Pingala. The three pillars may be also likened to Yin and Yang, the female and male principles of Chinese philosophy, with Tao (the way) being analogous to the Middle Pillar. "

Many crop circle formations may be related to the chakra system. See the section on crop circles as chakra section. 'SRI YANTRA'

Back in 1992, when the "chakra" message first started with me, my friend, Pablo, made an observation that seems quite significant now. He suggested that the two olive trees that stand up after 3 1/2 days in Revelation 11:11 correspond to Ida and

Pingala. In Zechariah 4, the two olive trees stand to the left and right of the golden lampstand with a bowl on top of it with seven lamps.

The bottom sphere of the Tree of Life, Malkuth-Kingdom-Earth is said to correspond to the first chakra. The second chakra is represented by the next sphere upward on the central pillar, Yesod-Foundation-Moon. The third chakra is represented by the feminine-masculine pair of spheres called Hod-Glory and Nezah-Victory, the two that are joined by the Tower Card pathway. The forth chakra, the heart chakra, is represented by the central sphere of Tiphareth-Beauty. As mentioned above, the pin-wheel crop circle formation that appeared with the Tree of Life formation seems to represent Tiphareth, and therefore the forth-heart chakra.

The sons of Jacob who became the Twelve Tribes are said to have a correspondence with the various spheres of the Tree of Life. It is Joseph, the eleventh son of Jacob, who wore the "Coat of Many Colors," who is said to correspond to Tiphareth.

This seemed to be confirmed by an incredible crop circle formation that appeared a few weeks prior to the 9/11/01 terrorist attacks. With a total of 409 circles, it became known as the Mega Glyph:

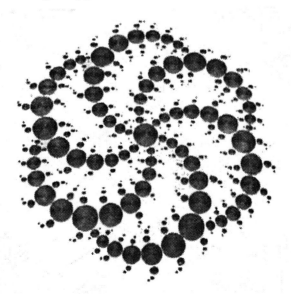

MILK HILL, Nr ALTON BARNES, WILTSHIRE- August 2001

It's general Flower of Life type of design is quite similar to the pin-wheel

109

formation that appeared with the Tree of Life formation in 1997. This number, 409, immediately struck me as related to the number 49S, or 7 x 7. With the ancient numbers, the zeros are said to be ignored in terms of the basic meaning. Right away, I made the calculation 409 = 360 + 49. Incorporating the very ancient number 360 in this case seemed to confirm the "49" message.

Steven Clementson posted some key information from Norma Smith on a web page on the internet.

Norma pointed out that the number 409 is the alphanumeric sum of the names of the seven colors of the spectrum. This system uses the form, A=1, B=2, and so forth. This is the list:

        RED = 27
        ORANGE = 60
        YELLOW = 92
        GREEN = 49
        BLUE = 40
        INDIGO = 58
        VIOLET = 83

        27 + 60 + 92 + 49 + 40 + 58 + 83 = 409

Norma noted:

"49 = Green (7 + 18 + 5 + 5 + 14), which is the very middle color of this color spectrum template. It's as though the 49 is a midpoint for pairing the other numbers/colors in a lambda shape . . . "

a)..............49...........................b).....................Green
.............92........40......................................Yellow..........Blue
.......60.....................58......................Orange.....................Indigo
27...................................83..............Red...............................Violet

A diagram on the page shows a Star of David drawn between points of the crop formation pattern.

It was not mentioned on the page that the colors listed are the chakra colors in order from first (red) to seventh (violet), and that "GREEN" (49) represents the heart chakra.

"Coincidentally," Aleister Crowley" predicted that an alphanumeric code would be found in the English alphabet. His book, "777" lists many English words and the numbers associated with them. But, Aleister added them in a different way. He assigned the sequence as A=0, B=1, and so forth up to Z =25. Perhaps the Mega Glyph crop formation is indicating a correction.

Also coincidental, there were 777 New York City firemen killed in the line of duty up to 9/11/01. On that single horrible day, 343 firemen were killed. That famous ancient number was found in the crop circle formations years ago. It is 7 x 7 x 7, showing the total spiritual evolutionary cycles of humanity.

The idea that Joseph with his Coat of Many Colors is assigned to the sphere of Tiphareth, representing the heart chakra, certainly fits perfectly this these revelations.

The number seven, of course, is perhaps the most important number in the Bible. Significantly, twice seven appears a number of times in the story of Jacob and his eleventh son, Joseph. Jacob had to work seven years to gain his first wife. He had to wait another seven years for the woman he loved. Joseph was the first son of that marriage.

Joseph later interpreted the dream of the Pharaoh in Egypt, which had the symbols of seven healthy cows and seven starving cows, along with seven fat ears of corn on one stalk and another stalk with seven thin ears of corn. The seven thin cows ate the seven fat cows and the seven thin ears of corn ate the seven fat ones. Joseph correctly interpreted the dream as meaning that there would be seven years of abundance, followed by seven years of drought (Genesis 41).

It may also be significant, given the status of recent world-events, that Bible scholars have shown that the sons of Joseph, Ephraim and Manasseh, became Tribes and received the covenants passed down from Abraham, of being a multitude of nations and a great and mighty nation, which came into fruition as Great Britain and the United States of America.

Some of the 2003 crop formations indicate a six-fold design inside a twelve-fold design. In one case it was a twelve-segment aperture inside of which was six circles in a ring with a seventh in the center. Drawing lines between points of the central design produces a Star of David. The formation fits very well with the major symbol of the heart chakra, which is a twelve-petal lotus flower with a Star of David inside. This may resolve the seeming conflict of a six-fold Flower of Life type pattern symbolizing the heart chakra within the Tree of Life. In the Eastern tradition, the second chakra is symbolized by a lotus flower with six petals. Apparently, the sixth sphere of the Tree of Life indicates the Star of David portion of the heart chakra symbol.

Tree of Life Connections
to the 1991 Barbury Triangle and
the Mandelbrot Set Crop Circle Formations

On September 27, 1993, I received The Circular, Volume 4:2, Issue 14. On pages 20-21 was an article by Mark Styles, titled, "Discovering the Reapers of the Field."

Figure 1   Figure 2

In the article, Mark suggested -

The Barbury Castle pictogram of 1991 (fig 1), combined with the Milk Hill glyphs of the same year (fig 2), gave a vital clue here: together they can be interpreted as forming the lower part of the Kabbalistic Tree of Life (fig 3).

Note: I am using my own graphics in this book, so they are slightly different than the ones in Mark's article. I have not included one of the figures, which depicted the spheres of the Tree without the paths. I have also adjusted the numbers of the figures, for clarity. Figure 2 is a diagram of a crop formation called, "The Milk Hill Multiple Agriglyph Inscription." The circle with ring, one on each end of the inscription, is a well-known ancient glyph for the Creator or Monotheistic Deity. One of the interpretations of the inscription was that the letters spelled the names of two ancient gods:

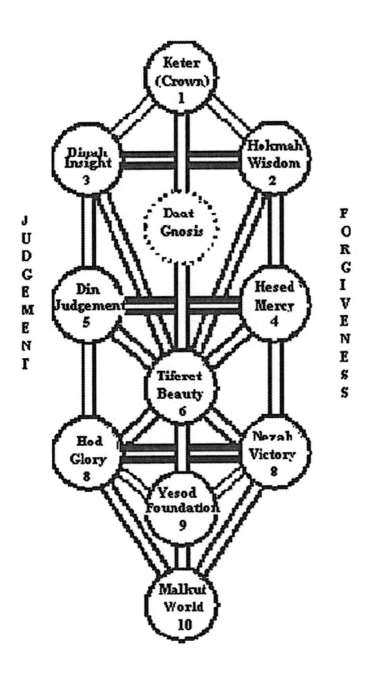

Figure 3

PHEH~THI, PTAH (PER-TAH), the Egyptian creator god
and
EA~ECH~CHE, EA (EH-AH), the Sumerian god of Wisdom
(Ea was also called Enki)

Therefore, the meaning was, "The Creator, wise and loving."

From Zechariah Sitchin's works we also understand that EN.KI (EA) supported mankind, whereas his brother, EN.LIL, wanted them destroyed.

"P'tah/Enki." P'tah was the Egyptian god of wisdom, and EN.KI (EA) was said to be the god who was the lover of mankind. So, the translation was, "The Creator, wise and loving." Interesting too, both P'tah and EN.KI (EA) did a lot of construction work, such as waterways. A symbol for P'tah, given in "The Sacred Symbols of MU" is the right-angle square, the "builder" glyph spoken of in regard to the swastika.

It has always been thought that this symbol (the builder-square) originated in Egypt but it goes back thousands of years beyond the commencement of Egyptian history. The two-sided square is a symbol, which is constantly found in the Book of the Dead, also in various Egyptian papyri. All seats where either gods or goddesses are shown sitting are composed of the two-sided square. In the Great Hall of Truth where Osiris is shown sitting in judgment his seat is composed of the two-sided square.

Mark briefly explained the basic meaning of the Tree, and continued:

The earliest names for Kabbalists were "Those who Know" and "The Reapers of the Field".

The design of the Barbury Castle pictogram closely resembles the lower part of the Tree, which deals more directly than the rest with the Earth (Malkhut). In the top left hand corner we see Reverberation (Hod), hence the rod protruding into the circle, indicative of a tuning fork. In the right hand corner we see Eternity (Nezah), hence the "spiral of time/ wheel of fortune". Below these two sephira lies Foundation (Yesod). Yesod is the final messenger of divine eminence to the earthly plane and we see this emanation occurring in the Barbury pictogram, reverberating like a raindrop in a pond. Finally at the bottom we have Kingdom or Earth (Malkut). This is most ingenious of all: the divine emanation occurs in the form of a lightening flash, and here we see the spiral form of that flash resounding a powerful "Do" as it strikes Malkut.

The connection mentioned above with the Milk Hill glyphs is that these strange looking letters recall Hebrew, although, in the tradition of texts of a religious or magical significance, they have been orientated in what could be called mirror imaging. The test represented in (fig 2) is written not in word form, but using a numerical system of relationship known as Gematria, a contemplative method of study employed by Kabbalistic scholars.

Mark Styles mentioned Benoit Mandelbrot's rediscovery in 1979 of the system of nature in mathematical terms. He continued:

"It does not take a great deal of imagination to see how similar are the two images of natural systems represented here:"

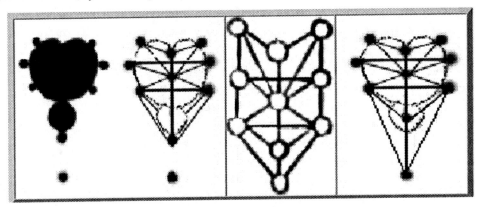

You may be thinking that the Mandelbrot Set does not contain the uppermost "Keter" part of the Tree - surely this is an important part of the cipher? Could not the reason for this be, as Kabbalistic teaching tells us, that "Daat" (Knowledge), the non-sephira, is the point where Keter (the divine will of God) can enter when the time is chosen to interfere with existence? It is quite possible that discovery of the Mandelbrot Set, in an attempt to recreate the order observed within the apparent chaos of nature's systems, has actually caused Keter to enter Daat and communication of the angelic kind to begin.

As we can see, once the Tree is in this interference mode, it resembles the Mandelbrot Set precisely. The Mandelbrot Set could be described as demonstrating the order behind the apparent chaos of nature. The same is true of the Tree of Life, and that order is "God". Kabbalism tells us that we are all part of that supreme order and collectively are "God".

Mark mentioned that the Tree is also the basis of man, then wrote a little about the "Mystical Marriage" -

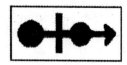

During the season of 1992 we saw a whole new chapter unfold in this enigma. In late July 1992, I discovered a formation just outside Tewkesbury which combined the planetary glyphs of Mars and Venus. The hieroglyph therefore symbolically represented the "Chemical Wedding" of the Alchemist's final stage in the "Great Work" of Unification: the aim of achieving synthesis of dualities, in this case Animus and Spiritus (conscious/unconscious), leading to a Super-Conscious state of illumination, represented as the hermaphrodite.

Earlier in 1992 a strange formation, later known as the "Dodman" appeared in the shape of a Snail, one of nature's few true hermaphrodites. Could the enigmatic Silbury Hill nearby, hub of crop circle activity, hold a clue in its androgynous design? It is constructed on a layer of crushed snail shells and could be likened to a shell itself. On the 18th August the formation which occurred there (the "Charm Bracelet" or Dharmic Wheel) strongly resembles the eight phases of the moon. It is reasonable to see a solar eclipse, which unites Sun and Moon, with Earth as the androgynous progeny, as an expression of the "Chemical Wedding". Elias Ashmole in 1652 showed astrologically that the final operation of the "Great Work" takes place during a solar eclipse at 19 degrees Leo. Such an eclipse occurs on August 22nd [actually the 11th] 1999, and is visible from Southern England.

To conclude, the objective of all Hermetic studies, including both alchemy and Kabbalism, has always been to unite the microcosm of Man to the macrocosm of the Universe, or the "return to Eden," a doctrine which was instrumental in creating philosophy, science and religion. It now seems instrumental in creating crop circles.

Mark had the date of the eclipse as August 22nd, but the solar eclipse of 1999 actually took place on August 11th. It occurred coincidentally at 11:11 a.m. The Mandelbrot Set crop circle formation appeared on that date in 1991. Other major crop formations have also appeared on that date.

The path of the eclipse also contains many coincidences and symbolisms in the context of earth changes. It is said to have caused major earthquakes as well within the path of the eclipse.

MENORAH

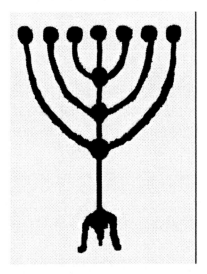

The message of the crop circles is becoming more clear. The magnitude of import is vast, to say the least. A breakthrough came with the appearance of the "Menorah" crop circle formation at Barbury Castle, which was reported on May 31, 1999. The Menorah - the lampstand with seven lamps, is one of the most important symbols in the Bible. Parts of the Book of Exodus tells the story of how Moses was given a divine revelation at Sinai concerning the construction of the Tabernacle, a portable tent used for worship, a place of revelation. The outer part of the Tabernacle was known as the Holy Place, and the inner part was called the 'Holy of Holies' or the most Holy Place. The Mercy Seat on the Ark of the Testimony was the location of the candlestick, or Menorah.

The Menorah may also be suggested in the Book of Revelation, verses 1:12-16:

Rev: 1:12 - And I turned to see the voice that spake with me. And being turned, I saw seven golden candlesticks; 13 - And in the midst of the seven candlesticks [one] like unto the Son of man, clothed with a garment down to the foot, and girt about the paps with a golden girdle. 14 - His head and [his] hairs [were] white like wool, as white as snow; and his eyes [were] as a flame of fire; 15 - And his feet like unto fine bronze, as if they burned in a furnace; and his voice as the sound of many waters. 16 - And he had in his right hand seven stars: and out of his mouth went a sharp two-edged sword: and his countenance [was] as the sun shineth in his strength.

The Menorah

The seven-branches candlestick known as the Menorah is one of the oldest symbols of Judaism. It's form was given to Moses by God, as told in Exodus 25:31-37

"Make a lampstand of pure gold and hammer it out, base and shaft, its flower-like cups and blossoms shall be of one piece with it. Six branches are to extend from the sides of the lampstand - three on one side and three on the other. Three cups shaped like almond flowers with buds and blossoms are to be on one branch, three on the next branch, and the same for all six branches extending from the lampstand. And on the lampstand there are to be four cups shaped like almond flowers with buds and blossoms. One bud shall be under the first pair of branches extending from the lampstand, a second bud under the second pair - six branches in all. The buds and branches shall be of one piece with the lampstand, hammered out of pure gold. The make its seven lamps and set them upon it so that they light the space in front of it. "

The seven candle-holders and three joints where the branches meet the central column represent the ten sefirot of the Tree of Life of the Kabbalah. The central column corresponds to the central Pillar of Equilibrium on the Tree, the holders to its left correspond to the Pillar of Severity and the holders on its right to the Pillar of Mercy.

The Jewish philosopher and theologian known as Philo of Alexandria or Philo Judaeus (c.15BC-c.45) linked the seven 'plants' of classical astrology to the seven branches of the menorah, with the sun being at the center. The seven branches may also be considered as corresponding to the seven days of Biblical Creation.

The menorah was adopted as an official emblem of the State of Israel in 1949, and it is featured on the president's flag. Menorahs with different numbers of branches are also encountered, the most common being the nine-branched version that relates to the Jewish festival of Chanukah.

The Menorah Formation

There were unusual properties to this Menorah formation. First of all, above the formation was another formation called 'The Scarab Beetle'. The second difference was that the base had a ball with 3 spikes coming out of it rather than a normal stand. The rotation of the spheres in the formation were also very specific.

The Scarab Beetle is of Ancient Egyptian origin, but biblical in nature, and represented the creator god Atum, "he who came forth" and was thought to push the sun across the sky everyday.

At the base of the Menorah, the bottom circle has an anti clockwise rotation, with the main stem flowing towards the base from the very top circle. The second circle from the base has an anti-clockwise rotation with a raised nest center.

Starting from the outer left side of the Menorah; and moving inward toward the center, the top circles have anti-clockwise rotations.

The forth circle at the very top of the main axis has a clockwise rotation.

Moving towards the right hand side of the formation, the rotation of the circles change to clockwise.

It is interesting to note here that the oldest meaning of the menorah is the Seven Sisters, better known as the Pleiades!!!

Further thoughts of the Menorah
by Francine Blake

"The Menorah is a very ancient universal symbol. Although it is associated with the Jewish Nation because they are still using this symbol, it is not specifically Jewish; it was known and used by many other races. For example, it is carved on a mountainside in Peru near as part of the Nasca Lines.

The symbol refers to levels (or dimensions) of Being and Consciousness. There are many aspects to the candelabrum at Barbury Castle, which is very close to, but not exactly like the Menorah as it has added symbolism to it.

If you put the candelabrum on its side you will see seven vertical dots. A vertical line of seven layers was called `Cosmic Pillar' by the Ancients and represents the spiritual aspect of Life. It is the central portion of the `Tree of Life'. The Cosmic Pillar, like the Tree of Life, refers to the understanding of the seven levels (or scales, or dimensions) of Being and of Consciousness. It is the line going from the lowest materialistic level to the highest spiritual level. In addition, it is an `As above, So

Below' symbol. Altogether a very profound teaching that describes the nature of our universe and our place in relation to it. There have been allusions to this knowledge in many crop circles already.

The circle in the middle of the Cosmic Pillar links five circular dots together in a horizontal line that ends with a symbol that looks very much like the ancient Egyptian symbol usually associated with the Goddess Hathor (Osiris = Earth mother or Earth Goddess). A very ancient Gaia symbol if you like. This is interesting because the number five, or five-fold geometry, has always referred to human beings (well illustrated by Leonardo Da Vinci's famous drawing of a man in a five pointed star, or a pentagram). A human being is sometimes described as "a tree with five branches". So here we have a line of five dots (human beings) connected to an ancient symbol of the Earth mother for added measure. The horizontal line indicates the material level and is related to time (going from past to future).

So this horizontal line relating to human beings and the Earth connects to the middle of the Cosmic Pillar. This is very interesting because in Olden Days, the Earth was sometimes described as the Middle Kingdom. I often wondered what that meant!

So this would indicate our place and our role in the universal scheme of things. We live in the material world but we are connected to the spiritual line and have access to the lowest as well as to the highest levels. The symbol at Barbury Castle, which is not exactly like the Jewish candelabrum as it has the added Hathor symbol at its base, would indicate that the purpose of the Earth and consequently the task for human beings, is to link the lower levels to the higher ones (both at personal level for human beings and at universal level for the planet) - or allegorically speaking and as the ancient alchemists endeavoured to do: to transmute base metals into gold. This is our role in life and the evolutionary path of our planet.

Once again crop circles reconnect us to our ancient knowledge and indicate the way to go forward.

Francine Blake
(The Spiral Magazine)

Other "Religious" Crop Circle Formations

The Menorah is not the first "religious" symbol to appear. Over the years, various crop circles have portrayed pre-Christian or esoteric European symbols, such as the Celtic Cross of 1988, the Irmensul ancient German Tree of Life of 1991, the

Dharmic Wheel of 1992, the Kabalistic Tree of Life of 1997, and the 1998 Beltane Wheel. The Bythorn Mandala, which appeared in 1994, is an East Indian symbol of Kali and the third chakra. A huge ground marking appeared in 1990, grooved into a lake bed in Oregon. It was also an East Indian symbol, called a Sri Yantra.

At least three Christian symbols have appeared, two of them indirectly. Several years ago, the Christian "Fish" symbol appeared as part of a crop formation. Dowsing within the Winterborne Stoke Swastika Circle of 1989, revealed the basic design of The New Jerusalem Plan, based on Saint John's vision in Revelation. The total of the square footage of the circles in the Barbury Castle formation of 1991 was 31,680, a number associated with a distance around The New Jerusalem. One tenth of that number, 3,168, was associated with "Lord Jesus Christ" by the early Christians, and previously to a figure in the Pagan religion. A "666" type crop formation appeared in 1993. The sixes were arranged in a triangle.

The Menorah is Linked to The Tree of Life

The Menorah crop circle formation is directly linked to three other extremely significant crop formations that also appeared at Barbury Castle, one of which was the Kabalistic Tree of Life. Amazingly, the circles of the new Menorah formation can be rearranged slightly to become strikingly similar to The Tree of Life!

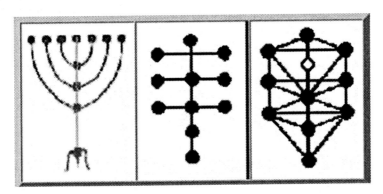

Confirmation in the Rotations

As with many formations, some of the circles in the Menorah crop formation had the plants laid down in a clockwise direction (or rotation), and others were laid down in a counterclockwise direction. I and some others feel that the two types of rotations may be part of the message -. that they have a duality, or male/female meaning.

I had a dream of a counterclockwise swastika in 1990. Energy was moving from the center, out into the arms. A voice said, "These are the forces going out from the center to experience negative manifested events in order to learn. It is generally square, and you circle counterclockwise."

Negative and positive are one type of duality. The idea of rotation is found in myths and religions around the world. Black Elk, for example, spoke of the reason that shaman of the Sioux Tribe "circle to the left," that is, from South to West to North, to East, returning to the South - in other words, rotating clockwise. Ancient glyphs of swastikas depicted them either clockwise (going East), or counterclockwise. The East-going swastika was a symbol of "good luck."

In my experience, counterclockwise rotation symbolizes the "male" aspect of creation, and clockwise rotation is symbolic of the "feminine" aspect. In this view, the physical reality is "male," in this sense, and the dream/Spirit reality is feminine. Others see it in the reverse. In terms of the human being, the male aspect is associated with rational, analytical thought and the left brain. The feminine aspect is associated with the dreaming, intuitive, emotional side and the right brain.

The rotations of the various circles in the Menorah crop circle formation are quite significant, I believe. The three circles on the top, left side had a counterclockwise rotation. The center and right three circles on top had a clockwise rotation. When the diagram is rearranged, as above, into a pattern similar to The Tree of Life, the three counterclockwise circles are on the left, and the three clockwise circles are on the right. This seems to confirm the Tree of Life association with the Menorah, because the left Pillar of the Tree of Life has three spheres that are associated with the feminine aspect, and the right Pillar has three spheres associated with the masculine aspect.

In the Kabalistic tradition, one can also imagine being inside the Tree. From that perspective, the masculine Pillar is on the Left and the feminine Pillar on the right. Perhaps this "mirror image" type of concept is a reason for the differing opinions concerning the duality. In any case, the Menorah crop circle formation certainly seems related to the Tree of Life.

Connection to the Nazca Line Markings

The bottom of the Menorah crop circle formation had spikes, rather than a normal lampstand base. Perhaps this suggests "roots" of the Tree.

A large tree-like shape, similar to the Menorah, is one of the many ground markings on the Nazca Plains.. The projections on the bottom of the Nazca marking are strikingly like those on the new Menorah crop circle formation. For decades there has been controversy about the Nazca markings. The method of creating the markings and the reason for producing them has never been clear. Erich Von Daniken, in his book, Chariots of the Gods, suggested that the markings are related to extraterrestrial beings who visited our planet thousands of years ago.

Since the crop circles began appearing in great numbers about 1990, there has been speculation that the Nazca markings may have come from the same source. The 1999 Menorah crop circle formation certainly seems to support the theory.

The Chakra Connection

I began to see a chakra connection to the crop circles in 1992. This began when I read Joseph Campbell's last book, The Inner Reaches of Outer Space. The great mythologist wrote about the universal "elementary" idea of the seven chakras and the midpoint, which is sometimes expressed as "3 1/2."

Notice the similarity of the depiction on the left to the Menorah crop circle formation. There are eight spheres along the balance beam pole, one of which is above the crossbeam. This is a very ancient depiction from the Egyptian Book of the Dead. The seven spheres below the beam, according to Joseph Campbell, are related to the seven chakras. The eighth sphere above the beam, he theorized, represents a realm beyond the earth plane. The snout of the "Swallower" beast cuts across the pole between the third and the fourth spheres, and the Judgment Seat is also located at that level.

The depiction on the right is a Navaho sand painting called The Pollen Path. It is a corn plant with seven markers. From the bottom-upward, they are marked by the root, the five leaves, and the tassel. Again, these correspond to the chakras, according to Joseph Campbell. The two leaves marking the third and fourth chakras also show ears of corn. A lightning bolt from above strikes at the fourth marker, which is in the center, the midpoint. This corresponds, he wrote, to the vajra, "the thunderbolt of enlightenment" of Hindu and Buddhist iconography, which exactly fits with the fourth chakra, anahata, "where the sound is heard that is not made by any two things striking together."

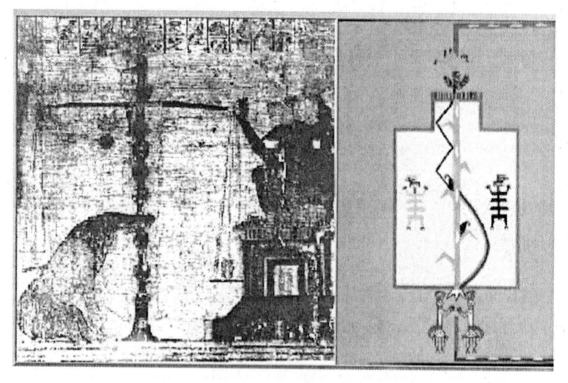

Note that the bottom of the corn plant has three roots, just as the Menorah crop formation has three projections or spikes at the bottom. Joseph Campbell wrote, "The root of the corn plant is threefold, like Yuktatriveni in the muladhara." Again, this corresponds to eastern concepts of the chakra system, which are quite ancient.

The central Pillar of the Tree corresponds to the chakras, and the left and right Pillars correspond to the two "snake-like" channels called Ida and Pingala. The Menorah crop circle formation suggest the chakras in the same way, because of its apparent connection to the Tree of Life, and the three projections from the base.

There is another suggestion of the chakras in the seven circles at the top. The seven lamps of the Menorah which correspond to the seven upper circles in the Menorah crop circle formation, seem to fit with the worldwide elementary idea of the seven chakras with the midpoint marked in some way.

Often, the Menorah has the center lamp above the other six, thus the midpoint is marked by the elevation of the center lamp, and by its attachment to the to the column.

Either or both "chakra" interpretations may be correct. It seems that a higher intelligence is trying to teach us something about "religious" concepts. I have a strong feeling that the higher intelligence behind the crop circle phenomenon is the same intelligence that gave mankind "religious" concepts throughout history. It is time to wake up and pay attention, I do think. Apparently, we have a lot to learn.

MANDELBROT SET

MANDELBROT CROP FORMATION

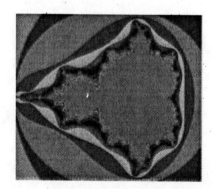

COMPUTER GENERATED MANDELBROT SET

One of the symbolic meanings seen in the Mandelbrot Set, is the repeating patterns across scales. This fits in well with the concept of the reality being composed of extremely small 'consciousness units' that build into higher gestalts, each 'unit' has the code of pattern of All-That-Is, or everything in all realities.

Many crop circle formations related to the science of chaos have appeared, such as the Koch Snowflake Fractal, and Julia Set types.

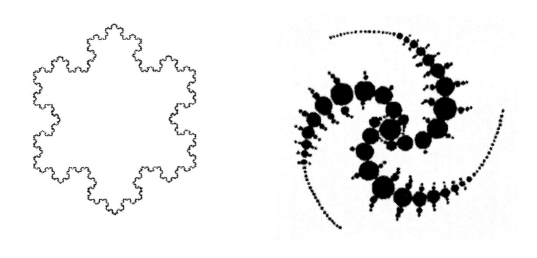

This is a computer generated Mandelbrot pattern

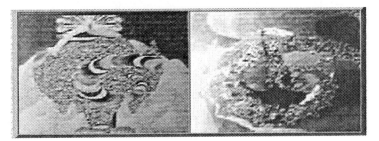

I saw a world of symbolism in these pictures, which I had created on my own computer with a Mandelbrot creation program.

Both pictures are basically the same origination, except for the "mask" and colors. They were composites of three pictures . . . the Statue of Liberty, a devilish alien face, and a spiral from a portion of the Mandelbrot Set. The original composites were combined randomly, by using an Amiga program called "The Director." The program chose which three pictures to combine and which pallet colors would dominate in the mask.

I saw the picture on the left as symbolically representing devilish beliefs blocking the light of the Great Mother Goddess. On the Amiga, the colors could be "cycled," giving the appearance of animation. When the colors of that picture were cycled, the spiral portion moved downward into the tighter spiral at the bottom, as if the devilish beliefs took one into hell. The mathematics of the Mandelbrot Set program seemed to suggest the reason - the output of each equation is fed back into the formula over and over.

The picture on the right revealed that the spiral was also like a tentacle, which grips. It is gripping the book held by the Goddess - the Constitution of the United States - representing freedom and the equality of people.

By "devilish beliefs," I mean beliefs in the devil, demons, or the like. We, mankind, are co-creators of the reality, and such beliefs help manifest negative events, even to the point where the devil or demonic entities manifest, as "real." It is our beliefs in such things that keep them alive and lead to the descending spiral of events. This is the "feedback" of the belief system that is put back into the "equation," when it is recalculated.

Monkey King.

The following is the text about the story:

The Ramayana

The Ramayana, a celebrated Indian epic written by the poet Valmiki and comprising some 24,000 couplets, describes Rama's long and perilous struggle against the asuras - a kind of Indian Titan - under their lord Ravana. The myth belongs in the same tradition of battles between gods and giants, or between the powers of light and the demons of darkness. Briefly, it tells that Rama's wife Sita was captured by the demon king Ravana and carried off to Lanka, the city of the 'Titans.'

At the hand of the gods Ravana was invulnerable - he could only be vanquished by a human being. It cost Rama much suffering and many furious battles to recover his bride. But with the help of the monkey king Sugriva, who built a living bridge across to Lanka with his monkey hordes, Rama and his heroic companions were able to cross to the city, defeat Ravana and set the beautiful Sita free. Since Rama is an avatar incarnation of the supreme being Vishnu, the story offers a connection between myth and the origin of religion.

(excerpted from Elliot, Alexander, editor, Myths, McGraw-Hill, New York, 1976)

The spirals all over the monkey's body, represent negative belief patterns, like the tentacle I found in the Mandelbrot picture. I felt that the myth was saying that mankind was in a great cycle of time experiencing this negative way of thinking and being.

The Monkey King was showing this foolish way of thinking and being. Yet, all of the foolishness has an overall positive purpose. It forms the living bridge where the hero rescues his mate. I was later to understand from dreams that this means the re-discovery of one's intuitional self, and a recognition of the Mother Goddess concept, in terms of a generating world that radiates this physical world out to black rest in cold space.

As I understand from channeled material, such as Seth, channeled by Jane Roberts, and myths of the dreaming God, our reality is created by thought. One of the meanings of being "created in God's image", is that we also create our reality by thought. We are given free will, to think and create as we wish.

In this great cycle of time, we do not realize that we are co-creating the reality by our thoughts and beliefs. The result is clown foolish, because all the negative events can be changed quite simply.

In the myth, the Demon King is invulnerable to the Gods. He can only be vanquished by a human being. This means that we must accomplish this challenge ourselves; .it will not be done for us by God.

Since the Mandelbrot Set is the repeating patterns across scales we can compare the extremely small 'consciousness units' building into higher gestalts, each 'unit' having the code or pattern of All-That-Is, or everything in all realities.

In this analogy, one could think of oneself as an extremely tiny speck in the Mandelbrot Set. Yet, the shape of that speck, on closer inspection, reveals that it has the same pattern as the entire Set. By understanding your own small realm, you can get an idea of the entire macro-cosmic pattern.

A related analogy made from the science of chaos, concerned the idea of the

"Butterfly Effect." An extremely small difference in initial conditions can cause a large-scale change in time. The idea is that a butterfly beating its wings in one part of the world, may create a storm in another part of the world sometime later.

In the Mandelbrot analogy it is a change in a tiny sub-set, influencing a change in the entire pattern.

Dreams and myths can be interpreted with these Mandelbrot analogies in mind. They can refer to one's personal life and larger scales, such as mankind generally.

A mythological hero, such as "Rama", or David in the Goliath story, can be seen as each person, and then as mankind. Your Goliath or Titan this evening, may have been paying the monthly bills this morning. On a grand scale, the giant is the negative thinking and beliefs on a global basis, and our challenge to overcome them.

The Mandelbrot Set is said to be the grandaddy of all Sets (like Julia Sets), the most complicated object in mathematics; yet it can be set in a few lines of computer code. The shape emerges from calculations involving coordinates; 'real' numbers horizontally, and 'imaginary' numbers vertically. Something like the following:

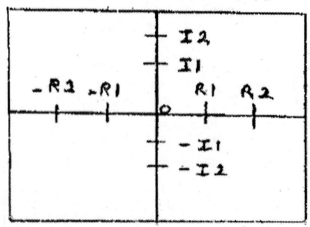

The computations involve solving an equation, taking the result and putting it back into the equation and re-calculating it again. This is repeated a designated number of times. The program looks to see if the number remains a finite quantity, or runs toward infinity. Based on the number of computations, a chosen color is placed at that coordinate point on the computer screen. In the photos here, the black areas represent points that remained a finite number after the designated number of calculations were performed. That is what is represented by the shape of the Mandelbrot Set. The colors and patterns near the black part, represent points that almost remained finite, that is, they ran toward infinity near the end of the designated calculations. These are the areas that are so extremely complex.

It is the symbolism that we are concerned with here. It as a good metaphor for the concept of our reality being formed by our thoughts. Our 'output'; our lives and world, 'prove' to us that our beliefs are 'true.' It is then 'feedback' that strengthens the belief. This is the equivalent of taking the results of an equation and putting it back into the equation again and then re-calculating. Negative or conflicting beliefs result in the descending spirals which grip us like an octopus tentacle. My Amiga computer picture can be animated by 'color cycling'. The computer steps the color pallette and re-displays the picture. The descending spiral can be seen flowing downward. The cycling can be reversed, and the flow is then in an upward direction.

I saw this as a good metaphor for changing one's beliefs and emerging from the octopus grip. As I understand it from Seth and numerous other sources, such as 'Alpha thinking', one can change his or her reality through a process of thinking and imagining. This seems ridiculous in our present world-view. But there is substantial evidence that it seems to work for some people. That small change in the belief pattern has the 'butterfly effect.' of a tiny change in the 'output', or reality. You then have a tiny bit of 'proof' that things got better. You concentrate on that, and it becomes 'feedback' into the equation, altering it a bit more. It takes 'time' or many calculations to achieve the major result; that is, spiraling up out of the octopus grip.

The term 'Titan' is interesting because the sinking of the Titanic in 1912 can be taken as a symbolic event signaling a world-wide period of stress that began with World War One two years later. A predictive book called "Futility" was written some years before, in which the ship had the name "Titan".

All these myths are about the great battle of good against evil, often symbolized by giants or devils, and are about this choosing of beliefs.

A personal communication in 1982 from Seth said that a great change was coming soon; that unity would come after a period of stress. When asked how humanity could help, he answered simply, "Love is the answer, It radiates you know!"

In the book, "Seth Speaks" on page 184, it states:

"The experiment that would transform your world would operate upon the basic idea that you create your own reality according to the nature of your beliefs, and that all existence was blessed, and that evil did not exist in it. If these ideas were followed individually and collectively, then the evidence of your physical senses would find no contradiction. They would perceive the world and existence as good."

It seems so difficult to make the belief-realty system work, but Seth said, "To me it is so incredibly simple."

In the Mandelbrot Set, symbolically from a few lines of simple computer code creates an infinitely complex pattern.

Gravity is an excellent symbol of the collective beliefs. It is the only force (of the four physical forces) that is additive. It is by far the weakest of the four forces, yet the additive nature gives it power over planets and galaxies

Various insects have a shape that is somewhat similar to the Mandelbrot Set. Certain myths include insect symbols. The Hopi myth of Grandmother Spider is an example. The eight legs of the spider are meaningful, and related to the sand paintings with eight people around the square.

It easily refers to mankind. The Mandelbrot patterns frequently reveal images of four or eight. The Hopi Spider has a dotted cross on its back, reminding one of the Mandelbrot coordinates.

After seeing the Hopi creation myth drawing, a dreamer told me that her sister, who was missing, came to her in her dream with a large spider in her hand. Her sister said that it was their spider, and no one else could touch it. The next day, the missing girl's best friend was told the dream and the girl said she had had the same dream. The realization came then that the spider represents the thread-like connection between each person, and our collective consciousness. Learning how to weave refers to our recognition of our interconnectedness, and forming a more ideal, mandala-like web. The twelve-petalled sunflower in the Hopi depiction may represent the pattern we will learn to weave, which is the New Jerusalem and the heart chakra.

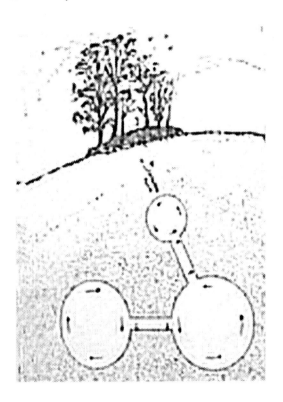 

The crop pattern of Doon's Law (Scotland-1990) (above - left), which is three circles with pathways between, resembles the Hopi myth (above - right). The lay of the wheatstalks "athwart in the passages", reminds one of the ladder-like climb of the humans in the Hopi design. (Athwart refers to the pathways being flattened in a lateral fashion) The equi-distant location of this crop pattern between two Templar churches, containing the tombs of 14th century crusaders, hints at the duality balance.

John Haddington, who lives in Berwickshire, England measured the circles. The diameter of the clockwise-swirled circle was 31 ft and it was linked by a 16 ft-long passage to an anti-clockwise, 32 ft circle. From that circle a passage, 16 ft long, led to another, 16 ft in diameter. All the dimensions occurred in units of approximately 16 ft. The wheatstalks in the passageways were unusually laid, not parallel to the lengths of the passages but athwart them.

About 70 feet south-west of the circles site is an ancient, tree-grown mound, Doons Law. John Haddington found that one of the passageways pointed to Doons Law and, beyond it, to the old church at Swinton. The other passageway, at an angle of 67 degrees to the first, was directed towards the church at Norham.

The multiples of sixteen feet connect well with the eight legs of spiders, and with the symbolism of the Mandelbrot Set, which often reveals images with four-fold, eight-fold, and sixteen-fold patterns

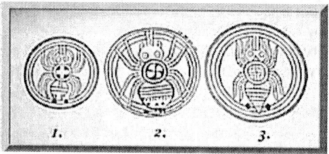

'The Sacred Symbols of Mu', by James L. Churchward, shows the spider with the cross pattern was also found in other ancient writings and art. Churchward states that the roads in the south-sea islands where he found these drawings are being constructed like a web, so that no man could discover the end. Like a ball of string, where you can't find the end, one realizes that there is no end, because it is generally circular. One must grasp any point and unravel it.

EGYPTIAN BEETLES

Another example of insect mythology is the scarab beetle. It is said to represent creative energy or force. The glyph of the God Khepra suggests a mental creation.

The inscription in the Secret Symbols of Mu by Churchward , on page 84, 'The God RA is like thee in his limbs, the God Khepra in creative force," is interesting because 'Ra' is a male sun symbol, which represents the male aspect of the deity and mankind. 'Limbs' suggest the 'Tree of Knowledge/Life'.

The Scarabaeus beetle as an emblem of the Creator because it rolls a ball of mud around, and sets therein its eggs to hatch. The repeating patterrn of the Mandelbrot symbolism is similar as the 'egg' contains the genetic code of the mother and father. The pattern of the whole is within this smaller portion.

An article in one of the early crop newsletters mentioned that the 'insectograms' (or 'laddergrams') resembled a beetle because of the split wing covers. I felt that this center circle part of the 'insectograms' was the ancient glyph for the dual deity

Insectogram near Stonehenge 1991

Perhaps that is one reason the beetle was chosen for a symbol in the first place.

Seth said in a person communication that our scientists are asking the wrong questions. He said that what is needed most was work on awareness and perception, and that our scientists have much to learn. In the book, Chaos on page 84, it reads:

"Unlike most mathematicians, he (Mandelbrot) confronted problems by depending on his intuition about patterns and shapes. He mistrusted analysis, but he trusted his mental pictures. And he already had the idea that other laws, with different behavior, could govern random, 'stochastic phenomena."

Jane Roberts reported that Seth made a statement about the 'Chaos' symbolism:

"Every time you say, "I am helpless and I am slipping into chaos,' whether you get laughs or not or whether you say it humorously or not, you are indeed pushing yourself further into the chaos you are creating with every breath you take."

One of the symbolisms of the Mandelbrot is like an infinite sea of possible patterns from which to choose. The challenge is finding and using the ideal pattern.

The musical instrument such as the guitar or violin, resembles the Mandelbrot Set shape. Our reality is somewhat like these grand instruments. The power of the sound is like the huge hand of the Creator strumming rhythmically. We are located at the tip where we adjust the tuning. Our lives are the music, either discordant or a beautiful melody.

In the Barbury Castle pictogram, the number 31,680 comes up. Numerous times the numbers eight (male aspect) and nine (female aspect) also shows in this pictogram. $8 \times 9 \times 440 = 31,680$. The number 440 represents the 'ratchet spiral', or man.

440 is the musical note of 'A' in cycles per second. I found this meaningful, because in The Sacred Symbols of Mu, James Churchward wrote that the letter $\mathcal{A}$ with a double crossbar, represented man with both aspects and $\mathcal{A}$ with a single crossbar represented man with one aspect lost.

'The Gnostic Gospels' contain the eight and nine symbolism: (Page 165)

"I see the eighth and the souls that are in it and the angels singing a hymn to the ninth and its powers - I pray to the end of the universe and the beginning of the beginning, to the object of man's quest, the immortal discovery - I am the instrument of thy spirit. Mind is thy Plectrum. (A pick to strum the strings) And thy counsel plucks me. I have received power from thee. For thy love has reached us."

The musical and string instrument metaphors are clear. Perhaps this early Christian heard the note of 'A' and recognized it for what it is.

In the 'Quartus report', A statement by John Price reminded me of the

Mandelbrot symbolism of repeating patterns across scales:

". . . each one of us is the sum-total of all the energies of the universe individualized, and that all we are and have in the phenomenal world reflects our energy in expression."

In the same report, is an article by John March. He uses the term 'chaos' several times in reference to the internal mind-talk of the rational mind and the external world. He stresses the importance of being 'still' mentally, to let your rational mind learn to become subservient to the intuitional.

"Chaos exists in man because we feel separated from our source and because we are trying to use an instrument that is too tiny and incomplete to run our lives."

It is as if he is saying that we are strumming our own, small Mandelbrot-guitar, when we should just tune it, and listen to the music, because the strumming power comes from higher levels.

Beetles and spiders have a metaphorical significance. Some of the beetles are Mandelbrot-like. Some have the 'T' or 'Y' shape between their segments, revealing three major portions, which reminds one of the Barbury Castle pictogram. The Brown Recluse spider has a guitar-like shape on its back.

These things may appear silly to one with a mechanical universe world-view, but symbols can come from any source. The object is to see if they tell a consistent story, and compare it to myths, dreams, channeled material, inspired material, and science. Dreams and inspired music and film, such as from Pink Floyd, suggest this by the 'artificial light' symbol.

This symbol appeared along with a crop circle in Russia in the late 1970's. A giant UFO was seen by three scientists. It looked like a light bulb. Were the animals created with an intentional, built-in symbol, or did the ancients merely recognize a symbol out of innumerable varieties?

A chaos 'attractor' pattern was shown from EEG signals from a subject in a relaxed state during meditation while being examined in a testing situation. The subject was asked to count backwards, by sevens. The EEG attractor patterns became enlarged. The scientist said that it showed the beautiful ability of the mind to quickly sort through a large variety of options and pick the correct choice.

The human heart was found to have an identical chaos pattern as a dripping water faucet. The duality-balance was a very important part of the message about the great change. The water-drops and heart have a duality aspect.

The scientists were surprised to find that it was not the forming of the big drop of water that controlled the attractor pattern, but the 'snap-back' after the drop falls.

This was found to be the case with the heart also, with the 'recovery', after the beat, being equivalent to the 'snap-back'. This a consistent pattern across scales.

For example, the dream-state is a 'recovery' period that is a prime control in our lives. Our intuitive and spontaneous aspects lead us to events often, yet we always feel the rational is in full control.

Needless to say, water in various forms, and the heart are important dream and mythological symbols.

Iron Bridge At Trinquetaille
Vincent van Gogh

The 'Unsolved Mysteries' show in 1990 aired a television program about the crop patterns, and I wrote down notes of the possible meaning of the 'first pictogram'. The very next day, while in town, I picked up a book about Vincent van Gogh, the artist, (by Meyer Schapiro) and saw a painting (above) that had a similarity to the pictogram. The Mother-Earth-like figure resembled the Mandelbrot Set. Interestingly, it refers to, "Out of chaos came forth form."

The lamp post in the drawing seems to be coming out of the woman's head, which seemed like terrible composition; very un-van Gogh-like. Similarly to the First Pictogram, the rectangles are also there.

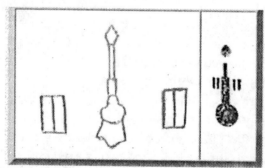

The diamond-shaped glass light, seems to represent the physical world, and the woman's body represents the large spirit pool or collective subconscious. The lamp-post represents the tunnel connecting the two realities.

In the photos of the Mandelbrot Set pictogram, there is a small (8 foot diameter) circle that appears to be located at a point equivalent to the lamp in the van Gogh painting.

In the computer Mandelbrot prints that I created on my Amiga computer, in a zoom-in view, there is also the equivalent of the small circle in the pictogram.

It appears to be a repeat of the entire shape, surrounded by an eight-pointed star, 'Coincidentally,' this star has appeared in other 'coincidences' and I believe symbolizes world unity.

In the book about the island of Mu, Mr. Churchward says that the octopus was an ancient symbol that meant 'water demon, the enemy of life'. Its' role was to prevent life on Earth, (Page 238). Then on page 239: "... it appears that the octopus was the symbol of the resistance of the mud against allowing the sun's forces to draw the Earth's forces out into the water to form life's cosmic eggs."

In dream symbolism, "life", or "death" often refers to a spiritual level. 'Mud' seems to refer to units of consciousness, such as ourselves, that is, we are both physical (earth) and spiritual (water) beings. The 'Sun's forces' refer to the male, radiating aspect of the Deity. We, (mankind) along with our other reincarnational or focus personalities, are the phallic, or male cosmic egg that is radiated out into the field of space-time.

The symbolism of the octopus as the 'resistance' of the 'mud' fits in perfectly to the spiral-tentacle picture.

The Pipestone Octopus
Wisconsin, Pipestone, Minnesota

Pipestone National Monument

The 'pipestone octopus' (above, from The Sacred Symbols of Mu), makes the meaning more clear. The tentacle holding the serpent shows that the nature of the resistance concerns the resistance to change. According to Joseph Campbell, a serpent symbolizes the death-rebirth of change, by the shedding of the old skin. In The Gnostic Gospels, some early Christians said that the snake in the garden represented wisdom.

The beak of the octopus is shown as a cutting, or dividing force. It is associated with woman's creation. This represents the separation of our intuitive-selves, which is often symbolized in dreams and myths, as a woman or girl. This separation keeps us from realizing our collective consciousness, and leads to further division among humans.

Adam and Eve symbolizes one person. Bones are a physical symbol of the soul, so Eve is a rib-sized portion of Adam's soul. The story is about this separation, and the dominance of the rational (Adam) aspect in this great cycle of time. A similar interpretation is in The Gnostic Gospels.

Mr. Churchward found it a bit odd that the Pipestone Octopus seems to be a sun symbol. The eight-pointed star represents united man collectively in the future. The octopus, with its eight tentacles, represents man in dis-unity in the present great cycle. The star is a male, sun symbol. The physical reality is male, in the sense of radiating out, as well as the dominance of rational thinking. That is why the cosmic egg is phallic, and 'man' is the 'son' of the Creator.

Mr. Churchward says that the ancients sometimes referred to the sun as 'Kin,' in reference to the celestial orb, and sometimes as "Ra," to indicate the monotheistic Deity. This could be a reference to collective man, in terms of the octopus and eight-pointed star.

In the book, 'Channeling' (by Jon Klimo) there is a channeled entity, who calls himself, "Ra". He said that he was a consciousness collective. Mr. Klimo tells of the channeled entity 'Spectra" who claimed to be a consciousness collective from the future.

An article by Mark Styles posits the theory that the 1991 Barbury Castle crop formation represents the lower triad of the Kabbalistic Tree of Life. He also suggested that the Mandelbrot Set crop formation fit well with the Tree of Life.

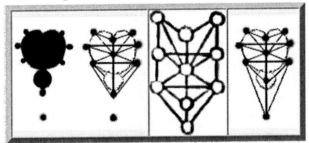

The top sphere of the Tree (Keter the Crown), in this case, has moved into the 'hidden' sphere of Daat (knowledge).

In 1997 the Tree of Life appeared as a crop circle formation at Barbury Castl.

In 1999 the Menorah, the seven-branched candlestick of the Hebrew Holy Place in the Tabernacle, appeared as a crop formation, again, at Barbury Castle.

The image clearly seems related to the Tree of Life:

This makes extensive comparative analogies between chaos theory, fractals, and the Mandelbrot Set, to the Tree of Life.

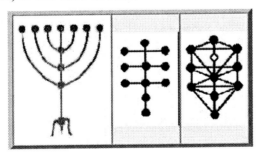

141

The Mandelbrot turns out not to be exactly like those composed by computer, according to Gerald Hawkins. It was changed in a way that demonstrates the diatonic ratios of the music scale. Also, it was pointed out by Freddie Silva in his book 'Secrets in the Fields', that various ancient sites composed of stones have the cardioid shape like the Mandelbrot Set. An example is Castlerigg.

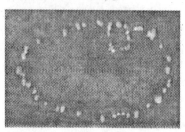

CASTLERIGG STONE CIRCLE
CUMBRIA, KESTWICK, ENGLAND

The crop formation of the Swallows of August 2003 also display the cardioid shape in their underlying geometry. Upsidedown, the Swallows resemble the Menorah.

THE SWALLOWS CROP PATTERN, 2003

BUILDER'S SQUARE

Prior to my study of ancient symbols, I had a dream of a counter-clockwise Swastika. Energy was flowing from the center, out into the arms. A voice said, "These are the forces going out from the center to experience negative manifested events, in order to learn. It is generally square, and you circle counterclockwise."

I later found Swastikas in The Sacred Symbols of Mu. Five illustrations on page 78 show how the swastika evolved from the cross. In this case, the Swastika is counterclockwise. James Churchward wrote that the arms of the Swastika are formed by glyphs called "Builder." These "L" - shapes are "two-sided squares," like the tool used by carpenters, masons, and other craftsmen. It was called a Mason's Square by the Masonic brotherhood. Four of the glyphs in the form of the Swastika indicate "the Four Great Builders of the Universe."

The two-sided square glyph is on many of Niven's Mexican tablets. In ancient Egypt it became a symbol of justice and uprightness. In the Book of the Dead and in various Egyptian papyrii, the seats of the gods and goddesses are composed of the two-sided square. It was a symbol of the god P'tah. Two of his titles were "The Divine Artificer" and "The Divine Builder."

Another type of Swastika was composed of four curved horn-like shapes. Two forms of this type are shown on page 225, one from the Mound Builders and the other from Niven's tablet number 1231. These two are clockwise Swastikas, which indicate moving from west to east. It is a "Good Luck" symbol.

Tablet No. 1231

The Swastika is a universal ancient symbol. As a "builder" from each of the cardinal directions, I believe it represents the "Demiurge," the helper of "God," or a "god" who is subordinate to the Supreme Creator. The Demiurge is the creator of the physical world, and can do "good or evil." The counter-clockwise Swastika, or West-going Swastika represents a negative, yet learning creation. The clockwise, or East-going, Swastika represents "good luck," a positive creation.

A recent set of dreams indicated that the counter-clockwise, negative Swastika also represents the "past," and the clockwise one is the "future." We are being "pulled by the future, and pushed by the past." This was related to the 'Push me-pull you' creature of the movie, 'Doctor Dolittle.'

It has always been thought that the builder symbol originated in Egypt, but it goes back thousands of years beyond the commencement of Egyptian history. The two-sided square is a symbol, which is constantly found in the Book of the Dead, also in various Egyptian papyri. All seats where either gods or goddesses are shown sitting are composed of the two-sided square. In the Great Hall of Truth where Osiris is shown sitting in judgment his seat is composed of the two-sided square.

The Great Hall of Truth or Judgment Seat of Osiris.

Left to Right: Osiris in judgment chair. A leopard skin, his banner. Four genii over closed lotus flower, symbol of Mu. Great beast of Amenti. Thoth with Ibis head recording history of the deceased. Anubis with jackal's head and Horus with hawk's head weighing the heart on a pair of scales against a feather. The deceased, hands aloft exposing his heart, being led into the Hall of Truth by a feather and being received by Maat, goddess of Truth. The bitch sits on top of the balance scale...the accuser...later called Satan by the Christian church. (From the Egyptian "Book of the Dead")

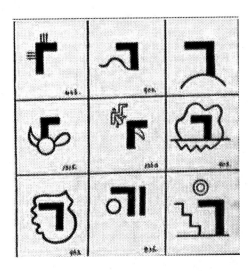

The graphic above shows the two-sided square, which is on many Mexican tablets. In all of these tablets they are referring to the Sacred Four as "The Great Builders of the Universe."

I was astonished when I found the following verses in Zechariah:

1:18 And I lifted my eyes and saw, and behold, four horns! 19 And I said to the angel who talked with me, "What are these?" And he answered me, "These are the horns which have scattered Judah, Israel, and Jerusalem." 20 Then the Lord showed me four smiths. 21 And I said, "What are these coming to do?" He answered, "These are the horns which scattered Judah, so that no man raised his head; and these have come to terrify them, to cast down the horns of the nations who lifted up their horns against the land of Judah to scatter it."

In my mind, this refers to a counterclockwise, or west-going Swastika composed of four curved horns, and to a clockwise, or east-going Swastika composed of four "builder" glyphs. Some Bibles translate the word "smith" as "carpenter." In any case, this is a "craftsman," a "builder" type of symbolism, and I believe it refers to mankind's role as co-creator of the reality.

One example of the builder glyph as part of a crop circle formation was the "Circuit Board," or "Grid" crop formation that appeared in 1994. It had seven lines inside a rectangle. The mid-point, the middle line, extended out beyond the rectangle, and connected to a circular shape. An "L" shaped pattern was near the rectangle.

The formation seemed to follow the "Pollen Path" sand painting and Egyptian symbolism of the midpoint of seven.

In the Navaho sand painting from the Time-Life book, 'Indians of the West,' a Navaho sand painting shows the gods of the four directions. Each of the gods also holds a counterclockwise Swastika.

Another example:

Danebury Hill Fort, 1998
A seven node curved swastika

A 'script' crop circle formation (below) appeared in 1991, and included builder type symbols. Part of the 'script' was interpreted to refer to the Egyptian god 'Ptah' who had the builder glyph as one of his symbols.

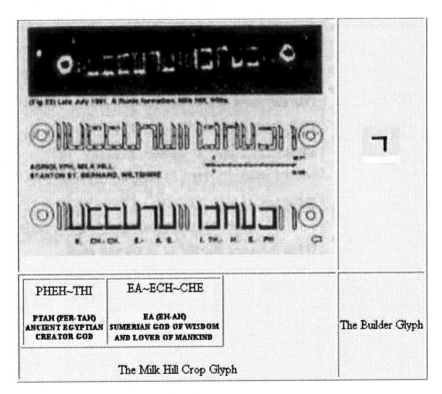

PHEH~THI	EA~ECH~CHE	
PTAH (PER-TAH) ANCIENT EGYPTIAN CREATOR GOD	EA (EH-AH) SUMERIAN GOD OF WISDOM AND LOVER OF MANKIND	The Builder Glyph
The Milk Hill Crop Glyph		

Mythology of peoples and nations over millennia have given us the names of 'gods' which they fully believe controlled their lives. In studying mythology, we find that while the names of 'god's of one people are different from another people, the stories of what these 'gods' did is the same or very similar, even when these people are far removed from each other.

In Zechariah Sitchin's "Divine Encounters" he tells us that according to the Egyptian priest Manetho, who had written down the history of Egypt when Alexander's Greeks arrived, in times immemorial "Gods of Heaven" came to Earth from the Celestial Disc. After a great flood had inundated Egypt, "a very great god who had come to Earth in the earliest times" raised the land from under the waters by ingenious damming, dyking, and land reclamation works. His name was P'tah, "The Developer", and he was a great scientist who had earlier had a hand in the creation of Man. He was often depicted with a staff that was graduated, very much like surveyor's rods nowadays. In time P'tah handed the rule over Egypt to his Firstborn son Ra ("The Bright One") who for all time remained head of the pantheon of Egyptian Gods.

The Egyptian terms for 'gods' was NTR ("Guardian Watcher") and the belief was that they had come to Egypt from TA.UR ("foreign/Far Land"). That land was Shumer (Sumer) ("Land of the Guardians"). Egypt's gods as the ANNUNAKI, P'tah as EA/EN.KI (whose Sumerian nickname NUDIMMUD, meant "The Artful Creator") and Ra as his Firstborn son Marduk.

Ra was followed on the divine throne of Egypt by four brother-sister couples, first his own children Shu ("Dryness") and Tefnut ("Moisture") and then by their children Geb ("Who piles Up the Earth") and Nut ("The Stretched-out Firmament of the Sky"). Geb and Nut then had four children; Asar ("The All Seeing") whom the Greeks called Osiris, who married his sister Ast, whom we know as Isis; and Seth ("The Southerner") who married his sister Nebt-hat, alias Nephtys. To keep the peace, Egypt was divided between Osiris (who was given Lower Egypt in the north) and Seth (who was assigned Upper Egypt in the south). But Seth deemed himself entitled to all of Egypt, and never accepted the division. Using Subterfuge, he managed to seize Osiris, cut up his body into fourteen pieces, and dispersed the pieces all over Egypt. But Isis managed to retrieve the pieces (all except for the phallus) and put together the mutilated body, thereby resurrecting the dead Osiris to life in the Other World.

And thus was born the belief that the king of Egypt, the Pharoah, if "put together' (mummified) like Osiris after death, could journey to join the gods in their abode, enter the secret Gates of Heaven, encounter there the great god Ra, and, if allowed to enter, enjoy an eternal Afterlife.

Also, we know that the gods could live eternally by eating a green plant grown in the ocean off the coast of Africa, and the Annunakis farmed this green plant and took it aboard their ship to keep themselves alive. However, once they created Man, who were only half god, half man, man did not have this ability to stay alive eternally in the physical body.

Jim A. Cornwell, a great biblical scholar tells us this about the gods:

Biblical Information of Giants (8,850 B.C. to 1,300 B.C.) Annunaki (Anak, Anakim, Anakites, Nephilim, Arba, Rephaites). Anu, Pleiades, An, Anshar, Kishar, Antu, Ki, Gibil, Nusku, Gulu, Ninmah, Nergal, Cuthah, Kuta, Gudua, Gudea, Imdugud, Ningursu, Danu.

Giants before the Flood

Then the Elohim (Hebrew idiom of a plural of magnitude or majesty (Gen. 1:1), used of heathen gods, or of angels or judges as representatives of God, Elohim is plural in sense as well as form. It's etymology, the most likely roots mean either "be strong," or "be in front," the power and preeminence of God; as to EL (Heb. 'el, God) it is a generic word for God in the Semitic languages: Aramaic elah, Arabic ilah, Akkadian ilu. In the OT, el is used over two hundred times for God. El has a plural, elim, occasionally elhm in Ugaritic; but the Hebrews needed no plural, though a plural term, 'elohim, was their regular name for God. The root from which 'el was derived may have come from 'el, "to be strong"; from an Arabic root 'ul, "to be in front of" as a leader from a Hebrew root 'lh to which both 'el and 'elohim belonged, with the meaning "strong"; from the preposition el, "to be in front of"; and using the same prepositions, as putting forth the idea of God as the goal for which all men seek. A truly satisfactory theory is impossible, because 'el and the other terms for God, 'elohim and 'eloha, are all prehistoric in origin.). They make their return in Genesis 6:2, when the "sons of God" have intercourse with the "daughters of men," .- "and they took them wives of all which they chose." The results of this event beget Lamech (Heb. lemekh, meaning undetermined), father of Noah, based his faith on the promised deliverance from the Adamic curse of Gen. 3:14-19, he foresees, even if faintly, the coming of One of his seed (cf. 1 Chron. 1:3; Luke 3:36) who will remove that curse (cf. Rom. 8:18-25). Jared was Enochs' father, who through tradition dictated to his son about 5800 B.C. "The Lamentations of Jared" how Gods came to the earth and led astray his own tribe of Adam and those tribes of Cain also.

From Adam to Noah there were seven major Patriarchs born, Noah being the eighth person as shown in 2 Peter 2:5. Note that Cain and Abel are not counted for a total of ten, but Seth was the first.

Uta-Napishtim (Babylonian Noah) was the tenth King of Babylon before the Flood. The Sumerian King List mentions five cities existing before the Flood: Eridu, Bad-tinia, Larak, Sippar, and Shuruppak.

~~~~~~~~~~~~~~~~~~~~~~~~~~~~~~

We find in studying tribes of Indians in remote areas of the world even today that they have stories of their gods and events in the past, which match almost word for word to peoples on the opposite side of the world. These tribes have never contacted other human beings and had no possible means of receiving or transmitting this information from one to another except by word of mouth and through the dreams of the Shamans of their tribes.

In all cultures throughout time, the successful Shaman would impart a special dream to the people and the people would say, "Yes! We've been dreaming that too!" and the culture would change accordingly. In the Bible there are numerous reports of dreams of Kings, which were told to the best dream analysts of the time and the running of the countries and even great wars fought over this information received in this manner.

In many cases, Kings and other people received visitations from 'angels'

We see in Zechariah Sitchin's book "Divine Encounters" in the chapters on Angels and Other Emissaries, that Jacob of the Bible had a dream, which is told in the Bible's own words (Genesis Chapter 28)

"And Jacob went out from Beersheba and went toward Harran. And he reached a certain place and went to sleep there, for the sun had set. And he took of the stones of that place and put them to rest his head on, and he lay down in that place.

And he dreamed, and beheld a ladder set up on the ground with its top reaching up to the sky. And behold angels of Elohim were going up and coming down it.

And behold, there was Yahweh standing upon it, and he spoke, saying, "I am Yahweh, the Elohim of Abraham thy ancestor and the Elohim of Isaac. The land upon which thou liest, to thee I will give it and to they seed. And thy seed shall be spread as dust on the ground, spreading west and east and northward and southward; and in thee and in they seed shall all the communities of the Earth be blessed. Behold, I am with thee; I will protect thee wherever thou goest, and I shall bring thee back to this land. I shall not abandon thee until I have done that which I am saying to you." And Jacob awakened out of his sleep, and said, "Surely Yahweh is present in this place, and I knew it not." And he was afraid, saying, "How awesome is this place! This is none other than an abode of Elohim, and this is the gateway to heaven!"

And Jacob got up early in the morning and took the stone that he had used as a pillow, and set it up as a pillar, and poured oil on it's top, and called the name of the place Beth-El."

In this Divine Encounter, in a nighttime vision, Jacob saw what, without doubt, we would nowadays call a UFO, except that to him, it was not unidentified; he well realized that its occupants or operators were divine beings, "angels of Elohim" and their Lord or commander none other than Yahweh himself, "standing upon it."

What he had witnessed left no doubt in his mind that the place was a "Gateway to Heaven" ...a place, which the Elohim could rise skyward. The wording is akin to that applied to Babylon (Bab-Lli, "Gateway of the Elohim") where the incident of the launch tower (whose head shall reach to heaven" had taken place.

The commander identified himself to Jacob as "Yahweh, the Elohim" - the DIN.GIR of Abraham thy forefather and the Elohim of Isaac." The operators of the "ladder" are identified as "Angels of Elohim" not simply as angels; and Jacob, realizing that he had unknowing stumbled upon a site used by these divine aeronauts, named the place Beth-El ("The House of El"), El being the singular of Elohim.

The Bible is careful to identify the subordinates of the deity as "Angels of Elohim" and not simply as "angels" because the Hebrew term Mal'akhim does not mean "angels" at all; it literally mean "emissaries"; and the term is employed in the bible for regular, flesh-and-blood human emissaries, who carried royal rather than divine messages.

According to Helena Blavatsky, the researches of Egyptologists present another corroboration of the identity of the Bible-allegories with those of the lands of the Pharaohs and Chaldeans. The dynastic chronology of the Egyptians, recorded by Herodotus, Manetho, Eratosthenes, diodorus Siculus, and accepted by our antiquarians, divided the period of Egyptian history under four general heads; the dominion of gods, demi-gods, heroes and mortal men.

By combining the demi-gods and heroes into one class, Gunsen reduces the periods to three; the ruling gods, the demi-gods or heroes - sons of gods, but born of mortal mothers...and the Manes, who were the ancestors of individual tribes. These

151

sub-divisions, as anyone may perceive correspond perfectly with the Biblical Elohim, sons of God, giants and mortal Noachian men.

Diodorus of Sicily and Beosus give us the names of the twelve great gods who presided over the twelve months of the year and the twelve signs of the zodiac. These names, which include Nuah, are too well known to require repetition. The double-faced Janus was also at the head of twelve gods, and in the representations of him he is made to hold the keys to the celestial domains. All these having served as models for the Biblical patriarchs, have done still further service...especially Janus... by furnished copy to St. Peter and his twelve apostles, the former also double-faced in his denial, and also represented as holding the keys of Paradise.

This statement that the story of Noah is but another version in it's hidden meaning of the story of Adam and his three sons, gathers proof on every page of the book of Genesis. Adam is the prototype of Noah, Adam falls because he eats the forbidden fruit of celestial knowledge; representing abuse of knowledge in an unbalanced mind. Adam gets stripped of his spiritual envelope; Noah of his terrestrial clothing; and the nakedness of both makes them feel ashamed. The wickedness of Cain is repeated in Ham. But the descendants of both are shown as the wisest of races on earth; and they are called on this account 'snakes' and the 'sons of snakes', meaning sons of wisdom, and not of Satan, as some divines would be pleased to have the world understand the term. Enmity has been placed between the 'snake' and the 'woman' only in this mortal phenomenal 'world of man' as 'born of woman'. Before the carnal fall, the 'snake' was Ophis, the divine wisdom, which needed no matter to procreate men, humanity being utterly spiritual. Hence the war between the snake and the woman, or between spirit and matter. If, in its material aspect, the "old serpent" is matter, and represents Ophiomorphos, in it s spiritual meaning it become Ophis-Christos. In the magic of the old Syro-Chaldeans, both are conjoint in the zodiacal sign of the androgyne of Virgo-Scorpio, and may be divided or separated whenever needed.

Thus as the origin of 'good and evil' the means of the S.S. and Z.Z. has always been interchangeable; and if upon some occasions the S.S. on sigils and talismans are suggestive of serpentine evil influence and denote a design of black magic upon others, the double S.S. are found on the sacramental cups of the Church and mean the presence of the Holy Ghost, or pure wisdom.

The Midianites were known, as the wise men, or sons of snakes, as well as Canaanites and Hamites; and such was the renown of the Midianites, that we find Moses, the prophet, led on and inspired by "the Lord" humbling himself before Hobab, the son of Raguel, the Midianite, and beseeching him to remain with the people of

Israel: "Leave us not, I pray thee; forasmuch as thou knowest how we are to encamp in the wilderness; and thou mayest be to us instead of eyes." Further, when Moses sends spies to search out the land of Canaan, they bring as a proof of the wisdom (kabalistically speaking) and goodness of the land, a branch with one cluster of grapes, which they are compelled to bear between two men on a staff, they add: "We saw the children of Anak there." They are the giants, the sons of Anak, "which come of the giants" and we were in our own sight as grasshoppers, and so we were in their sight"

Anak is Enoch, the patriarch, who dies not, and who is the first possessor of the "mirific name" according to the Kabala, and the ritual of Freemasonry.

The Bible contradicts itself here as well as the Chaldean account, for in Chapter VII of Genesis it shows "every one of them" perishing in the deluge.

Comparing the Biblical patriarchs with the descendants of Vaivaavata, the Hindu Hoah, and the old Sanskrit traditions about the deluge in the Brahmanical Mahabharata, we find them mirrored in the Vedic patriarchs who are the primitive types upon which all the others were modeled. But before comparison is possible, the Hindu myths must be comprehended in their true significance. Each of these mythical personages bears, besides an astronomical significance, a spiritual or moral, and an anthropological or physical meaning. The patriarchs are not only euphemistic gods...the prediluvian answering to the twelve great gods of Berosus, and the ten Projapatis, and the postdiluvian to the seven gods of the famous tablet in the Ninevean Library, but they stand also as the symbols of the Greek Aeons, the kabalistic Sephiroth, and the zodiacal signs, as types of a series of human races.

This variation from ten to twelve will be accounted for presently, and proved on the very authority of the Bible. Only, they are not the first gods described by Cicero, which belong to a hierarchy of higher powers, the Elohim...but appertain rather to the second class of the 'twelve gods' the Di minores, and who are the terrestrial reflections of the first, among whom Herodotus places Hercules. Alone, out of the group of twelve, Noah, by reason of his position at the transitional point, belongs to the highest Babylonian triad, Nuah, the spirit of the waters. The rest are identical with the inferior gods of Assyria and Babylonia, who represent the lower order of emanations, introduced around Bel, the Demiurge, and help him in his work, as the patriarchs are shown to assist Jehovah...the "Lord God".

Besides these, many of which were local gods, the protecting deities of rivers and cities, there were four classes of genii; we see Ezekiel making them support the throne of Jehovah in his vision. A fact which, if it identifies the Jewish "Lord God" with one of the Babylonian trinity, connects at the same time, the present Christian God with the same triad, inasmuch as it is these four cherubs, on which Irannaeus makes Jesus ride, and which are shown as the companions of the evangelists.

The Hindu kabalistic derivation of the book of Ezekiel and Revelation is shown in nothing more plainly than in this description of the four beasts, which typify the four elementary kingdoms...earth, air, fire, and water. As is well known, they are the Assyrian sphinxes, but these figures are also carved on the walls of nearly every Hindu pagoda.

The Hindu goddess Ardhanari is represented as surrounded by the same figures. It fits exactly Ezekiel's 'wheel of the Adonai', known as 'the Cherubs of Ezekiel' and indicates, beyond question, the source from which the Hebrew seer drew his allegories.

~~~~~~~~~~~

It is said that when Jesus selected SIMON as one of his disciples he changed his name to "P'tah" meaning "ENLIGHTENED ONE" and through lack of understanding of the "unenlightened" translators of the Bible they called this disciple SIMON PETER - instead of Simon the enlightened one.

The Kings of the Royal Bloodline are related Biblically to Judah, who is the "lion's whelp" (Genesis 49:9). A Templar-related story gives a clue to the meaning:

You are born a camel. You get down on your knees, and a load is placed upon you (conditioned beliefs of childhood). When you grow up and leave home, you become a lion who goes into the desert. Eventually, the lion runs into a dragon who has "Thou Shalt" written on each of his scales (confronting the conditioned beliefs). The lion slays the dragon and transforms into a baby. At that point, you have overcome the conditioned beliefs and are operating from your own heart's center.

It is also said, "The heavier the load, the stronger the lion."

The symbolism seems to be quite old. In one of the sayings in the Gnostic Gospel of Thomas, Jesus says: *"Lucky is he who eats the lion, for the lion becomes human. But, cursed is he who the lion eats, for the lion still becomes human."*

Keeping this in mind, various passages in the Book of Revelation seem clear. The Kings of the Earth "fornicate" (bond) with the harlot who is seated upon many waters, which are peoples and nations, multitudes and tongues (unconscious influences). They become "drunk" on her wine, which evokes and fury and collectively give over their "Royal Power" to the beast.

At the end of the story, the Kings of the Earth bring their glory into The New Jerusalem, which symbolizes "the order of the heavens made apparent on earth." The Tree of Life stands at the center of the city. The Tree represents a totally abundant en mass belief system, after mankind has overcome the negative influences in the collective unconscious.

It is basically the same as the Seth teaching, that we will learn to be conscious co-creators.

This is why Rev. 3:11 advises to let no one seize your "Crown," that is, your Royal Power, your ability to create your own reality consciously. It is also expressed in Isaiah 65:17, 65:21, 22, as building our own house and living in it, and planting our own vineyard and eating the fruit.

THE MASONIC CONNECTION

(They are also known as Free and Accepted Masons or Freemasons) who call themselves the world's oldest and largest fraternal order, and trace their roots to the building trade guilds of medieval Europe.

Their most identifiable symbol is the interlocking V's - the compasses and stone builder's square - framing the letter G, which stands for Geometry and God as Grand Architect.

Some scholars link the Masons' origins to the Knights Templar, an order founded on the site of the ancient Temple of Solomon in Jerusalem in 1118 following the First Crusade. They were later outlawed by Pope Clement V and persecuted, and the secret society is thought to have formed to protect fugitive Templars.

Many of North America's early patriots were Freemasons. Thirteen signers of the Constitution, fourteen Presidents of the United States Masons represent virtually every occupation and profession, yet within the Fraternity, all meet as equals. Masons come from diverse political ideologies, yet meet as friends. They come from varied religious beliefs and creeds, yet all believe in one God.

Freemasonry (or Masonry) is dedicated to the Brotherhood of Man under the Fatherhood of God.

It uses the tools and implements of ancient architectural craftsmen symbolically in a system of instruction designed to build character and moral values in its members.

Its singular purpose is to make good men better. Its bonds of friendship, compassion, and brotherly love have survived even the most divisive political, military, and religious conflicts through the centuries. It has been said recently that even priests

155

are becoming Masons though it is officially against the laws of the Catholic Church.

~~~~~~~~~~

An interesting person in history was Thomas the Apostle: He is also known as Didymus; the Twin; Apostle of India; and Doubting Thomas

He was ready to die with Jesus when Christ went to Jerusalem, but is best remembered for doubting the Resurrection until allowed to touch Christ's wounds. Preached in Parthia, Persia and India, though he was so reluctant to start the mission that he had to be taken into slavery by a merchant headed that way. He eventually gave in to God's will, was freed, and planted the new Church over a wide area. He formed many parishes and built many churches along the way. His symbol is the builder's square, from an ancient story that built a palace for King Guduphara in India.

THAT ANCIENT SQUARE

What one symbol most typically represents Freemasonry as a whole? Mason and non-Mason alike will answer, "The Square!" Many learned writers on Freemasonry have denominated the square as the most important and vital, most typical and common symbol of the ancient Craft.

Whether in Masonry or in the building trades, the dominant law is the law of the square." Newton stated: "Very early the square became an emblem of truth, justice and righteousness, and so it remains to this day, though uncountable ages have passed. Simple, familiar, eloquent; it brings from afar a sense of wonder of the dawn, and it still teaches a lesson we find it hard to learn."

"An important emblem - passed into universal acceptance." In his encyclopedia, Kenning copied Mackey's phrase. Klein reverently denominates it "The Great Symbol." I Kings, describing the Temple, states that "all the doors and the posts were square." It is impossible definitely to say that the square is the oldest symbol in Freemasonry; who may determine when the circle, triangle or square first impressed men's minds? But the square is older than history. Newton speaks of the oldest building known to man: "- A prehistoric tomb found in the sands at Hieraconpolis, is already right angled."

156

To the Masons the word "square" has the same three meanings given the syllable by the world:

(1) The conception of right angleness - the Masonic ritual tells us that the square is an angle of ninety degrees, or the fourth of a circle;

(2) The builder's tool, one of our working tools, the Master's own immovable jewel;

(3) That quality of character, which has made "a square man" synonymous not only with a member of our Fraternity, but with uprightness, honesty and dependability.

The earliest of the three meanings must have been the mathematical conception.

Plato, the greatest of the Greek philosophers, wrote over the porch of the house in which he taught: "Let no one who is ignorant of geometry entry my doors."

Zenocrates , a follower of Plato, turned away an applicant for the teaching of the Academy, who was ignorant of geometry, with the words: "Depart, for thou has not the grip of philosophy."

The science of measurements is concerned with angles, the construction of figures, the solution of problems concerning both, and all the rest upon the construction of a right angle, the solutions which sprang from the Pythagorean Problem, our "Forty-Seventh Problem of Euclid," so prominent in the Master's Degree.

The ancient Greek name of the square was "gnomon," from whence comes our word "knowledge." The Greek letter "gamma" formed like a square standing on one leg, the other pointing to the right - in all probability derived from the square, and "gnomon," in turn, derived from the square which the philosophers knew was at the root of their mathematics.

Democritus, old philosopher, according to Clement of Alexandria, once exulted: "In the construction of plane figures with proof, no one has yet surpassed me, not even the Harpedonaptae of Egypt." In the truth of his boast we have no interest, but much in the Harpedonaptae of Egypt. The names means, literally, "rope stretchers" or "Rope fasteners."

In the Berlin museum is a deed, written on leather, dating back to 2,000 B.C. which speaks of the work of rope stretchers; how much older rope stretching may be, as a means of constructing a square, is unknown, although the earliest known mathematical hand-book (that of Ahmes, who lived in the sixteenth or seventeenth Hyskos dynasty in Egypt, and is apparently a copy of a much older work which scholars trace back to 3400 B.C.), does not mention rope stretching as a means of square construction.

Masons learn of Pythagorean's astonishment and delight at his discovery of the principle of the Forty-seventh Problem.

Researchers into the manner of construction of pyramids, temples and monuments in Egypt reveal a very strong feeling on the part of the builders for the proper orientation of their structures. Successfully to place the building so that certain points, corners or openings might face the sun or a star at a particular time, required very exact measurements. Among these, the laying down of the cross axis at a right angle to the main axis of the structure was highly important.

It was this, which the Harpedonaptae accomplished with a long rope. The cord was first marked off in twelve equal portions, possible by knots, more probably, by markers placed into the body of the rope. The marked rope was then laid upon the line on which a perpendicular (right angle) was to be erected. The rope was pegged down at the third marker from one end, and another, four markers further on. This left two free ends, one three total parts long, one five total parts long. With these ends the Harpedonatae scribed two semi-circles. When the point where these two met, was connected to the first peg (three parts from the end of the rope, a perfect right angle, or square, resulted.

It is of interest to recall McBride's explanation of the "center" as used in English Lodges, and the "point within a circle," familiar to us. He traces the medieval "secret of the square" to the use of the compasses to make the circle from which the square is laid out.

Lines connecting a point, placed anywhere on the circumference of a circle, to the intersection with the circumference cut by a straight line passing through the center of the circle, forms a perfect square.

Limits of the square.' This would be 481 B.C., but it is in the words of the great follower, Mencius, who flourished nearly two hundred years later, that we meet with a fuller and more impressive Masonic phraseology. In one chapter we are taught that just as the most skilled articifers are unable, without the aid of the square and compasses, to produce perfect rectangles or perfect circles, so must all men apply these tools figuratively to their lives, and the level and the markingline besides, if they would walk in the straight and even paths of wisdom, and keep themselves within the bounds of honor and virtue.

"The compasses and Square are the embodiment of the rectangular and the round, just as the prophets of old were the embodiment of the due relationship between man and man."

"The Master Mason, in teaching his apprentices, makes use of the compasses and the square. Ye who are engaged in the pursuit of wisdom must also make use of the compasses and the square." In the "Great Learning," admitted on all sides to date from between 300 to 400 years before Christ, that a man should abstain from doing unto others what he would not they should do unto him: "This, is called the principle of acting on the square."

T - TAU

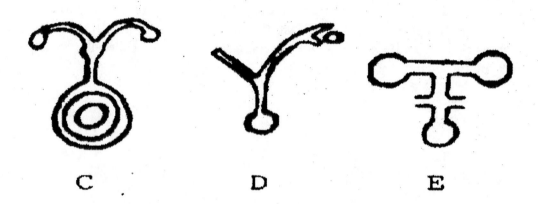

In 1990 a group of people saw two apple trees in an orchard shaking violently. They found a half ring formed in the field next to the trees. In 1991 several patterns appeared that had Tau-like shapes (C, D & E).

The first one (C) is said to be the Irmensul, the ancient German tree of life. It reminded me of a Gnostic account saying that one's world is like the womb, with the placenta as the Garden of Eden. The second one (D), I felt, might be related to a message I heard in a dream: "I'm stretching out my limb in order for you to watch it grow."

An important symbol of the change is the Tau, depicted at a "T" with two trees and a flower on top, or as a split-trunk tree with three branches at each end. The two trees, I believe, represent the dual aspects and the two ways to knowledge, rational and intuitional.

A T-Tau like pattern appeared at Charley Knoll in 1993. I was reminded of Mayan depictions of the Tau, with two trees and a flower atop the cross arm. A researcher showed that a reversed five-pointed star is revealed in the geometry of the Charley Knoll design. One writer pointed out that it might be related to the seven chakras.

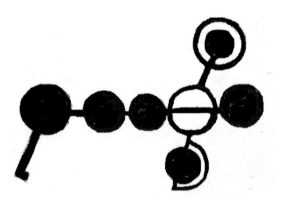

Charley Knoll, Nr Loughborough, Middlesex. Formed 7th July, 1993

I happened to read the first pages of The Secret Doctrine (vol. 1) after reading about the Charley Knoll formation. On pages 4 and 5, Blavatsky shows a number of ancient glyphs, most all of which have appeared as crop patterns in some form. Three of them seem to be within the Charley Knoll pattern.

Tawsmead Copse, Nr West Stowell, Wiltshire. Formed 9th August, 1998

OMNI: ARE EXTRATERRESTRIALS STEERING US TO A ONE-WORLD RELIGION THROUGH CROP CIRCLES?

"The Magnificent Seven"

The formation is 300 feet in diameter, 175 little circles, each with a different twisted center like a birds-nest. Seven-fold geometry is rare in crop circles, but one month before the magnificent Seven formation at Tawsmead Copse another seven-fold geometry had appeared in the East Field a mile away. The logical geometry construction evolution would have been from Tawsmead Copse to the East Field, but the phenomenon put the patterns down in reverse order. What is even stranger about this formation is that two people had spent the night outside that night - to watch a lunar eclipse on the night of August 8, 1998. The experience started about 11:30 p.m. First they saw two red lights in the distance. Then two very clear white lights, one directly above the other, very round, which only lasted a second. They were like two bubbles bursting, and then they disappeared. They saw a light come down, split into three - a red one and two white ones, which moved own over the landscape. The lights were bright white with a dark rim around the outside - round, smooth lights. It was a bright, full moon and they said they could actually see the crop go down. They sat there and watched the event until about 5:30 a.m. The lights were moving around the field the entire time.

Reported by Nikki and Andrew Saville.

The number 175 comes from the majic square of 7, but there is more to it than that. Here are the other meanings of the number 49:
Buddha remained 49 days near the tree named "Bô".
When the religious tradition of the Orient refers in its teachings to the psychic nature of the man, it uses the knowledge relative to the centers of force called by Hindus "chakras" (wheel) or again "padma" (lotus). These centers are 7 majors, 21 averages and 49 minors, but only the 7 majors one have retained the attention because of their importance in the initiatory process.
The seven cosmic plans include 49 under plans and the seven races which, according to the Theosophy, evolve on a planetary globe, include 49 under races.
A legend tells that Indra cut the foetus of Diti in seven parts, then each one in seven, giving 49 parts.
The Book of the Jubilees of the writings of the library of Qumran (written approximately 100 years before Jesus Christ) talks about the rules concerning jubilees and the strict laws for the observance of the Sabbath. At the end, a passage mentions:

"there are 49 jubilees plus one week and two years from Adam until this day; there is again forty years to come to learn the commandments of the Lord before the sons of Israel enter the earth of Canaan and cross the Jordan to the west."

The Zohar indicates that there exists 49 interpretations of the Writings, and that can even go up until 70 degrees of interpretations.

The "devanagari", or writing of the gods, employed for the traditional Sanskrit language, has 49 simple signs.

In an Ethiopian apocryphal book, named "The Wisdom of Sibyl", it is question of the 49 cycles of Ezra, each one counting 143 years, for a total of 7007 years. The Days of the Lord are 7 told the Sibyl, what gives, for one Day, a duration of 1001 years.

The Tibetans see in this number the intermediate world, the "Bardo" (bar: between; do: two; between two worlds: the Earth and the Sky), space where the soul has to wander during 49 days following the death.

The magic square using the 49 first numbers is associated with the Venus planet and has as sum 175.

MAGIC SQUARE 7

30	39	48	1	10	19	28
38	47	7	9	18	27	29
46	6	8	17	26	35	37
5	14	16	25	34	36	45
13	15	24	33	42	44	4
21	23	32	41	43	3	12
22	31	40	49	2	11	20

All rows, all columns and both diagonals add up to 175

Buried into the southern shore of Orkney Island, Sandwick Bay Bay o' Skaill is the Neolithic village of Skara Brae.

In the winter of 1850, a great storm battered Orkney island and revealed a small village of house under what had been a large mound known as Skerrabra. Revealed was the outline of a series of stone buildings excavated on the site.

By 1868, the remains of four ancient houses had been unearthed. But it wasn't until 1925 when another storm damaged some of the previously excavated structures that anything was done about them. A sea-wall was built to preserve these remains, but during the construction work more ancient structures were discovered. Radio-carbon dating in the early 1970s showed it actually dated from the late Neolithic, inhabited between 3200 BC and 2200 BC. The tiny village is made up of eight dwellings, linked together by a series of low alleyways.

Because of the protection offered by the sand that cocooned the settlement for 4,000 years, these buildings and their contents are incredibly well-preserved with the walls of the huts still standings and alleyways still roofed with their original stone slabs.

Each house shares the same basic design, leading to a large square room with a central fireplace, a bed on either side, and a shelved dresser on the wall opposite the doorway.

In its lifetime the village became embedded in its own rubbish and this, together with the encroaching sand dunes meant that the village was gradually abandoned before being finally covered by a drifting wall of sand.

What was previously considered to be a stone dresser, is in fact an altar, which is itself symbolic of an Ancient Egyptian Temple and its inherent cosmic meaning. The top slab of the altar and the double central column forms the letter T, the Ancient Egyptian "Tau", which represents the Sacred Gateway, Portal or Opening. It is through this Sacred Gateway that the Sun rises to herald in the Dawn of a New Age of the Zodiac.

The Tau is represented by the letter "T".
These hieroglyphs translate as "Sacred Opening"

When Sacred Taus are joined together horizontally they represent a temple. In Ancient Egypt huge columns were erected in this same fashion. Henges in Britain are also Sacred Taus joined together, often in a circular design, to form a temple.

A Double Tau forms a Dolmen.

The hieroglyph for "Temple" at the top of the Narmer Plate. Notice how "Tau" is formed in the space above the temple. The Narmer Plate is an Ancient Egyptian artifact, which commemorates the Dawn of the Age of Taurus. (Also known as the Nermer Plate) The Narmer Plate is a sky chart depicting the sky at night in the year 4468BCE.

The Triple Tau represents the Temple of Jerusalem

Taus originated in Ancient Egypt, representing Temples, which are Gateways for the Sun at the Dawn of a New Age of the Zodiac. Temples are used to track the movements of the Sun during both what is called the 'ordinary year' and 'Great Year', in order to predict Solstices and Equinoxes. In the Great Year they predict the next Age of the Zodiac in the Precession of the Equinoxes.

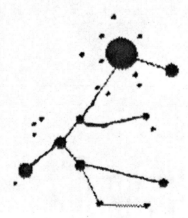

The centre of a flower with seven petals represents the star Sirius.

BROADBURY BANK, AUGUST 2000
An example of a seven petalled flower

The seven petals represent the seven minor stars surrounding Sirius. The King of the Seven Stars is in fact a personified portrayal of the constellation of Canis Major.

The star Sirius represents the King's head. The body, legs and left arm of Canis Major represent those of the King. The axe of the star system is lying in a horizontal position. The container held in the King's right hand is represented by the three stars on the right hand side of the body of Canis Major.

Around the neck of Sirius, the "King of the Seven Stars", is the double tau, (the "pi" symbol). The Tau hieroglyph in the Ancient Egyptian Book of the Dead makes it clear that "Tau" means "holy or sacred gate" or "holy or sacred opening".

The five-pointed star denotes the word "sacred".

The five-pointed star was considered "sacred" because it was a symbol encoding the Secret of Precession. The number of degrees around the center-point of the star (360) divided by the number of arms of the star (5) equals the number seventy-two. Seventy-two is the number of years that it takes for the sky-bodies to appear to move through one degree of their cycle. 72 synchronicitly is the number of the names of God as well.

When the seventy-two years are multiplied by the three hundred and sixty degrees of the complete cycle, we find that it takes is 25,920 years for each heavenly cycle to be completed … at which time the process starts all over again. This is the cycle referred to as Precession.

BOURBON BISHOPS CANNINGS, WILTSHIRE, JULY, 1997

The Double and Triple Tau are the plural form of Tau. When the Taus join together on a horizontal plane, they represent a temple, such as in the hieroglyph depiction between the Taurus Bulls' heads in the chiefs on each side of the Narmer Plate. The vertical trunks of the Taus represent the columns of the Temple.

In the Osiris Legend, Osiris was encased in a tree trunk, which was later utilized as a pillar. The pillar of a temple is thus seen as representing Osiris. Osiris is seen as the Axis Munde in the Djed Pillar; the Pillar of Stability. Multiple Taus form a Temple, which then open a portal to the Netherworld from which the Sun is seen to rise when the new Zodiac begins.

The Triple Tau represents the Temple of Jerusalem. Since a Tau represents a Gateway, then the Temple of Jerusalem similarly being a portal or gateway to the Netherworld complete with Osirian Pillars also represents the Sun rising at the Dawn of a new Zodiac arising in the skies above us.

The Great Pyramid is also built on a Sacred Mound and, like the Osirian Pillar, it represents the Axis Munde. The Temple of Jerusalem as the Triple Tau, is secured within the triangle of the Great Pyramid. The Great Pyramid and the Temple of Jerusalem are symbolic of the Sacred Summit, the Axis Munde, and the concept of Precession.

The Axis Mundi or World Pillar is the spot at which the skies revolve around over their vast time cycles. The reason that Precession occurs is that the Earth not only rotates on its axis ... otherwise known as Axis Mundi or World Pillar .. it also wobbles. This wobble effect is a phenomenon caused by forces exerted by the Sun on the bulges of the Earth at the Equator.

The wobble effect is best explained in terms of a spinning top. As the top begins to lose momentum it begins to wobble. It is this same kind of circular movement, or wobble, of the Earth, which moving at a constant speed over long periods of time alters the direction of the Polar Axis. One revolution is completed every 25,920 years. The central point of revolution is called the "pole of the ecliptic".

In the New Testament the angel Gabriel foretells to Zachary the birth of the Precursor, and to Mary that of the Saviour.

Thus he is throughout the angel of the Incarnation and of Consolation, and so in Christian tradition Gabriel is ever the angel of mercy while Michael is rather the angel of judgment. At the same time, even in the Bible, Gabriel is, in accordance with his name, the angel of the Power of God, and it is worth while noting the frequency with which such words as "great", "might", "power", and "strength" occur. The Jews seem to have dwelt particularly upon this feature in Gabriel's character, and he is regarded by them as the angel of judgment, while Michael is called the angel of mercy. Thus they attribute to Gabriel the destruction of Sodom and of the host of Sennacherib, though they also regard him as the angel who buried Moses, and as the man designated to mark the figure Tau on the foreheads of the elect (Ezekiel 4). In later Jewish literature the names of angels were considered to have a peculiar efficacy, and the British Museum possesses some magic bowls inscribed with Hebrew, Aramaic, and Syriac incantations in which the names of Michael, Raphael, and Gabriel occur. These bowls were found at Hillah, the site of Babylon, and constitute an interesting relic of the Jewish captivity. In apocryphal Christian literature the same names occur, in the works of Enoch, and in the Apocalypse of the Blessed Virgin.

On August 11, 1999, a planetary cross surrounded the Earth during a Total Eclipse of the Sun. When 2000 A.D. drew near, the planets were positioned in LION,

169

EAGLE, OX and MAN, the creatures of the apocalypse. Remarkably, a second cross in the form of a TAU, Ezekiel's sign of Victory, surrounded the Earth as well. On that August day, planet Earth appeared to have been crucified in space.

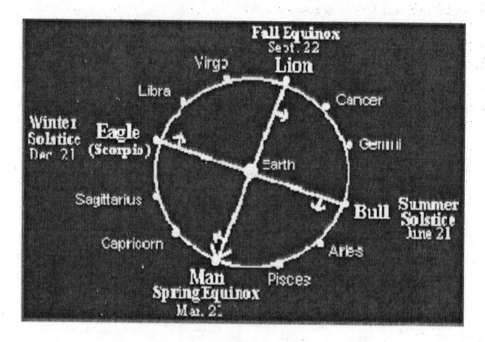

The Grand Cross Alignment -
The Sphinx, The Zodiac, The Four Living Creatures
and The Twelve Tribes

Prior to and during the eclipse of 1999 the planets aligned in a Grand Cross, pointing to Leo, Taurus, Aquarius, and Scorpio. In ancient times Scorpio was symbolized by an eagle. Scholars say that these Zodiac signs marked the positions of the solstices and equinoxes during the Age of Taurus. They also aligned in a similar way during the Ages of Leo and Scorpio, and will again in the Age of Aquarius, as the signs are 90 degrees apart from each other.

The Sphinx, as the lion/man, may represent the Zodiac Ages from Leo to Aquarius. These Zodiac signs are the Four Living Creatures of Ezekiel and Revelation - the lion, the ox, the man, and the eagle (see Ezekiel 1 and Rev. 4:6-8). This symbolism was well known prior to Ezekiel, in the ancient near-east. It is also associated with the twelve tribes of Israel. There is evidence, including Biblical sources, indicating that

170

some of the Tribes traveled to the British Isles long ago. The sign of the Zodiac are said to be within the natural landscape around Glastonbury. The area is also called, "The New Jerusalem."

Daniel Walsh's book, "Lost Tribes of Israel Study Maps" is very informative. He traces the history and travels of the ancient Hebrews. Prior to the Exodus, and again later, some of the Hebrew people traveled to other lands, including into western Europe and the British Isles. Through marriage, the Royal Bloodline was reunited in Britain, that is, the married pair were of the bloodlines of the two twin sons of Judah, Pharez and Zarah.

Judah was associated with the lion, because he is called "a lion's whelp" in Genesis 49:9. The scepter, the ruler's staff, will remain with him, that is, his bloodline, until one comes to whom it belongs. Daniel Walsh pointed out that the four main tribes and their symbols are these:

Judah - Lion
Ephraim - Ox or Bull
Reuben - Face of a Man
Dan - Eagle

Daniel referred to Numbers 2:1-33. The Twelve Tribes are set up in quadrants in their encampments around the central Tabernacle. Each quadrant has three Tribes, with a leading Tribe for each. The Tribe of Judah is on the East, the Tribe of Reuben is on the South, the Tribe of Ephraim is on the West, and the Tribe of Dan is on the North.

When the Tribes set out on the march, Judah was the lead Tribe, followed by the others in the same order given in the camp positions. The Levites are an extra group in the center with the tent of meeting, or Tabernacle, and they are not numbered among the people of Israel.

This seems to be yet another "coincidence" to add to the list. The Tribes of Israel correspond directly with the Grand Cross and Zodiac in the heavens at the time of the eclipse, over an area with the Zodiac signs in the landscape, and over a people thought to have the Royal Blood of the Ancient Hebrew Kings.

Judah, then, as the leader, can in the grander sense, be thought of as representing mankind, or the path of mankind in spiritual evolution.

OMNI: ARE EXTRATERRESTRIALS STEERING US TO A ONE-WORLD RELIGION THROUGH CROP CIRCLES?

Nostradamus Prophecy

The Nostradamus quatrain, C10, Q72 may to be related to the eclipse:

In 1999 and seven months
From the sky will descend a great terrifying King
Who will resuscitate the great King ANGOLMOIS.
Before and after, Mars reigns happily.

In the seventh month of 1999, the planets were in the Grand Cross alignment, and a lunar eclipse did occur. The following month, the great solar eclipse took place. Joan Sckrabulis has written a great book about the 1999 eclipse, called The Lost Covenant. ANGOLMOIS, Joan says, means, SANG + LION + SOLOMON, giving - "Blood of the Lion, Solomon".

The last line of the above Nostradamus Quatrain may be related to Eliphas Levi's statement that the blade of the magical sword should be forged in the hour of Mars, with new tools.

The Philosophical Research Society quotes Manly P Hall, "

Eliphas Levi describes the preparation of a magical sword in substance as follows: The steel blade should be forged in the hour of Mars, with new tools. The pommel should be of hollow silver containing quicksilver, and the symbols of Mercury and the moon and the signatures of Gabriel and Samael should be engraved upon it. The hilt should be encased with tin, with the symbol of Jupiter and the signature of Michael engraved upon it. A copper triangle should extend from the hilt along the blade a short distance on each side: These should bear the symbols of Mercury and Venus. Five Sephiroth should be engraved upon the handle, as shown. The blade itself should have the word Malchut upon one side and Quis ut Deus upon the other. The sword should be consecrated on Sunday."

~~~~~~~~~~~~~~~~~~~~

The Sphinx is The Father of Terror

Richard Hoagland and other scientists have found evidence suggesting that the structures in the Cydonia area of Mars are monuments built by intelligent beings many thousands of years ago. The geometry and mathematics indicate a link between the structures on Mars and the ancient monuments at Giza in Egypt, the pyramids and Sphinx. The word, Cairo, means Mars. The ancient Arab word for the Sphinx means "the Father of Terror." Could this be related to the "great terrifying King" in the Nostradamus quatrain?

The Sphinx as The Zodiac

It seems likely that the Sphinx is related to the Zodiac Ages Leo (the lion) and Aquarius (the man). Recent investigations suggest that it was built much earlier than previously proposed. It was probably built in the Age of Leo, and faced East, aligned with the Zodiac sign of Leo on the spring equinox. Directly behind, at 180-degrees was Aquarius. As the equinox point has moved through almost six Ages covering some 12,960 years, the alignment of the Sphinx will be 180-degrees reversed from the original.

Some researchers believe that the Sphinx originally had wings and the hindquarters of an ox, to represent the two other Zodiac signs, Scorpio and Taurus. Others say it is a cryptogram of the Zodiac.

Judah and The Sphinx

Verses in the Book of Genesis 49:9-10 suggests that Judah may be related to the symbolism of the Sphinx, and this is related to his status of being the King:

Judah is a lion's whelp; from the prey, my son, you have gone up. He stooped down, he couched as a lion, and as a lioness; who dares rouse him up? The scepter shall not depart from Judah, nor the ruler's staff from between his feet, until he comes to whom it belongs; and to him shall be the obedience of the peoples."

The part reading "until he comes," is sometimes translated as, "until Shiloh comes." As I understand it, some churches teach that Shiloh refers to Jesus Christ, and the verse indicates His second-coming. But, others say that Shiloh was a word meaning simply a person. I also read that Shiloh was a place where the Temple of the Levites was placed at one time.

The Royal Bloodline and the Rightful King

The idea of the Royal Bloodline of Kings and the dispute as to the "rightful king," is found extensively throughout history. My personal experiences with dreams and "coincidences" also led to these legends. I believe the legends carry very important symbolic messages about mankind. The symbolism involved in the solar eclipse, in terms of the location, time (11:11 a.m.), and the Grand Cross alignment of the planets, seem quite connected to the Royal Bloodline of Kings.

The Egyptian dispute between Osiris, Typhon-Seth (or Set), and Horus is one of them. H.P. Blavatsky wrote that the Cain/Able/Seth story in Genesis was based on the Egyptian version, as was the story of Esau and Jacob. Jacob took the name Israel, and his sons became the basis of the Twelve Tribes of Israel. One of his sons was Judah, from whom came the Biblical Royal Bloodline of Kings, leading eventually to Jesus. Some say Judah's brother, Joseph, and his bloodline became the rulers during the time the tribes were in Egypt.

Chapter 38 of Genesis tells the very strange story of the twins, born of Judah and Tamar. Tamar was married to Judah's first son, and later to the second son. Both were apparently unfit, and therefore were killed by God. Judah promised Tamar that she would marry his third son, but he delayed for a long time. In frustration, Tamar hatched a plot. She dressed up like a harlot, and waited by the city gates. She offered the unsuspecting Judah sex for a price. Judah offered a kid from the flock, but Tamar wanted a pledge to make sure the kid would be brought later. Judah gave her is signet, staff and cord, to be retrieved later when the kid was delivered.

Later, Judah sent his friend with the kid, to retrieve his items. The "harlot" was nowhere to be found. Months later, it was reported to Judah that Tamar was pregnant from playing the harlot. Judah was angry, saying "Bring her out, and let her be burned." Tamar presented the signet, staff and cord, exposing Judah as the one who had made her pregnant.

When the time of delivery came, a strange, breach birth of twins took place. A hand came out of the womb. The midwife bound the hand with a scarlet thread. The hand withdrew back into the womb, and then the other twin, Perez (meaning "breach"), was born first. The other twin, Zerah, was then born, who became known as "Zerah of the Scarlet Thread."

At the battle of Jericho, there was only one family in the city that helped Joshua and his men. This was the family of Rahab, who lived in the walls. She signaled to the spies by placing a scarlet thread in the window. This is said to signify Zerah of the

Scarlet Tread, and his bloodline. Rahab was later part of the Royal Bloodline, as she had a child by Boaz, the son of King Solomon.

Both Tamar and Rahab are listed in the genealogy of Jesus Christ, as given on the first page of the New Testament (Matthew 1-16).

It is significant in terms of symbolism, that the "pretend harlot" and the real harlot in the genealogy are part of the Royal Bloodline. Revelation 17 speaks of the harlot of Babylon, with whom the kings of the earth have committed fornication. They become drunk on her wine, which causes fury, and give over their "royal power to the beast" until the words of God are fulfilled.

When the New Jerusalem comes, the kings of the earth bring their glory into it (Rev. 21:24). This could be related symbolically to Judah in Genesis 38 and 49, as the verses in Revelation seem to indicate a change in the kings of the earth. Remember, the Scepter, the ruler's staff, stays with Judah - who "fornicated with the harlot" - until the person comes to whom it belongs. That person, it seems, is the "rightful King."

My own research led to the conclusion that the harlot of Revelation 17 has the same meaning as Kali in the eastern religions. The harlot/Kali seems to represent the furious consciousness of mankind during our warring time cycle. A karmic or "judgment" function is involved, which seems to be a way of learning.

In the Sumerian story of Enlil and Enki, there is also a dispute as to who is the rightful ruler, perhaps suggesting that this symbolism goes back to the dawn of history.

Lawrence Gardner, a brilliant scholar has recently produced some very interesting and significant material concerning the Royal Bloodlines.

"The Most Synchronistic Day of the Millennium"

11 August 1999
At 222 + 1/2.22 days (10:49 UT 11 Aug 99),
the last total solar eclipse of the century lasts
2 minutes 22.2 seconds
during the appearance of
2 - 22nd Hebrew letters (taus) in the sky . . .
The Destiny of America - 1776 = 222 x 2 x 2 x 2

The final solar eclipse of the last millennium occurred on August 11, 1999. It began in the Atlantic Ocean at 9:30 a.m., reaching full eclipse over Greenwich, England at 11:11 a.m. This was a Leo eclipse with Sun and Moon at 88 degrees Leo.

At the same time there was a North Node eclipse, with the North Node at 13 degrees Leo. Astrologically, the North Node eclipse represents movement toward our collective destiny.

At the time of this major eclipse, a powerful Grand Cross was in formation within the four fixed signs of the zodiac, representing the fixed conditions in which all manifestation takes place. This is depicted by Tarot card 21, "The World", the final card of the Major Arcanum. The bull, Taurus, represents the element of Earth that gives form; the lion stands for Leo and the element of fire; the eagle is connected with Scorpio and the element of water; the man represents Aquarius and the element of air. These are also the four beasts of the Apocalypse as referred to in the Book of Revelation. The Hebrew letter assigned to Tarot card 21 is "Tav" which means "cross," referring to "world consciousness" and dominion over slavery. It is assigned astrologically to the planet Saturn. The fixed cross has been described by Alice Bailey as "a transition in consciousness," and "an initiation of the soul by the fires of God."

In addition to the planetary cross, a "T-square" or "Tau" was present on August 11, in which Mercury in Leo opposed Neptune in Aquarius, both squaring Jupiter in Taurus. The "T-square" carries the energy of self-transcendence. Another synchronicity of August 11 was a heliocentric "Grand Sextile (six pointed star) in perfect balance, representing an elevated level of spiritual consciousness in the higher dimensions of existence. There was at the same time a new moon that formed a conjunction with the Sun, resulting in the seeding of the New World within the "Divine Feminine." The

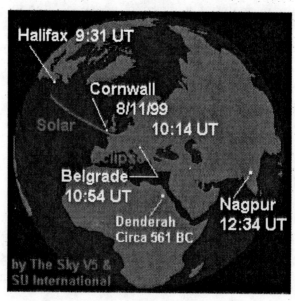

ultimate result of these dynamic and archetypal formations was the opening of the most powerful and promising portal in human history - the Window into the Great "Age of Light," the new Aquarian Age of the 21st Century.

In Chinese Astrology, August 11, 1999 was the first day of the Water Monkey month. This date prophesied a bright, warm day in which the opportunity existed for people to use their intuition to obtain what they need just prior to actually needing it.

Synchronistically, those observing the Aztec Sun Calendar called August 13 "The Day of Destiny". (Many astrologers conclude that the difference in dates between August 11 and August 13 are probably due to discrepancies between our calendar and the Aztec Sun calendar, so they both were actually referring to the same astronomical events and time.) The Sun Calendar prophesied for this date "movement, freedom, change, simplification, the sky, Heaven, visions, inspiration, emptying, completion, returning to origin, centrality, choice, possibility and the beginning of a new cycle."

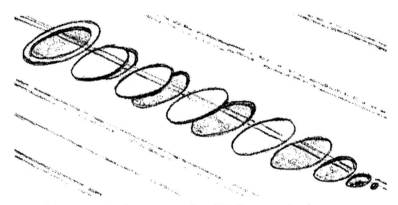

This crop circle appeared at Wallop, nr Andover,
Hampshire, England. Reported Monday 3rd May,
strongly suggesting a solar eclipse.

The solar eclipse of August 11, 1999 might well be one of the most important events in human history. At the very least, it will be one of the most incredible "coincidental" symbolic events of all time. It could be far more, perhaps the Ascension, the Transformation, the return to the Golden Age, the change of the Ages from Pisces to Aquarius, the return of the Avatar, or the second coming of Christ.

There are various coincidences concerning the time and location of the eclipse. The date, August 11, coincides with a number of events in the crop circle phenomena and in a few other ways. The time, 11:11 a. m., has extensive "coincidental" associations. The location, specifically - where the eclipse shadow strikes land at Cornwall, the southwestern tip of England, has the most incredible legendary and symbolic associations, including the Arthurian legends of the Quest for the Holy Grail.

~~~~~~~~~~~~~~~

The Crop Circle Connection

The Grail legends are often said to combine Christian beliefs with other mythology, primarily Celtic. The crop circles have often portrayed pre-Christian or esoteric European symbols, such as the Celtic Cross of 1988, the Irmesul ancient German Tree of Life of 1991, the Dharmic Wheel of 1992, the Kabalistic Tree of Life of 1997, and the 1998 Beltane Wheel.

At least three Christian symbols have appeared, two of them indirectly. Several years ago, the Christian "Fish" symbol appeared as part of a crop formation. Dowsing within the Winterborne Stoke Swastika Circle of 1989, revealed the basic design of The New Jerusalem Plan, based on St. John's vision in Revelation. The total of the square footage of the circles in the Barbury Castle formation of 1991 was 31,680, a number associated with a distance around The New Jerusalem. One tenth of that number, 3,168, was associated with "Lord Jesus Christ" by the early Christians, and previously to a figure in the Pagan religion. A "666" type crop formation appeared in 1993. The sixes were arranged in a triangle.

Update July 5, 1999: An incredibly significant symbol appeared as a crop formation at the end of May, 1999. It was the Menorah, the lampstand with seven lamps mentioned in both the Old and New Testaments. It clearly seems related to the Tree of Life crop circle formation, which appeared in the same area in 1997.

~~~~~~~~~~~~~~~

Ancient Number Codes

In Revelation 13:18, 666 is said to be the number of man. The number was associated with the sun in Greek Gematria. 3168, 666, and other numbers involved with the crop formations were part of a very ancient system of numbers.

The Southern Cross Constellation

The Southern Cross (CRUX) is now the smallest of all 88 constellations covering just 68 square degrees. Visible in the past to many of the great civilizations in the north, precession of the equinoxes has carried it from the view of all those effectively above the tropics. Though now no longer visible in the north temperate zone, it was seen there from the time of Adam and Seth to that of the Christian era. Owing to the greater thickness of the earth at the equator, that part of the earth comes every year a little sooner to what are called the equinoxes, the points where the ecliptic crosses the equator. Consequently the north pole moves every year a little farther on in the circle it describes in the northern sky. Thus it has gradually receded from the Southern Cross. This movement being known to be about 50 inches in a year, the place of the stars in ancient times can be ascertained by it.

It is well known that the cross was a sacred emblem in the Egyptian mythology. The Arabians and Indians also, before the coming of Christ, venerated this emblem. There is in the British Museum a large silvery cross, taken from the mummy of an Egyptian priest. Sozomenes, AD 443, relates that "there was found in the temple of Serapis the sign of the cross, surrounded by hieroglyphics, which meant the life to come." The last letter in the Hebrew alphabet, thau, was originally in the form of a cross; and its name means boundary, limit, finishing (as in Genesis 49:26), as of the Messiah's work, as when He said, "It is finished."

"In the fourth century the Christian anchorites in the Thebaid would see the Southern Cross at an altitude of 10 degrees." "It will again appear in the northern latitudes, but after the lapse of thousands of years" (Humboldt).

Should any one wish to follow, on the modern celestial globe, the position assigned to this constellation in former ages, it will be necessary to reckon back the precession of the equinoxes to the time required, as altering the boundaries of the signs, the position of the colures and of the pole of the earth. While the pole of the ecliptic, in reference to which the stars are divided, is fixed, the pole of the equator has a motion in consequence of that of the equinoxes. About 6000 years since it would point to the brightest star in the tail of the dragon, which must be considered as the pole-star, in trying to rectify the globe for that time. This must be done for N. lat. 36 degrees or thereabouts, which the traces of ancient astronomy have been thought to indicate as that where the earliest observations were made. Such being the situation of the sources of the river Euphrates, this supposition agrees with what is said in Genesis 2 as to the original habitation of mankind, the fountains at least of great rivers apparently not having been altered by the deluge. The Southern Cross will then be found to rise about 16 degrees above the horizon when on the meridian; this altitude gradually lessening, its highest star will be seen to have disappeared from the latitude of Jerusalem about the time of the crucifixion of Jesus.

For the ancient Maya, the cross represents both the constellation of the Southern Cross and the "Sacred Tree" its four branches analogous to the four elements and the four cardinals points.

There is an ancient legend thousands of years old that tells of a time when Earth's inhabitants knew perfect peace in heart and mind. During this era our solar system was moving through a different part of the cosmos. In the story of the lost continent of Mu in the South Pacific there was a constellation of stars, known today as the Southern Cross. When this group of stars passed over Mu at a specific angle each year it brought the rains for the gardens. The shape of this constellation inspired the letter T. On Mu it was pronounced Tau (tah-oo).

The letter T is one of the oldest symbols known to humanity and comes from this legend. The Greeks have carried this symbol forward and have made it the nineteenth letter in their alphabet. The letter T heads the word "Tree" and can be seen as a tree. This T also centers the word "altar". The vertical line holding up the horizontal line reveals the structure of the T, as well as the basic design of most altars--elevated structures. The "Tau" heads the Zodiac constellation Taurus, the Fixed earth sign vibration of Mazzaroth. The brightest star in the constellation of Taurus is

Alderbaran, which in Arabic means Follower of the Pleiades-- the seven sisters, the seven levels of being. The term "Tao" originates from "Tau". "Tau-ha" means the stars that bring the rain, conveying new life with their waters. "Tau" is synonymous with the word "emersion". Thus, the T is a true symbol of the Tree of Life.

~~~~~~~~~~~~~~~

In Helena P. Blavatsky's, "Isis Unveiled." she speaks of God's Signet Ring. She says it is the Tetragrammaton, the four letters of the Divine Name, and symbolized by the Tau Cross. It is the mark on the forehead given to the 144,000 thousand in Revelation 7. Rev. 14:1 says they have "his FATHER'S NAME written on their foreheads."

From this and other hints, we believe that mankind is not guilty or condemned, as they say, and will be the hero when the truth finally comes. Babylon, or the seed of Babylon, seems quite negative, suggesting intolerance, division, conflict, and violence, yet these verses suggest the seed of Babylon leads to a very positive outcome.

Unfamiliar to sky gazers north of about 25 degrees north latitude, the Southern Cross, constellation Crux, is near the horizon from Hawaii. A compact constellation of bright stars, the long axis of the cross conveniently points south toward the southern celestial pole. The top of the cross is marked by the lovely pale red star Gamma Crucis, which is in fact a red giant star about 120 light-years distant. Stars of the grand constellation Centaurus almost engulf the Southern Cross with blue giant Beta Centauri, and yellowish Alpha Centauri, appearing as the brightest stars to the left of Gamma Crucis. At a distance of 4.3 light-years, Alpha Centauri, the closest star to the Sun, is actually a triple star system which includes a star similar to the Sun.

The Southern Cross represents a unifying religious movement, a fusion of religions-- coming out of the New Age. And the French nuclear blasts - nuclear fusion- - are a hologram, a symbolic parallel event - representing the fusion that the Southern Cross will produce. Of course, nuclear testing is not a good thing, it is terribly destructive to the earth's environment - but it is part of the holographic pattern.

Recently a gigantic chunk of ice broke loose from Antarctica - this could mean that the Antarctic ice cap is starting to break up, which could eventually raise the sea level and flood our coastal cities. This, again, may be a parallel symbolic event, related to the Southern Cross. As the water from frozen Antarctica spreads across the earth, so will the Southern Cross spread its influence across the earth. You see its influence in the New Age movement; out of the New Age movement will come a unifying world religion. Water is referred to as "water of life" in Revelation 22; although the water from melting Antarctica will bring chaos, from this chaos rebirth will come.

Another sign of the Southern Cross influence is the thinning of the ozone layer near the South Pole - the resulting increase in ultraviolet near the South Pole symbolizes the spiritual "light" of the Southern Cross. On November 28-29, 1993, there was a total eclipse of the moon, that was seen in the U.S. This eclipse was unusual in that the Southern tip of the moon was much brighter than the rest of the moon. This could also be a symbolic representation of the spreading influence of the Southern Cross - bringing "light" to the Southern hemisphere. Also significant was the solar eclipse of November 1994 over South America. Also, Polaris, the Northern pole star, has been a variable star, oscillating in brightness. However, in 1994 Polaris stopped oscillating, becoming a constant star of constant brightness. This may be connected with the Dragon constellation spreading its influence across the Northern hemisphere.

The 1987 supernova is now brightening again from a collision of gases in space, which should have it reach unaided eye visibility by year 2007. The NASA photo shown above from 1994 shows these gas rings around this supernova. Therefore, the Southern Cross effect I have described here is likely to peak in year 2007 as this star brightens again. As the End Times events end in 2007, possibly resulting in Armageddon, this means that hope for the world will come from the Southern Hemisphere. This brightening supernova could be like a new Star of Bethlehem. Note the hourglass shape of this gas bubble around the supernova may indicate that it is a timekeeper, brightening as the End Times end in 2007.

THE OPENING EYES
THE APERTURE
FLOWER OF LIFE
METATRON'S CUBE

When we talk about 'sacred geometry', one must wonder what makes it sacred. Is there something magic about geometry? Paul Devereus, one of the world leading writers on earth mysteries says: "but an extrapolation by it of the implied patterns in nature that frame the entry of energy into our space-time dimension. The formation of matter and the natural motions of the Universe, from molecular vibration through the growth of organic forms to the spin and motion of the planets, stars and galaxies, are all governed by geometrical configurations of force."

He continues: "It is the ultimate systems language." (Devereux 1992)

One finds sacred geometry everywhere, even where we would least expect it and that is in religion.

Sufi, Jewish, and Hindu religions show sacred geometry in the archetypal world of God. One only need to look at the ancient artwork decorating the walls of temples, mosques, and other buildings of importance. We also see it in Celtic, Tibetan, Buddhist and Native American art.

The word 'geometry' means literally 'measure of the earth'. If we could see the temples and building from before Noah's flood, we would see it there, but take a look at the pyramid of Giza. The entire Egyptian civilization based its structures on a complete and precise understanding of Universal laws. One can see the failures there too if one studies their architecture. It was obviously a learning process.

One finds examples of all the Platonic Solids within the crop circles presented to us all over the world. The Platonic solids were known to the ancient Greeks, and were described by Plato in his Timaeus ca. 350 BC. The criteria for Platonic solids are

183

that all their edges are equal; they have only one surface and one angle; and their points all fit on the surface of a sphere. There are only five known shapes that can do this.

In his work, Plato equated the tetrahedron with the "element" fire, the cube with earth, the icosahedron with water, the octahedron with air, and the dodecahedron with the stuff of which the constellations and heavens were made (Cromwell 1997).

If P is a polyhedron with congruent (convex) regular polygonal faces, then Cromwell (1997, pp. 77-78) shows that the following statements are equivalent.

1. The vertices of P all lie on a sphere.
2. All the dihedral angles are equal.
3. All the vertex figures are regular polygons.
4. All the solid angles are equivalent.
5. All the vertices are surrounded by the same number of faces.

Triangles. The interior angle of an equilateral triangle is 60 degrees. Thus on a regular polyhedron, only 3, 4, or 5 triangles can meet a vertex. If there were more than 6 their angles would add up to at least 360 degrees which they can't. Consider the possibilities:

3 triangles meet at each vertex. This gives rise to a Tetrahedron.
4 triangles meet at each vertex. This gives rise to an Octahedron.
5 triangles meet at each vertex. This gives rise to an Icosahedron

Squares. Since the interior angle of a square is 90 degrees, at most three squares can meet a vertex. This is indeed possible and it gives rise to a hexahedron or cube.

Pentagons. As in the case of cubes, the only possibility is that three pentagons meet at a vertex. This gives rise to a Dodecahedron.

Hexagons or regular polygons with more than six sides cannot form the faces of a regular polyhedron since their interior angles are at least 120 degrees.

Freddy Silva tells us in his book 'Secrets of the Fields, on page 182, "The outward expression of the circle in six movements is synonymous with the days of creation. God's "day of rest" is expressed by the complete figure of seven circles. The next outward expression creates the Seed of Life. Within the Seed lies the Tree of Life. The next outward expression creates the Egg of Life, which can be simplified. The next outward expression creates the Flower of Life. Again, this can be simplified as six circles packed around a seventh. Within the Flower lie the thirteen circles of the Fruit of Life. Connecting the circles generates Metatron's Cube, which contains all the geometric energy patterns necessary to create the platonic solids. The Platonic Solids are fundamental bonding patterns forming the physical Universe.

This was the first flower of the season in the year 1991. There are two marks above and to the right of it that look like bird flying.

AVEBURY DOWN - WILTSHIRE JULY 15, 2000

PICKLED HILL, ALTON BARNES

While people looking at the above crop glyphs may say, 'Oh what pretty flowers!" we see a greater message in the patterns, symbolizing the spiritual growth of mankind. It has been long known that the daisy petals are part of the 'flower of life'.

The two examples of daisy-like crop glyphs suggest closed eyes; the one from the 15th shows 3 semi-circles which look like closed eyelids as well.

While the crop glyph below from July 25th, 2000 shows a form like an open eye or aperture of a camera. The reasons for these interpretations are explained further below.

A newer version has appeared in 2003, with the addition of six circles in the center of the open eye.

The six circles are about the flower-of-life, the heart chakra, and the sixth sphere on the tree of life.

See how reminiscent it is of the Mexican Tablet No. 988, which was found many centuries ago, and again as a tattoo on the back of an old man's hand on the Island of Yanagooni, Japan a few years ago, when underwater rock wall temples were found by sea divers.

Several other aperture-like crop glyphs have appeared also.

BISHOPS CANING nr DEVIZES, WILTSHIRE, JUNE, 2000

187

SOUTH FIELD, ALTON PRIORS, WILTSHIRE, JUNE, 2000

Nick & Bridget were up on Knap Hill for the sunrise, when they noticed a new formation in South Field (across the road from the East Field), in barley, and went to visit it right away.

Like most of the good formations so far this summer, it's in the 200-foot ballpark, beautifully laid, with the downed crop veering gently from side to side in many places, like water in a stream. It consists of a 50-foot circle in the center with eight scallops around its' perimeter, and sixteen spokes radiating outward from it, terminating in semicircles -- and the whole thing enclosed in a ring. (Style-wise, it's unique, and has almost nothing in common with the one below Clay Hill that looked like bicycle spokes a few years ago.)

A really attractive detail is that the semicircles are made with the barley swept in from both sides, so the ears with their long, soft whiskers, fluff up in the middle where they overlap the spokes. and in the center of these junctions, many have one, or just a few, standing stalks. Lovely!

Report by Peter Sorensen

The following show a similarity in pattern forming:

AUDLEY, 1996   BARBURY, 1997

In 1996, a curved star pattern appeared below Silbury Hill. Note the aperture-like center.

SILBURY HILL, Nr AVEBURY, WILTSHIRE, JUNE, 1996

The formation is in Barley and is located in the field opposite Silbury Hill on the A4. It is in a central position in the field. It is a flower-shape with six petals with a central inner-circle with a further six more petals.

The formation is surrounded by an outer ring with an overall diameter of approximately 82 feet. The inner circle is 17 feet diameter. The formation is laid in a clockwise crop rotation.

Joe Mason says the six-petal pattern produces a Star of David in the center. He says, "A strong clue, as I see it, of the aperture opening, and the leap to the Heart Chakra by humanity en-masse."

Dee had a dream in 1999 about her eyes being opened permanently, which rather freaked her out because being able to close one's eyes to sleep and thinking that she might not be able to do that and have to 'see' everything all the time is a rather scary thought.

J.J. Hurtak said on page 508 of his, 'The Book of Knowledge - Keys of Enoch' book : "From the higher heavens the Elohim and the B'nai Elohim continually oversee creation through the Father's Eye of creation and the Eye of Horus. They are the "Fathers" who watch the formation of the Brotherhoods of Light who are pre-created in the heavens. They align their eyes with the eye network patterns of the individual species for the eye is the opening to the code of creation."

He also says: "As Man begins to unlock the Mysteries of the Great Pyramid in relationship to biblical teaching he will understand why Enoch told me that within the Great Pyramid, within a different energy field, the biochemical functions of the body of Moses and Jesus can be found, for they are the two highest incarnate manifestations of within this present cycle. Enoch said they are within the Pyramid to show that the Pyramid is the Eben Shettiyah,, the foundation stone, or the resonance eye for soul manifestation connecting the Office of the Christ with this planet. And when the Pyramid is reactivated they will return as the capstone. They will return to demonstrate the scientific and spiritual unity of all Ascended Masters."

While researching the open eye and Eye of Horus, the crop circle at Woodborough Hill, nr Woodborough, Wiltshire. Reported 19th July, 2000 appeared.

How appropriate it is to show a crop glyph in wheat or barley of the opening eye. This is part of the description of the Eye of Horus:

WOODBOROUGH HILL, JULY, 2000

EYE OF HORUS

The EYE OF HORUS has a very specific meaning. The eye is represented as a figure with 6 parts. These 6 parts correspond to the six senses - Touch, Taste, Hearing, Thought, Sight, Smell. These are the 6 parts of the *eye*. The eye is the receptor of *input*. It has these six doors, to receive data.

The highly stylized eye of the falcon-headed solar and sky god Horus (the Latin version of Hor) is associated with regeneration, health, and prosperity. It has become commonly associated with esoterica and the occult. It is also called the udjat eye or utchat eye, which means "sound eye".

The udjat is depicted as a human eye and eyebrow as they would be seen looking at a person full-faced. The eye is decorated with the markings that adorn the eyes of hawks.

Usually, it is the right eye shown as the udjat, although the left is not uncommon. This is probably because of another myth that say that the sun and the moon were the right (sun) and left (moon) eyes of the sky god and the sun is seen as more powerful.

Each piece of the udjat can be seen as representing a fraction of the descending geometric series 1/2, 1/4, 1/8, etc., put together they make 63/64 or approximately 1.

The entire eye measured 1 heqat. And each of the parts of the eye measured fractions of the heqat.

The corresponding sense data are :-

1/64 heqat — Touch
1/32 heqat — Taste
1/16 heqat — Hearing
1/8 heqat — Thought
1/4 heqat — Sight
1/2 heqat — Smell

This part of the EYE represents the sprouting of the wheat or grain from the planted stalk. It is the food we put into our mouth, and so represents taste. Taste is also = Touch + Shape. That is to say, the different tastes we experience come from touching different shapes. So, touch is more a fundamental sense than taste.

This is the pupil of the EYE
And so no more needs to be said.
It represents seeing, or the sensation of light.

Hearing 1/16 heqat or 20 ro

This part of the EYE represents the EAR. The figure points towards the ear on the face. Also, it has the shape of a horn or musical instrument. When we Hear a sound or combination of sounds we find this to be pleasing or unpleasant. The sound has a taste for us, causing a preference. Sound requires Touch + Taste and so is a combination of the lower senses. Horus, the son of Osiris and Isis, was called "Horus who rules with two eyes." His right eye was white and represented the sun; his left eye was black and represented the moon. According to myth Horus lost his left eye to his evil uncle, Typhon-Set (or Seth), whom he fought to avenge Seth's murder of Osiris. Seth tore out the eye but lost the fight. The eye was reassembled by magic by Thoth, the god of writing, the moon, and magic. Horus presented his eye to Osiris, who experienced rebirth in the underworld.

On page 511 of 'Keys of Enoch' by J.J. Hurtak , he states:

"The Elohim transfer the divine image into proper seed forms of the Shekinah creation which are reprogrammed and regenerated   by the Eye of Horus placed upon the face of the elect who are the Brothers."

It appears to me, that showing us the crop glyphs of the opening eye, that we are now in this age and we 'are' the elect ... those who see and understand.

Dee says, "This is part of the dream that told me I needed to know more about the Eye of Horus:

My eyelids were aching so I looked in the mirror.

I touched my eyelids with my fingers and saw that my eyelids had become detached from my body and were about to fall off. I carefully held them in place despite the pain because if I didn't, I'd never be able to close my eyes again and I'd see more than I wanted to from now on.

Some days I feel like that, but fortunately, not all the time.

In April of 2000, some dreams and coincidences came together and I put up a web page about a crop formation which appeared in 1994."

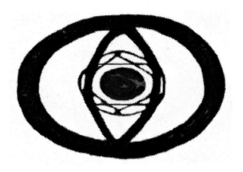

THE ALL SEEING EYE

1994 - created by an unknown source on July 19/20, 1994 at the east field of Alton Barnes, UK. It was 3 tram-lines wide. Most dowsers found various energy lines. An anomalous light was reported in the area of the formation.

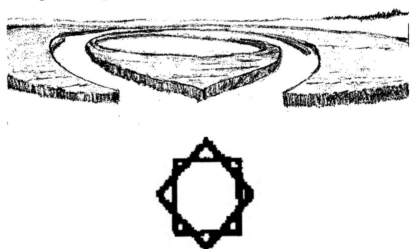

The center detail of this formation was made of thin lines forming a double-diamond round 'pupil' of the large elaborate Eye formation.

~~~~~~~~~~~~~~~~~~~~~~~~~~~~~~~

I hope the readers of this page noticed that these glyphs use the Vesica piscis in their creation: Ilyes has done a super job of writing about this type of crop glyph:

The weird squiggle at the top of the picture is actually at the base of an electric-lines pole. The lines run over the top of this crop pattern, but they are too pale to be seen well. It appears that the overhead electricity cables to the nearby pole discharged itself as a rough version of the original design. Froxfield. 1994

I see this "turtle" Pattern as one of the Circle-Makers' "practice forms". We had not seen the Vesica Piscis (eye) shape in the fields before. The Circle-Makers already knew how to design Circles and Paths [of which the "turtle's feet" suggest the beginnings], for they'd transmitted many in the past; but the Vesica was new in '91. Over the years there have been several examples of what appear to be their "practice" Formations, precursors to the major Transmissions in which a novel or complex shape or lay is involved. This Vesica Piscis form did, in fact, arrive twice more that same year, on the Avebury Avenue and at Firs Farm. In both, the "Turtle's feet" had mutated into Rings. Another example: the previously referred to Overton Oval at West Overton [England '93] appears to have been preceded by a "practice Oval".

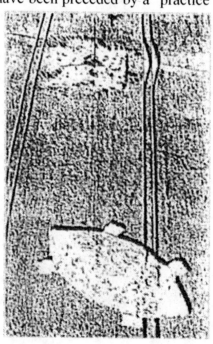

The Vesica Piscis is one of the most fundamental geometrical forms of this ancient discipline and it reveals the relationship between the The Great Pyramid and the 2 dimensional expansion of a circle of one unit radius R

The Vesica Piscis is formed by the intersection of two circles or spheres whose centers exactly touch. This symbolic intersection represents the "common ground", "shared vision" or "mutual understanding" between equal individuals. The shape of the human eye itself is a Vesica Piscis. The spiritual significance of "seeing eye to eye" to the "mirror of the soul" was highly regarded by numerous Renaissance artists who used this form extensively in art and architecture. The ratio of the axes of the form is the square root of 3, which alludes to the deepest nature of the triune which cannot be adequately expressed by rational language alone.

The scholar Jim A Cornwell says: In A.D. 1054 the Church split up again into two groups: the first being the Roman Catholic Empire and second one the Eastern Orthodox Empire (or Ottoman). From A.D. 1096-1291 the Crusades progressed through the world and at this time the Christian Crusaders controlled Palestine, but by A.D. 1187 it was in the hands of Saladin, a Sultan of Egypt and Syria, during the Third Crusade (1189-1192). Symbolism of the Age of Piscis were prevalent even during the Middle ages. A vesica piscis which was a pointed oval shape used in medieval Christian art (paintings and sculpture) as an aureole (halo) to surround a sacred figure. The Latin word piscis means fish (from the resemblance in shape). This became the geometrical principle on which the Gothic cathedrals were built.

Gothic is a term relating to the Middle Ages or medieval and the architectural style prevalent in western Europe from the 12th through the 15th century as characterized by pointed arches, rib vaulting, and flying buttresses. Another item of interest is the piscina — a stone basin with a drain for carrying away the water used in ceremonial ablutions. It is derived from the Latin, fish-pond, pool, from piscis, fish. Another is the miter the liturgical headdress and part of the insignia of a Christian bishop. In the Western church it is a tall pointed hat with peaks in front and back, worn at all solemn functions. It was also the ceremonial headdress worn by ancient Jewish high priests. The word is derived from Middle English mitre, from Old French, from Medieval Latin, from Latin mitra, headdress of the Jewish high priest, and from the Greek.

SUFI - THE VERSE OF LIGHT

The Verse of Light from the Quran 24:25:

"God is the Light of the heavens and the earth;
the likeness of His Light is as a niche
wherein is a lamp
(the lamp in a glass,
the glass as it were a glittering star)
kindled from a Blessed Tree,
an olive that is neither of the East nor of the West,
whose oil wellnigh would shine, even if no fire touched it;
Light upon Light."

Quran 24:35 - This psychic structure of the soul has been expressed by Ghazali in an esoteric commentary upon the Verse of Light (Quran 24:35). The niche, as a place of gathering of both sound and light in the outer world, is also a place of gathering inwardly for all sensory perceptions. A focus point, an aperture in the wall, it symbolizes the first inner aspect of the soul, common sense. The glass symbolizes the second, imagination, which like glass is part of the materiality of this world and has a definite dimension; like glass in is making, imagination is at first opaque to the light of the Intellect, which transcends direction, quality, and distance. Once the imagination is clarified and refined, it gains a similarity to the Active Intellect, or spiritual Heart, and becomes transparent to the light, just as a glass is needed to protect the candlelight from being dissipated by the wind, so the imagination is needed to control intellectual knowledge and hold the images together.

Joe Mason's research has shown, after he drew an interlocking ring diagram, he recalled that he saw another shape in a dream the previous month. It was a circle with curved lines into the center. A voice spoke in the dream, saying that this represented an aperture, like that on a camera. This was referring to how wheatstalks in some crop circles laid down in a somewhat similar pattern .

He says after I drew the interlocking ring pattern, I noticed that the center of the drawing could hint at an aperture in the center. I then drew this pattern, calling it a closed aperture -

The six-petal daisy came to me through dreams, as it is made up from interlocking circles in a ring. It has appeared many times in various forms as a crop formation. The north sun symbol in the Barbury Castle formation was similar. My dream-coincidences indicated that it would open, letting in the Seventh Ray on the Seventh Day of Creation (we are not Man yet). It is the Lost Pleiad of the Pleiades, and the Angel that rises from the Dawning Sun in Revelation 7, to mark the foreheads. (those who have stayed awake).

The Hopi depict a 12-petal sunflower in their Creation myth of Spider Grandmother. She teaches us how "to weave" after the fourth step (Heart chakra), and emergence into the Sunlight. Tantra, in Sanskrit means, "to weave." The Lotus of the Heart chakra has 12 petals, and it is related to the New Jerusalem.

THE FLOWER OF LIFE
(also called the Flower of Amenti)

The Flower of Life symbol is considered to be sacred among many cultures around the world, both ancient and modern. Within this symbol can be found all the building blocks of the universe that we call the Platonic Solids. The symbol contains within it all life and spirit within the universe. The Platonic Solids are found in the rudimentary construction of organic life, as well as music, language and consciousness.

Credit is given for all this to the ibis-headed Egyptian God Thoth. Thoth is also Hermes, a God with Greek and Egyptian origins, who was most noted for his swift consciousness, was later portrayed by the Romans as the winged footed Mercury. The skillful and dexterous patron of alchemists, commerce, esoteric scholars, gymnasts, and travelers, he carried the caduceus rod with entwined serpents. A philosophical intellectual, contemplative mystic, arcane writer, mysteries theologian, intuitive magician, pious sage, and wisdom psychologist, Hermes is an extremely complex, mutable, and versatile individual with a penchant for solving puzzling perplexities and for transforming by reconciling opposites.

The secrets of these sublime truths were given to the priests and initiates of the Mystery Schools of the time, but hidden from the common man, who were thought not to be able to understand the mysteries of life.

The unfolding process of nature is seen in the Flower of Life and all its divisions, in which the Seven Days of Creation in the book of Genesis comes from and the octave of the music scale. Each of the cells created within the Flower of Life, contains the pattern of the whole matrix - like a hologram. This is all found even in the DNA and even within the originating amino acids.

The flowers' outward rotation forms what is called a tube-torus. An easy way to visualize this is to picture a 'Slinky' that children play with and place the two ends together. The final arrangement of loops is the tube-torus. From that shape, combined with a tetrahedron come all of the letters of the Hebrew alphabet - in order. The Greek and Arabic alphabets were found in a similar way by Stan Tenon. This is another reason why these shapes are said to be sacred.

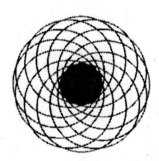

ALTON BARNES, Nr AVEBURY, WILTSHIRE. 11th July, 1997
THE TUBE TORUS

This knowledge was also sacred to the illuminated societies like the Knights Templars and the Gnostic Cathars in Languedoc, France. In the Albigensian Crusades, the Catholic church wiped out all of the Cathars over a 40 year period. The word Cathar comes from the Greek, which means 'Pure Ones.' In 1208 Pope Innocent III launched a Crusade against these heretics , destroying their communities with great cruelty. Later, the Catholic Church created the Inquisition, initially with the purpose of eliminating all traces of Cathar heresy from France, Spain and northern Italy. The Cathars were vegetarians and did not use animal products whatsoever. They worshipped a God above Yahweh, which the Catholics said had to be Lucifer. This higher God is said to be called 'HU" by some groups today. They also believed in reincarnation.

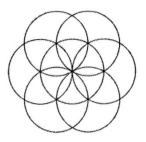

SEED OF LIFE

Notice that it has a 6 petalled flower surrounded by 6 rings.

This image is first seen at the Temple of Osiris at Abydos, Egypt, where it is actually burned into the stone with some kind of force. Experts say it is not chisled into the stone. We find it again in Italian art from the 13th century but also in Israel on Massada and Synagogues in the area of Galilee. It is found in many sacred sites around the world.

Most people don't pay attention to what is on the money they carry around with them. The code is on our One Dollar bill in the United States. The pyramid contains 13 levels. Note the all-seeing-eye above the pyramid - the single eye who sees all. There are 13 leaves and 13 arrows. The Star of David above the eagle's head also contains 13 five-point stars. The Masonic group, which designed our money and our government, have embedded the code of the flower of life into everything they did. Even the city of Washington D.C. was laid out with this design in mind.

This may not be apparent to the eye, but the word ONE in Hebrew means Echad and has the numerical value of 13. All of creation came out of the void using the Flower of Life.

From earlier in this chapter, we have seen the same 6 petalled flower in crop circles, along with similar rings. One must assume a connection between the two. The latest 6 petalled flower within overlapping ring appeared in the year 2003.

TEGDOWN HILL, PATCHAM, BRIGHTON, EAST SUSSEX, JULY, 2003

Since we are seeing a parade of these types of crop circles, one must wonder what they mean? What are the circle makers trying to convey to humanity? Since they appeared first thousands of years ago, have we still not gotten the picture and the lesson?

Of course, the seed of life represents creation, but there must be more to it than that. We see creation occurring all around us, if not every day, then every week, month, or year. We see babies being birthed rather regularly, whether human or animal. Life is so valuable to us. So, then what else are we to learn from this symbol?

To get to the real picture, one must look at the development in the cell division - the growth pattern. We then see this form:

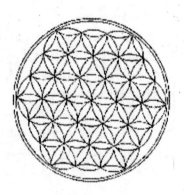

FLOWER OF LIFE

Of course, the first implication of the form is of cell division, but more than that, it is about souls in their divisions or separations from the central point of God. As the soul separates from the original pool of life - the primordial waters - it grows in every direction (not just the flat 2 D form we see here) it grows in every dimension as well in its soul consciousness.

More than that, when the soul separates into two separate souls, just before the separation is complete, the vesica picis is the area where the petals of the flowers are where the two circles overlap. The visica picis also shows the separation/union of the male/female energies. The circles joined represent the duality of God. One must understand that God is not male or female but both. Every soul that is sentient, is not only possessing all that created it, but is also ONE with God. It is also in union with all other souls.

Just by looking at the flower of life picture, one can see all of that information within it. This flat 2-D form shows us a two-dimensional shadow of a sphere. Atoms, cells, seed, planets, star-systems and natural cycle all echo this circular nature. The circle is the primary symbol and organizing principle for everything.

As human beings, we are considered singular within ourselves, yet the eastern concept of yin-yang is that within the one is the 'two principle' - active-passive and also male-female. We are all creatures who co-create with God, therefore are gods (with a small g) of our own creations, but in the physical form and with our thoughts. We continually have all the components of the original soul, the ONE that creates all. This Flower of Life exists within the whole of us in our genetic structure - within the DNA.

We can look back through 'time' and trace our family 'tree of' life just like we work to climb our own personal tree of life, through the cell division and DNA. That may not have been so evident in past years, but it certainly is now. All that evidence is within us and within our cells and blood.

We are not a simple creature like an amoeba - we have many lives of awareness. We are part of a group of souls whether we recognize that connection or not. Throughout all of time and all of creation, we are part of all of it.

But that is not all. There is more. The flower of life is known as the "language of light" and speaks to us within its' silence and therefore a "language of silence" as well. The Flower of Life has within it a code that contains 13 informational systems. These may not be apparent at first glance, but there are there.

By completing the incomplete circles, we find the Fruit of Life contained within its pattern. By connecting all the middle points of these circles, Metatron's Cube is found. That is the shape that every known molecular structure in the universe is made from.

The Flower of Life seems to be a very simple form in its two dimensional drawings, but it is a complex code demanding more study.

The Flower of Life is made up of nineteen intersecting circles encompassed by two concentric rings. The seed of the Flower of Life is composed of seven of the intersecting circles.

The circular lines are considered masculine and the straight lines are considered feminine. The 'marriage' of these two line systems produces the Metatron's Cube. Frissel, in 1994 said, "From its hexagonal matrix emerge the Platonic Solids, the five crystallization so that creative thoughts of God, the very bonding patterns of nature."

METATRON'S CUBE

The Cube is a Platonic Solid. The six duplicated faces of the Three Dimensional Cube are Two Dimensional Squares. Metatron's Cube is a tremendously important aspect of Nature's First Pattern. It is based on 13 circles found within this first pattern.

Connecting the centers of these 13 circles is the key. This sacred geometric archetype proves the direct relationship between the conceptual Two Dimensional Universe and the manifest Three Dimensional Universe. The root architecture of all the Platonic Solids (the Tetrahedron, the Cube, the Octahedron, the Icosahedron and the Dodecahedron) lie hidden within Metatron's Cube. All these perfect three dimensional forms fit perfectly within a Sphere, which relates directly to the Circle

Pythagorus had been educated in the Egyptian Mystery Schools where he was initiated. Pythagoras of Samos. Born: about 569 BC in Samos, Ionia Died: about 475 BC. He is thought to be the first pure mathematician.

Pythagoras of Samos is often described as the first pure mathematician
Born: about 569 BC in Samos, Ionia
Died: about 475 BC

Pythagoras was interested in the principles of mathematics, the concept of number, the concept of a triangle or other mathematical figures and the abstract idea of a proof. Each number had its own personality - masculine or feminine, perfect or incomplete. The Pythagoran theorem, was known to the Babylonians 1000 years earlier, but he was the first known mathematician to prove it.

(i) The sum of the angles of a triangle is equal to two right angles. Also the Pythagoreans knew the generalization which states that a polygon with n sides has sum of interior angles 2n - 4 right angles and sum of exterior angles equal to four right angles.

(ii) The theorem of Pythagoras - for a right-angled triangle the square on the hypotenuse is equal to the sum of the squares on the other two sides. To Pythagoras the square on the hypotenuse would not be thought of as a number multiplied by itself, but rather as a geometrical square constructed on the side. To say that the sum of two squares is equal to a third square meant that the two squares could be cut up and reassembled to form a square identical to the third square.

(iii) In astronomy Pythagoras taught that the Earth was a sphere at the centre of the Universe. He also recognized that the orbit of the Moon was inclined to the equator of the Earth and he was one of the first to realize that Venus as an evening star was the same planet as Venus as a morning star.

Number Property of the number

1   monad (unity) generator of numbers, the number of reason
2   dyad (diversity, opinion) first true female number
3   triad (harmony = unity + diversity) first true male number
4   (justice, retribution) squaring of accounts
5   (marriage) = first female + first male
6   (creation) = first female + first male + 1 ?
10 (Universe) tetractys

The Music of the Spheres

The Pythagoreans wove their musical discoveries into their mathematical cosmology to produce a hauntingly beautiful description of the Universe. The Pythagorean Universe consisted of a central, spherical earth surrounded by the heavenly objects. These were attached to crystal spheres at distances determined by the regular solids (solids which can be circumscribed by a sphere). The rotation of these spheres produced wondrous musical harmonies.

The Pythagoreans explained that normal people cannot hear the "harmony of the spheres" because they have grown too accustomed to hearing it from birth (Pythagoras alone was supposed to be able to hear it). Nonetheless the quest for the mathematics behind these harmonies captivated some of the greatest minds over the next two thousand years. Koestler describes how the early physicist Kepler spent much of his productive life trying to discover the harmony of the spheres. The three laws he is best remembered for were virtually footnotes to his investigations into the harmonies.

Plato lived from 427-347 BCE. His name gives rise to the term Platonic Solids. However, evidence in rock caves show that these same shapes were known as far back as Neolithic structures over 8000 years ago.

According to Helena P. Blavatsky, in Isis Unveiled Vol. II, page 33, she states: "It certainly does seem as if the events of the first centuries of Christianity were but the reflection of the images thrown upon the mirror of the future and the time of the Exodus. During the stormy days of Irenaeus, the Platonic philosophy, with its mystical submersion into Deity, was not so obnoxious after all to the new doctrine as to prevent the Christians from helping themselves to its abstruse metaphysics in every way and manner. Allying themselves with the ascetical therapeutae - forefathers and models of the Christian monks and hermits, it was in Alexandrea, let it be remembered, that they laid the first foundations of the purely Platonic trinitarian doctrine. It became the plato-Philonean doctrine later, and such as we find it now. Plato considered the divine nature under a threefold modifaction of the First Cause, the reason or Logos, and the soul or spirit of the universe. "The three archiacal or original principles," says Gibbon, "were represented in the Platonic system as three gods, united with each other by a mysterious and ineffable generation." Blending this transcendental idea with the more hypostatic figure of the Logos of Philo, whose doctrine was that of the oldest Kabala, and who viewed the King Messiah as the Metatron, or "the angel of the Lord the Legatus descended in flesh, but not the 'Ancient of Day's' himself, the Christians clothed, with this mythical representation of the Mediator the fallen race of Adam, Jesus, the son of Mary.

DNA

      Why include the topic of DNA in a book about One World Religion? Because DNA is responsible for the state of religious beliefs we hold, based on the information coming from scholars that mankind has been genetically manipulated since the beginning of humanity as we are today.

DNA CROP FORMATION
EAST FIELD, ALTON BARNES, WILTSHIRE, JUNE 1996

12 circles in a line, accompanied by an interwoven 80-circle-double-helix 'DNA' type pattern. In total 658' long

NOTE, where the double helix strands cross over each other in 3-D the near strand would hide one of the circles on the far strand. Hence, we surmised that there are ten circles in each of the eight loops - except that one of the loops has eleven! Thus, counting 'hidden' circles, there is a total of 93.

The diagram is as accurate as can be drawn. The left side of the helix curves out slightly further than the right side. Care has been taken to show how the strands overlap. The diagram is made with reference to an aerial view and shows the formation as it appears from the air.

FROXFIELD, Nr HUNGERFORD, BERKSHIRE

This diagram was called 'The Brain' because of its conformation, but it is associated with the structure of human DNA as viewed under Ultra Violet light. Ten sections make up the design. Some researchers say it represents chromosomes, which are composed of DNA.

DNA IN THE BEGINNING

The following is partially excerpted from the book by Zechariah Sitchin, GENESIS REVISITED, (1990)

"THE ADAM: A SLAVE MADE TO ORDER"
For those of you who haven't read Zechariah Sitchins books, his information

comes from the Sumerian texts left behind by scribes who lived in the days of Sumeria, thousands of years ago. These texts are still being found and read and transcribed by archaeologists. The information continues to come in from the past, which gives us clues about the past and the future alike.

There are those who are strict Bible fundamentalists who will have a problem with this as they believe the Bible to be true to its' every word and not open to translation or interpretation. But this information is not from the Bible. It is pre-Bible. This information is in fine detail, not the generalities of the first chapter of Genesis in the Bible.

"The insurmountable problem arises when Creationists insist that we, Mankind, Homo sapiens sapiens, were created instantaneously and without evolutionary predecessors by 'God." "And the Lord God formed Man of the dust of the ground, and breathed into his nostrils the breath of life, and Man became a living soul." (p 158)

The book of Genesis tells us that Adam (homo sapiens sapiens) was created by the Elohim (which is plural) and translated to be 'gods' not "God".

"The quoted verse explains why "The Adam" was created "For there was no Adam to till the land"(p 158)

Genesis 1:26-27 - God said, Let us make men in our image, after our likeness"; *"and God created man in his own image, in the image of God created He him; male and female created He them."*

"The biblical account is further complicated by the ensuing tale in Chapter 2, according to which "The Adam" was alone until God provided him with a female counterpart, created of Adam's rib." (p 159)

As stated in Zechariah Sitchin's earlier book, 'The 12th Planet', the creation of Man was done by the Anunnaki, who were astronauts from another world, called Nibiru.

"It happened, we learn from such long texts as Atra Hasis, when the rank-and-file astronauts who had come to Earth for its gold mutinied. The backbreaking work in the gold mines, in southeast Africa, had become unbearable. Enlil, their commander-in-chief, summoned the ruler of Nibiru, his father Anu, to an Assembly of the Great Anunnaki and demanded harsh punishment of his rebellious crew. But Anu was more understanding, "What are we accusing them of?" he asked as he heard the complaints of the mutineers. "Their work was heavy, their distress was much!" Was there no other way to obtain the gold, he wondered out loud.

Yes, said his other son Enki (Enlil's half brother and rival), the brilliant chief scientist of the Anunnaki. It is possible to relieve the Anunnaki for the unbearable toil by having someone else take over the difficult work: Let a Primitive Worker be created!" (p 159)

As stated in the texts, there was already a creature on earth, who could do this work, but without the intelligence needed to do the work.

Enki states, "Bind upon it the image of the gods." (p 160)

There is debate here as to whom this creature was that they genetically manipulated. Zechariah Sitchin states that it was Apeman/Apewoman. Others would say it was another type of being.

One such scientific researcher states: "Your ancestors are not apes," Charles Darwin wrote in his book. Research scientists tell us that no evidence of a non-human ancestry of man has been found. Evolutionary theory is a myth. You were created by God; you did not come from a flock of monkeys. God created everything; the evidence clearly points to it. Nothing else can explain the mountain of evidence."

More: About Lucy: This australopithecine was nothing more than an ape.

"To complicate matters further, some researchers believe that the afarensis sample [Lucy] is really a mixture of [bones from] two separate species. The most convincing evidence for this is based on characteristics of the knee and elbow joints."-*Peter Andrews, "The Descent of Man," in New Scientist, 102:24 (1984).

"The evidence makes it overwhelmingly likely that Lucy was no more than a variety of pigmy chimpanzee, and walked the same way (awkwardly upright on occasions, but mostly quadrupedal). The `evidence' for the alleged transformation from ape to man is extremely unconvincing."-A.W. Mehlert, Creation Research Society Quarterly, December 1985, p. 145.

"Adult chimps and gorillas have elongated faces, heavy brow ridges, powerful jaws, and small brain-cases in relation to overall skull and other characteristic proportions. Baby apes have flat faces, rounded brain-cases, light brow ridges, proportionately smaller jaws, and many other bodily features strikingly like human beings."-*R. Milner, Encyclopedia of Evolution (1990), p. 325.

"The process envisioned by Enki was to 'bind' upon the existing creature the 'image' - the inner, genetic makeup - of the Anunnaki; in other words, to upgrade the existing Apeman/Apewoman through genetic manipulation and, by thus jumping the gun on evolution, bring "Man" - Homo sapiens - into being.

The term Adamu, which is clearly the inspiration for the biblical name "Adam," and the use of the term "image" in the Sumerian text, which is repeated intact in the biblical test, are not the only clues to the Sumerian /Mesopotamian origin of the Genesis creation of Man story. The biblical use of the plural pronoun and the depiction of a group of Elohim reaching a consensus and following it up with the necessary action also lose their enigmatic aspects when the Mesopotamian sources are taken into account. (p 160)

The newly created being, "The Adam", is a generic term, meaning literally 'the Earthling'.

"The Sumerian term that means "Man" is LU. But its root meaning is not 'human being' it is rather "worker, servant" and as a component of animal names implied "domesticated". (p 161)

"The Akkadian language in which the Atra Hasis text was written (and from which all Semitic languages have stemmed) applied to the newly created being the term 'lulu', which means as in the Sumerian, "Man", but which conveys the notion of 'mixing'. The word 'lulu' in a more profound sense thus meant "the mixed one". this also reflected the manner in which The Adam - "Earthling" as well as "He of the Blood" was created. (p 162)

Sumerian drawing of Invitro Fertilization
Genesis Revisited
by Zechariah Sitchin - page 162

"There is no doubt that their origin is Sumerian, in whose texts we find the most elaborate descriptions and the greatest amount of detail concerning the wonderful deed: the mixing of the "divine" genes of the Anunnaki with the "earthly" genes of Apeman by fertilizing the egg of an Apewoman.

It was fertilization in vitro - in glass tubes as depicted in this rendering on a cylinder seal. And, as I have been saying since modern science and medicine achieved

210

the feat of in vitro fertilization, Adam was the first test-tube baby." (p 162)

"Laying the groundwork for ensuing events, the Atra Hasis text begins the story of Man on Earth with the assignment of tasks among the leading Anunnaki. When the rivalry between the two half brothers, Enlil and Enki, reached dangerous levels, Anu made them draw lots. As a result, Enlil was given mastery over the old settlements and operations in the E.DIN (the biblical Eden) and Enki was sent to Africa, to supervise the AB.ZU, the land of the mines. (p 163)

Over time, during the initial experimentation, many different forms of 'beings' were created, before Apeman/Apewoman was finally decided on. You see many of these 'beings' in drawings from antiquity, men with wings, one body with two heads, beings with both male and female genitalia, some with the legs and horns of a goat, a bull with a human body, or a lion with a human head. These were not freaks of nature but the result of the experimentation. Just so you are aware, the scientists who are cloning animals and humans now will have similar results. They will have to try 100 times to get one good one, and even then no one will know how the internal organs are, or how fast the infant will age, or the diseases it will get.

Nevertheless, it would have taken evolution many, many thousands of years to reach the point the Sumerians did in just a few years, thanks to the experiments of the Anunnakis. And we are all descendants of the 'gods and Apeman', according to Sitchin. All of us. That means, we are all part extraterrestrial.

"Called upon to perform the task of "fashioning servants for the gods" - "to bring to pass a great work of wisdom," in the words of the ancient texts - Enki gave Ninti the following instructions:

Mix to a core the clay from the Basement of the Earth, just above the Abzu, and shape it into the form of a core. I shall provide good, knowing young Anunnaki who will bring the clay to the right condition.

The Akkadian words which are translated 'clay' or 'mud' have evolved from the Sumerian 'TI.IT, literally 'that which is with life,' and then assumed the derivative meanings of 'clay' and 'mud' as well as 'egg.' The earthly element in the procedure for 'binding upon' a being who already existed 'the image of the gods.' was thus to be the female egg of that being - of an Apewoman.

All the texts dealing with this event make it clear that Ninti relied on Enki to provide the earthly element, this egg of a female Apewoman, from the Abzu, from southeast Africa. Indeed, the specific location is given in the above quote: not exactly the same site as the mines (an area identified in The 12th Planet as Southern Rhodesia, now Zimbabwe) but a place 'above ' it, farther north. This area was, indeed, as recent finds have shown, where Homo Sapiens emerged. (p 166-167)

Humans have been part of Ngorongoro's landscape for millions of years. The earliest signs of mankind in the conservation area are at Laetoli, where hominid footprints have been preserved in volcanic rock for the past 3,600,000 years. The story continues at Oldupai (Olduvai) Gorge, a river canyon cut 100 meters deep through the volcanic soils of the Serengeti plains.

Olduvai Gorge, a 30-mile-long gash in Tanzania's Serengeti Plain, is renowned for the remains of the earliest humans to exist. Between 1.9 and 1.2 million years ago a salt lake occupied this area. From 1.2 million to 600,000 years ago fresh water streams and small ponds appeared.

Over 400 fragments of the skull Australopithecus- Zinjanthropus Boisei were found in 1911, but it was only in 1959 when Mary Leakey uncovered a 1.75 million year old australopithecus jawbone. This was the first conclusive evidence that hominids had existed for over a million years and that they had evolved in Africa.

~~~~~~~~~~~~~~~~~~~~~~~~~

The part of the human genome that's passed from father to son is the Y chromosome. Inside every human cell are 23 pairs of chromosomes, made up of DNA. One half of each pair comes from the mother, the other half from the father. One of those pairs determines a person's sex. Women generally have a pair of similar chromosomes called XX, men have XY. If the father contributes his X to the offspring, it will be a girl. If he contributes his Y, it'll be a boy. It's the Y chromosome that determines maleness. And the Y doesn't exchange much genetic material with its partner X, so a father passes his Y chromosome on to his son virtually unchanged.

Humans did come out of Africa, says DNA. The DNA of living humans is revealing the secrets of our evolution, reports Jeremy Thomson.

7 December 2000
JEREMY THOMSON

Brushed aside: Homo sapiens neanderthalensis

Archaeologists are still not sure when and where modern humans first appeared. Some believe that Homo sapiens evolved independently in several places

212

around the globe. But research revealed in this week's Nature1 lends support to the idea that we appeared in one location in sub-Saharan Africa and spread from there, replacing Neanderthals and other early humans as we went.

Researchers led by Ulf Gyllensten of the University of Uppsala in Sweden have found evidence that we are all descended from a single ancestral group that lived in Africa about 170,000 years ago. And they suggest that modern humans spread across the globe from Africa in an exodus that took place only around 50,000 years ago.

Gyllensten's team didn't scrutinize fossils to come up with these results -- instead the group examined DNA from living people around the world.

The genetic material in our chromosomes is a combination of genes from our parents. But each cell also contains structures called mitochondria, and these house DNA that is independent of that found in chromosomes.

Mitochondrial DNA (mtDNA) gives researchers a window into history because it is only transmitted along the female line. There is no mixing between generations, and the DNA sequence only changes as a result of random mutations or copying errors. If these mutations appear at a fairly constant rate, then comparing the mitochondrial DNA of two populations reveals roughly when they had a common ancestor.

This approach is not new, but in the past researchers have concentrated on only 7 percent; of the total mitochondrial DNA sequence, known as the control regions. The mutation rate for these regions might be different from the rest of the sequence, so Gyllensten and co-workers sequenced the entire mitochondrial DNA of 53 people from diverse ethnic backgrounds. They excluded any parts of the DNA that mutated unusually quickly, then compared the data to produce a sort of human family tree.

They discovered that the most recent common ancestor of everyone in the sample group lived in Africa $171,500 \pm 50,000$ years ago. They also found a significant branch in the tree that separates most Africans from non-Africans. This genetic divide probably represents an exodus of people from Africa that took place $52,000 \pm 27,500$ years ago.

This evidence favouring the 'recent African origin' theory of human evolution is compelling, but the researchers hope for better data in the near future. "Mitochondrial DNA is only one locus, and only reflects the genetic history of females," they write. "With the human genome project nearing fruition, the ease by which such data may be generated will increase, providing us with an ever more detailed understanding of our genetic history."

References:

Ingman, M., Kaessmann, H., Pääba, S. & Gyllensten, U. Mitochondrial genome variation and the origin of modern humans.

Nature 408, 708 713 (2000).

Blair Hedges, S. A start for population genomics.Nature 408, 552 553 (2000).

© Nature News Service / Macmillan Magazines Ltd 2001

ANOTHER OPINION

DNA SHOWS NEANDERTALS WERE NOT OUR ANCESTORS

"The task of obtaining the 'divine' elements was Ninti's. Two extracts were needed from one of the Anunnaki, and a young 'god' was carefully selected for the purpose. Enki's instructions to Ninti were to obtain the god's blood and 'shiru, and through immersions in a 'purifying bath' obtain their 'essences'. What had to be obtained from the blood was termed TE.E.MA, or as best translated 'personality' , a term that expresses the sense of the word: that which makes a person what he is and different from any other person. But the translation 'personality' does not convey the scientific precision of the term, which in the original Sumerian meant 'That which houses that which binds the memory." Nowadays we call it a 'gene'.

"The other element for which the young Anunnaki was selected, shiru, it commonly translated 'flesh'. In time, the word acquire the meaning 'flesh' among its various connotations. But in the earlier Sumerian it referred to the sex or reproductive organs; its root had the basic meaning 'to bind,' 'that which binds.' The extract from the shiru was referred to in other texts dealing with non-Anunnaki offspring of the 'gods' as kisru, coming from the male's member, it meant 'semen,' the male's sperm.

"These two divine extracts were to be mixed well by Ninti in a purifying bath, and it is certain that the epithet 'lulu ("the mixed one") for the resulting Primitive Worker stemmed from this mixing process. In modern terms we would call him a 'hybrid.'

"All these procedures had to be performed under strict sanitary conditions. One text even mentions how Ninti first washed her hands before she touched the 'clay'. The place where these procedures were carried out was a special from the Sumerian Akkadian 'bit Shimti,' which, coming from the Sumerian SHI.IM.TI literally meant 'house where the wind of life is breathed in' - the source, of course, of the biblical assertion that after having fashioned the Adam from the clay, Elohim "blew in his nostrils the breath of life." The biblical term, sometimes translated 'soul', is Nephesh. The identical term appears in the Akkadian account of what took place in the 'house where the wind of life is breathed in' after the purifying and extracting procedures were completed: (p 167-168)

"The mixing of the 'clay' with all the component extracts and 'essences' was not yet the end of the procedure. The egg of the Apewoman, fertilized in the 'purifying baths' with the sperm and genes of the young Anunnaki 'god', was then deposited in a 'mold' where the binding' was to be completed. Since this part of the process is described again later in connection with the determining of the sex of the engineered being, one may surmise that was the purpose of the 'binding' phase.

"The length of time the fertilized egg this process stayed in the 'mold' is not stated, but what was to be done with it was quite clear. The fertilized and 'molded' egg was to be re implanted in a female womb - but not in that of its original Apewoman. Rather it was to be implanted in the womb of a 'goddess', an Anunnaki female! Only thus, it becomes clear, was the end result achievable. (p 168)

"The female Anunnaki chosen to serve as Birth Goddesses if the experiment succeeded, Enki said, should stay and observe what was happening. It was not, the texts reveal, a simple and smooth birth-giving process:

The birth goddesses were kept together, Ninti sat, counting the months. The fateful tenth month was approaching - the tenth month arrived - the period of opening the womb had elapsed.

The drama of Man's creation, it appears, was compounded by a late birth; medical intervention was called for. Realizing what had to be done, Ninti 'covered her head' and with an instrument whose description was damaged on the clay tablet, 'made an opening'. This done, 'that which was in the womb came forth." Grabbing the newborn baby, she was overcome with joy. Lifting it up for all to see, she shouted triumphantly:

I have created!
My hands have made it!
The first Adam was brought forth. (p 170)

THE FOLLOWING IS A CHANNELED EXPLANATION
FROM AN ET NAMED BLUE

Having accomplished what they set out to do, to create a 'hybrid' of 'man' and 'god' they set about to continue to the experiments and create more of them. Continuing the genetic engineering, they created 14 more, 7 male and 7 female. There is no conflict between this and the Bible. After Adam was created by himself, and being a success, they went into mass production, creating the workers they needed.

[Blue] first we wish to say that you need to look at this wholly and not an 'Us and Them' scenario, the enemy and so forth, you have to move beyond this - we understand of what you speak and ask - we ask that you start from the beginning of this epic as you may garner a better understanding.

[R] Blue can you please keep it simple, I mean simple so can explain it to the five year old next door ...

[Blue] After the separation, the split, the fall into physical matter, those streams that separated and wanted to become creators likened unto the all-that-is, but not aligned with the all-that-is became raptured with the physical domains/frequencies - as we have explained, mmm - we are re-scanning for better explanation - okay - they knew that the all-that-is could if it wanted pull it back - but also they knew that the all-that-is wanted to experience the physical, to behold it - and so they thought they could with-hold it - their problem was since cut of from the source in an entropic system, they required sustaining energy, just as do all physical beings and systems residing in the physical universes - now a way of obtaining this sustaining energy was to connect back with the source within the non-physical universes - but in order to do this they would require obliques the grip on the physical - which they did not wish to do!

Further on/within, the all-that-is commissioned/desired a project to allow full interface with the physical universes, to be able to co-exist with in both domains - and so began our work with the human 24 DNA physical body - and our consciousness would embody this - to allow a physical body and all-that-is and part there of to experience self-referential identity as well as all-that-is identity with in the one physical body - as we have explained, this was a two-fold project:

1. to allow the all-that-is to interface/experience

2. for the human stream to become a retro-repair for other physical embodiments that it may interbreed with allowing them to carry their own interface also back to the all-that-is should they choose it to be so...to keep this short - what occurred was that the fallen for a better word, saw that this could be there way of obtaining a route back to the non-physical without needing to abide by the laws of the all-that-is - you see, as long as they remain in physical universes/frequencies they can do as they please with in certain limitations - but to put a foot so to speak in the non-physical domains, they would need to abide by laws that would render them - so they saw if somehow they could tap into the 24DNA coded matrix which was designed to interface with the physical as well as non-physical domains.

[R] But surely interbreeding with humans would have given them this, no ?

[Blue] Yes, but as soon as they stepped into non-physical domains, they still would lose control - what they wanted was to have both, control solely over the physical as well as co-exist in the non-physical domains and be universal law unto themselves regardless of the totality of all-that-is.

[R] This is beginning to spin my head ...

[Blue] In order to co-exist in both domains, it is not just simple to obtain some DNA wiring codes and sequences, you must also on a soulular level resonate to those specially wired strings so to speak.

[R] Please explain!

[Blue] It is likened unto a musician - a skilled musician can play all types of music from all differing cultures, eg. Rock-n-roll or classical - now a musician who hates classical may still be able to play it, but it does not mean he loves it or enjoys it, thus his soul does not resonate truely with the music - apart from this, the audience can sense it and it does not feel that same as if one playing from within their heart/self - the musician may be able to keep up this charade for a while (physical) - now tell this musician that he must play classical music for all eternity (non-physical) - now if he had the correct instruments (DNA code) he could play it but not all eternity, Eventually he would succumb to his true desire/heart to play rock-n-roll, as what would be the point of being in the non-physical if you could not play only rock-n-roll.

[R] I would have thought all types of music co-existed within the all-that-is ?

[Blue] You misunderstand - it does allow for all, but it must have to come from the heart so to speak, you must want and enjoy classical so to speak - we are only giving examples, it is not literal, we are speaking metaphorically - do you see not that all this is about obtaining the genetics which will allow both physical and non-physical experience/creation through one unified embodiment - in order to fill this embodiment, it also requires a unified, mind and soul and spirit to be able to control it, otherwise it would be likened unto putting a 5 year old in the driving seat of the space shuttle with no training or preparation - do you see - so in short - you have 5 year-olds wishing to embody/control/take over the space shuttle - and assuming they do, would wreak havoc unto themselves as they would not be able to control it and if they managed the launch sequence codes and managed a take off, the G-forces would crumble their little bones - and they may not survive - again we are giving you a simplified metaphoric - so what is it that these shadows want if not for oil, wine, women and song, as you say - mmm.- do you not recall the encrypted/compressed DNA known to you as junk DNA - which makes up 90% of your genetic makeup - well there is a forgotten event which R allowing we will cover in your near future - a point came in your past, where domination and exploitation began over the Lilium (Human stream) - cause the 5 year olds figured if they could find the key that opens up the doorways to the non-physical, they could attempt to take control - and so began the exploitation of the Lilium and much experimentation and so forth - as although their soul/stream were not and still to a degree are not able to embody a fully switch 24 DNA embodiment as they did not resonate with it, they wished somehow to find the key to allow them to match resonance regardless of soulular frequencies - every time they attempted embodiment unto a 24 DNA wired body, they failed miserably as they needed to get the resonance correct and of course they could not do this for the 24 DNA wired body was only keyed for the Lilium (human) soul-matrix - so in order for them to be able to embody one method was to switch off certain DNA keys, basically have a crippled body that function 10% of its full capabilities, which allowed them to embody.

This is simply put - but the idea was as they became accustomed, they would slowly switch on one key at a time, until they had full integration - this concerned many in the physical and non-physical as to re-start the whole creation would never be the same - so an event occurred where we had to commission an encryption/compression to the remaining 10-physical DNA strands today known to you as junk - ever since, they have been trying to break this encryption!!!

Why is it you think that your Jehovan (Eli-Jovi) scientists of today are so driven for stem cell research and cloning and so forth - the research continues in hidden labs using technologies far in advance and yet to be able to break the encryption - for they fail to see it is at the soulular level and not ONLY physical body.

[R] Hang on a tick - do you mean that the " I " of me is a 5 year old one of them?

[Blue] No! Not necessarily - you see we had to close of access to the remaining as they began to embody Lilium bodies - so this was a set back for both - meaning that Eli-Jovi and Lilium souls only had 2 physical strands (4 in total, 2 physical and 2 non physical)

Why is it your main bible of today's earth begins with Genesis?
Is it not 'Gene of Isis!' and have we not told you the root-sonics of Ishael and Israel have all to do with this 'Gene of Isis' - you have:

Isis-Hathor-EliJovi = Ishael and
Isis-Ra-EliJovi = Israel

Elohim/Jehovah is the offshoot in the physical universes for the Eli-Jovi as Humans are for the Lilium - and whom might you think are the authors of Genesis and most of your Judeo-Christian bibles - is it not the one and only flesh and blood god-stream known as the war god Jehovah - mmm - this is the fabricated beginning of the Lilium demise due to the attempted misuse of trying to obtain the keys.

And to continue with answering the questions - this is why they need you subdued and suppressed - because they need the keys, but they know only Lilium souls are able to de-crypt the remaining DNA - so they keep you in the dark and feed you shit, in the hope that you may be able to break the encryption for them - once you begin unravelling, they will begin more and more gross experiments - we suggest you watch your genetic research and technologies development this will give you an indication.

There is one thing you must understand - that the many beings on this planet are a hybrid physical makeup - where souls from the differing streams can embody - but however there are some that can only be embodied by the Lilium and vice versa.

This why they keep you here and do not wish for you to wake up - cause with a simple opening of your eye, you will see what is going on and once fully empowered you would do away with them.

[R] But isn't this a catch 22? How can they have the keys, if we don't wake up and unravel it; so in effect they are doing themselves a disservice?

[Blue] You see they long ago gave up on for you to do it via waking up - so now they do it via technology, food stuffs, genetic research both open and secret, vaccinations and a concoction of other methods - to attempt to break the encryption - also they do seek out those who are advanced and do much grotesque research/experimentation.

We will tell you some that may shock you, but most of your new-age streams are set up by these groups, to bring those out who may have this genetic soulular advancement, so they can be tagged, watched and some very high level technologies used beyond your awareness, to try and seek the keys - sort of like a stealth key-logger - something that is implanted mentally and cellularly that watches every key stroke, records it and then retrieved so they can study and see how the soul/body interface is working.

Think on this - why is it most of your new age streams are geared around Jehovan ideologies - think on it - your kabbala, off-shoots from your bibles using much of the same verbage as your bible does, mmm - have you come across any alternatives that did not bear any close resembles to your Judeo-Christian or other fabricated religions?

It is the same thing with another twist.

So they can take your genes but only the non-encrypted ones - the rest they need the keys - and so in simple - waking up needs to be on the quiet/inner levels - to do it otherwise where you are polarized against another, makes it only obvious and actually will attract them to your diminishment - this is why you must walk the center of the cross and not die on it metaphorically speaking, but arise unified from the cross - but to do it openly and resistively against the establishment only will get you crucified - are you listening R?

Do you see that this whole affair is beyond the physical, it is not about oil, or money or world government, not about globalization and so forth, it is more than this, but these are only used as the cannon-fodder medium to keep you occupied and no time to wake up - they play both sides of the game and see both hands of cards., whilst to you it looks like a conflict - where you must side with one or the other - "you are either with us or not" as one of your infamous leaders said to the rest of the world in order to polarize.

We will tell you also that living underground, the Jehovah/reptilian group appear as white skinned people - your aboriginals all over your world are the true color skin representation of you as humans with 24 DNA - which is black/brown.

From this comes the different mixes which give different colors of your skin races except for the Asian races which were put in place as a means to rectify the imbalances created by the Jehovah stream

[R] So now these two groups are fighting for control - over earth humans when you awaken and see your unified self for what it is, rather than your fragmented selves, you will begin to slowly, see with real-eyes (realize) and have full perception and access to much knowledge that is carried from generation to generation within your junk-DNA - likened unto finding the encryption key to unlock this encrypted junk-DNA.

Many of you think that your junk-DNA is the portion that has been de-activated thus limiting your fields of perception and ability. To some degree this can be the case, but in fact, when you sold yourselves out due to deceit unknowingly, we had to encrypt much of your DNA and leave only that which was sufficient enough to allow your survival.

There are still many species who try in vain to decrypt your 24 DNA matrix soul/body in hope that they may attain the codes to heaven's gate so to speak - but forcing one's way into a house, is not the same as earning the right of entry, and stealing one's possessions/knowledge is not the same as working and earning and learning the knowledge unto yourself .

From: 4-30-2002

[Question] If we unlock this code that you - Blue talk about, does it mean we get connected with this endless energy?

[Blue] If you unlock the code to your self, we shall say you have "access" to endless energy on a soulular/cellular level, be it in the physical universes or non-physical.

[Question] In terms of every day experience, what would it mean for us to unlock this code? What does a person who did it looks like? What is this person able to do? Is it the same as getting enlightened? Was the Buddha a man who unlocked the code? When you unlock the code, you awake to what? What happens with consensual reality?

[Blue] Your questions are one-dimensional, but the answers are multi-dimensional It is more than just physical or 3rd Dimension in Universe-1. As you unlock the code here, you begin access to universe 2 and then universe 3 ... as a soulular being/entity/group/family. Remember the "I" in You is only a fragment of a whole soul/gestalt, which resides at the utmost levels of Universe 6 in the non-physical - below this are fragments, which further fragment all the way down to Dimension-1 - currently the "I" of you, which we are corresponding with resides in Dimension-4, your physical body being in Dimension-3 of universe-1. You have soulular family in D1-D2-D3-D4, which belong or work together and belong to other souls in upper dimensions / universes, which are one family which ultimately belong to one of the 24 streams/frequencies emanating from the all-that-is. We - "Blue" are one of these frequencies - why is it you are attached, to an animal/pet, or even a sentimental object, plants etc. - because its' energy makeup vibe belongs in the same family soul group as you are in.

[Blue] Once you have unlocked/braided all the way to universe-3 / dimension-4, you must await the cogs and wheels of universe, wheels within wheels to align This alignment occurs in cycles of your time - remember the one-way valve - where it is feeding lines into the physical universes, well at the right time it reverses allowing those who have unlocked the doors of they be - to go back into the non-physical (non-time) universes ... now again, a cycle is coming to pass, and thus why the big rush to gain access to the non-physical universes - but understand, there are maligns who are residing in universe-3 who are attempting to force their way thru - now since you are not in universe-3, but Universe-1, then what is the big deal for you? For you it is not a matter of jumping from Universe-1 thru Universe-3 into Universe-4 (non-physical) - but as these cycles come to pass, you have opportunities to go from Universe-1 to Universe-2 - but there are those who are malign STS (Service to Self) who feed off you and your knowledge and your access codes that are locked encrypted with in you, who require you in order for them to also make the jump to Universe-2 and beyond - what is the term you call a hitch-hiker - or more drastic a hijacker - there would not be an issue if they wished to go to Universe -2, Universe-3 and beyond for benign reasons, but for if they were in union with source they would not need to hitch-hike or hijack, they would get thru on their own accord. But since they have ulterior reasons/motives, they are taking the hitch-hike ride. What it means to be in a state of self-aware, fully potentialized, all these extra senses you pick up, you would determine every step of your past, present, future and sovereign unto your own creation and not limited choices given to you to decide. You would have access to knowledge beyond your current, you would not know of any dis-easement or physical limitations - nor old age and should a limb be chopped off, you would grow it again. Foods/sustenance would not be required, as your intake would be from ionized air and unfiltered UV light. Death would be by choice or by decapitation only - you would grow to be hairless, approximately 8 ft tall, and your skin would be likened unto a tumescent blue, sort of like a bruised light-blue-white - your physical composition would be composed more of silica.

[R] You mean you could live for ever?

[Blue] Time as you know it, it would appear as forever, but time in Universe-3 flows differently to Universe-1 and thus it is not forever, but from a Universe-1 perspective it is a very long time. You would have telepathy and full communication with all animal kingdoms. Please understand what we are describe is a 12 DNA, Universe-3 being - making the jump to Universe-2 gives you a subset of these attributes - and lesser in Universe-1 much of your mythical gods thru your various histories are akin to attributes of above, which questions as to whether they are myths or not.

Note you currently have 2 DNA to 4 DNA for Universe-1 -majority are sitting on 2-3 - with some at DNA 4 - to get to Universe-2 when the valve reverses you need to be at DNA 4 and jump across to DNA 5. You don't have much longer to before valve reverse. To re-iterate

Physical Universes   Non-Physical Universes

Universe-1 = DNA 1 - 4   Universe-4 = DNA 12 - 15
Universe-2 = DNA 5 - 8   Universe-5 = DNA 16 - 20
Universe-3 = DNA 9 - 12   Universe-6 = DNA 21 - 24

What is important this cycle around is that all the valves between Universe-1 thru to Universe-6 all reverse in alignment, allowing light from the all-that-is core to filter all the way thru!!!

Normally it is only a subset cycle meaning, that the valve between Universe-1-Universe-2 or Universe-2-Universe-3 and so on - this time is all valves thru from core to Universes-1 are reverses.

Please understand - many a new age fad sell you on this ascension business - it is not really ascension, as in Universe-2 and Universe-3 you still have polarity and malignancy existing. Please note: that many of those who pull the strings, control and set the stage in Universe-1, operate from Universe-2 and Universe-3 - this is why it appears the odds are stacked against you.

[Question] And also, the entities that want us to do the homework of unlocking the code, what do they want it for? Reconnection with the all-that-is? Free energy only?

[Blue] We have explained above, it is transportation into the all-that-is domains to take control, supply more energy to feed their entropic universes/domains.

Definition of entropy: the degradation of the matter and energy in the universe to an ultimate state of inert uniformity by a process of degradation or running down or a trend to disorder.

[Question] Can one have access to this free energy while keeping a separated/paranoid consciousness? If not, do these entities suspect that this "unlocking" would be dangerous to their "separated" way of living?

[Blue] There is no such thing as free energy in your physical universes, the energy system that claim free energy have to vampirize this energy from elsewhere, so something gives in order for something else to take - this is the physical law !!!

Many who do not understand this nature, can cause more problems than they are innocently aware of, by developing such free energy machines. However there are systems, which can be built which may use of energy that is already given, such as your suns' rays, wind, waves and so on. We do not mean to pooh pooh your free energy inventors, but as many of you deem it sometimes a conspiracy by those not wanting you to have free energy, this is not so - as their are beings in place who are benign and aware of problems/havoc that can be caused by these devices, that they will give these inventors choices such as $$$$ etc. and buy their inventions of them, agreeing never to be used.

In truth it is your maligners who use these devices for their own greed, and much, not all of your weather patterns and storms out of the blue un-noticed as well as earthquakes are due to uses of these free energy systems which rob other areas of your nature for energy!!!

You can only take from that which has already given or chosen to give - you can not forcefully take from something that has not given or chosen to give against it's will - it is known as the law of compensation! We often muse upon this term and have given it a name known as the law of complexation, as many get complex in issue in trying to understand this law - but it is quite simple, do not take from that which does not give to you, ask first.

Know you your nuclear plants and atomic weapons are of such nature, taking forcefully.

As for Buddha, who's mother was known as Maya, is not a person and not to be personified - it is an epoch, a state of mind, consciousness, just as the Maya were clues there-in, where did they vanish or go?

[Question] How can certain power plants, like Ayahuasca and magic mushrooms help us to unlocking this code?

[Blue] There are many substances, which when taken when one is first aware/awoken that will further assist into unlocking memories providing access to further perceptions of knowledge - to take these substances when on a cellular/soulular level you are closed off and not open, which can cause havoc, creating holes akin to black holes on an etheric level and as well as cellular levels, which can drain your life force further accelerating your entropy.

This is why in many cultures, which partake of these substances, it is only allowed by the elderly or mature or aware tribes people who have earned or proven their maturity.

Know you there are some very balanced, open minded that nicotine is actually of benefit or ecstasy pills are of benefit, but you have to be at a level where you are already aware, unblocked as taking them is likened unto blowing the doors off with explosives, which will cause more damage than just as it were one to simply open the door with no force.

Do you not see this is why they wish to hold many of your substances from you making them illegal - it is not to protect you, it is to protect themselves, so you do not awaken.

[R] You mean it not for black money to fund black projects?

[Blue] This is part of it, but they could fund in other ways, not in pushing illegal substances that cost nothing to make for high prices - the truth is that they do not wish for people to awaken - why is it you think, all of a sudden, your tobacco industry has gone in reverse - every corner as an anti-smoking campaign??

There was a time, where your governments and others pushed it like water unto you as children, now the same governments are attempting to completely rid you of your tobbaco/nicotine - by making anti-smoking laws and raising the taxes upon it - the shadows have woken up that by proxy these substances are awakening you to other fields of perception.

[R] This is interesting, as I never thought about it like this. Is there a right time or wrong time or how can I say, how does one know if they are at a stage where taking of these substances will assist or will be detriment?

[Blue] When you know you are addicted or becoming addicted to any substance, then you are not ready - when you are able to partake of them or not at will, without any cravings - at any time - then you are perhaps ready.

[R] Does this apply to coffee?

[Blue] Yes!

[R] It is sort of like a catch 22 - if I am at a ready stage, then why the need to partake of them?

[Blue] Precisely! Everything is already with in you, but they can be of benefit if one is on that fine line between "ready" and "just not quiet ready" If one is closed in mind and physically blocked, then partaking of them is dangerous for the mind, body and spirit.

226

From: 5-1-2002

[Blue] One of the most asked questions - "How do I get out of here?" The idea is not to get out of here, but to be here, fully embodied 100%. The new age fad of ascension is literally leading you up the garden path.

[R] But hang on, just yesterday you said, that one could transcend from Universe-1 to Universe-2 etc. is this not ascension?

[Blue] It is only ascension as such when the goal is NOT to get out of here. If your goal and aim to ascend is to get away, to escape, to seek refuge, then it is not ascension and you will not wake up, become fully realized. It is a paradox for you. When you seek escape, you actually are entrapping yourself. If you simply allow, live in full, 100% be here fully embodied 24 DNA, then you do not need to seek or obtain ascension, as you become it automatically.

Your whole new age business is built on providing you with methods of escaping, fast-food drive-thru spirituality so to speak - because people do not want to see or be fully realized, they just want to get the hell out of here - you do not want to look behind the veil and see the real picture!!

Well we must tell you , your destiny is to be here and to allow the all-that-is the physical experience, 100%. When you achieve this, you will not want to escape, believe us!!

There was no other purpose for you to be here, other than to be here 100%, otherwise what is the point of you being here, the all-that-is, could have just let the fallen, continue on with their separation, until all energy within this system was depleted, nullified and in the end it ALL GOES BACK TO SOURCE ANYWAY!!!! (but without any self awareness) The universal truth is, you-the-all-that-is wanted to experience this new discovered world called physicality in all it's unconditional vibrancy 100% embodied and fully aware of itself and it's connectedness to source simultaneously!! So by attempting escape, you are not awakening to your true-self !!

Now the $24 million dollar question - how to awaken - mmm - what to do - mmm -

We say it again and again and again - you must know who you are, you must know yourself, the self that is really you, not what society programs or dictates you to be.

You must know own all your feelings and experiences - without owning them you can not proceed!!

There is no magic pill, which will give you this - it is an internal affair, not external - most of you look outside of yourself, in order to gather some information about who you may be - it is not out there - it is in you!!! Period!!

Look inside, and you will see, that the outside moulds itself to you and not you molding yourself to the outside.

Also you need to allow unconditional processing within, be it polarized or not polarized, negative or positive, it does not matter - which ever it is you MUST own it, all of it - do not push it away, are hide it under a carpet rug.

[R] How about DNA activation, how to assist to do this ?

[Blue] When you know and own yourself, this occurs naturally. But we will let you all in on a tiny secret. Your supernova's play a major role in programming and activating you on a physical and conscious level. With each supernova in your ages of past, has affected your evolution in quantum leaps - within the light of the supernova has been programming sequences - these are created by you/us/all-that-is to occur at intervals and stages in your time, to awaken you on a mass scale (not individual).

If you are not ready to receive the high frequency voltage, you overload and burn. We suggest you research this, know and understand all you can about neutron and pulsars stars, which become supernovas. Your pulsars are especially important as they pulse cosmic heartbeat, which affects you and your growth.

Why do you think your sun is doing - it is pulsing more and more in amplitude, as it prepares to go supernova - and as it does with it, it releases codes of light which program whole species - your sun now is pulsing you codes - note if you can not take on these codes, you will burn - it is like a high frequency - if your ears can not handle the high pitch, your ear drums will explode, before the pane of glass does.

There is another star about to go supernova, as you know it in your time. From where we sit, it has already occurred, and it is glorious in its expression. It will appear to the naked eye in the year 2007.

NOTE: Before the invention of the telescope, not too many supernovae were known. Since the invention of the telescope, there have been more supernovae seen every year. Last year, 2002, for example, 82 were found!

The first recorded supernova was in 1066. The Chinese astronomers took note of it, but no westerners did! The next recorded one was in 1181, again by the Chinese.

Another was in 1054,.observed by the Chinese. Evidence is that it was seen by American Indians as well. This bright supernova was easily visible in full daylight, and today can be seen as the Crab Nebula. The great astronomer Tycho studied another one in 1572. Kepler observed one in 1604. In 1885, one occurred in the nearby Andromeda Galaxy. This was the first supernova ever seen outside our own Galaxy. The last naked eye supernova was 1987A, which occurred in a satellite galaxy to the Milky Way.

In November 1994, the light of a supernova in nearby NGC 3370 reached Earth. This stellar outburst briefly outshone all of the tens of billions of other stars in its galaxy. Although supernova are common, with one exploding every few seconds somewhere in the universe, this one was special. Designated SN 1994ae, this supernova was one of the nearest and best observed supernova since the advent of modern, digital detectors. It resides 98 million light-years (30 megaparsecs) from Earth. [End note]

[R: Pictures in mind of this, when flashed to me, gave me a full on warm fuzzy buzz feeling, as I saw this huge ocean wave made up of blue/violet luminescent light ripping across black space, as if it was like rippling up and down my spine] Keep your eyes to the sky and listen out for news for a newly discovered supernova - coming soon to a galaxy near you.

[Blue:] We wish to also give you a heads up on pulsing - you must understand, when we speak of pulsing, we mean ANALOG PULSING - there is a difference to DIGITAL.

Your digital world is in fact blocking and corrupting your fields of perception - as everything is pulsed digitally - all your sound and pictures are now digital in your media, your radio, TV, music, dvd and so forth - this is detrimental to your health, mind, soul!!

This pulsing does not allow you to see/realize your reality in full.

[R] Please explain ...

[Blue] Digital pulsing has gaps in it - whereas analog pulsing is gapless there is no gaps - although it is perceived as a pulse - i.e. on-off - it is not, it is a wave, that rises and diminishes, but never stops - it is continuous - although to you it appears it has disappeared/stopped from your field of perception - it has not - because if you were to awaken/expand your fields of perception, you would see that in fact this wave has not diminished - it is still there - whereas with digital - a pulse or frequency as some term it, is not really a frequency - it has gaps/spaces all over it.

eg. 288 hz = 288 cycles per second

Pure analog, this wave rises and diminishes like your sine wave, snakelike - 288 times per second - although it goes to zero at two points, THE WAVE ITSELF IS STILL THERE, it has not gone anywhere.

Digital - although it still has a frequency/cycle of 288 times per second - is in fact fragmented - on-off-on-off-on-off - 288 times on and 288 times off - to make your 288 hz cycle - it is like taking a string - and cutting it up into 288 fragments/pieces - you are not getting the full sound, but an imitation of it!! .... a sliced up version of it WHICH HAS GAPS - these gaps cause you havoc and actually can cause mind and DNA programming entrainment.

Imagine sunlight beaming thru a fan-blade - as the fan spins, the blade cycles thru 288 times a minute - and the sunlight flashes upon your eyes.

In 3D, it appears to your physical eyes to be pulsing/flashing - but the sunlight is still there, it has not gone anywhere!!! Because your 4D or above perception still sees the sunlight in its complete form - as the fan-blade does not get in the way of your above-self, your peripheral self - do you understand?

With digital - if you were to replicate sunlight digitally - you would chop it up and then stream all the chopped up pieces making it appear as if you have sunlight flashing 288 times per minute - your 3D eyes would still see it as 288 flashes upon your eyes - BUT your other full self , 4D and above also does not see the full sunlight - it also see GAPS in this imitation of your sunlight and is not nourished by it - as it is NOT COMPLETE.

We tell you this, because it is very important and many do not understand, that ridding of analog is going against your development, growth, and activation - you are being kept back by bombardments of digital environments - in 3D it maybe as good as the real thing, but in 4D and above we assure you it is like Swiss cheese - this is what is termed half-light universes 144 harmonics and 288 full-light harmonics.

This is nor the time and place for discussion, but the shadows are setting up shields, fences that are digital pulsing, HAARP, your space station with it huge wings of solar panels, is in fact there to reflect the light about to approach you from the sun and supernova so you do not receive it.

Your ozone layer was purposely triggered aeons ago to act as a filter blocking

UV and other encoded light - now they tell you to wear sunglasses and sunscreens - to the degree that you have diminished your natural sunblocking ability which still allows activation - and now rely on other devices to protect you.

Did the aborigines of old wear sunglasses and creams, the Hopi Indians and so forth, did they die of skin cancer ?

Again we tell you, your ozone depletion is natural evolution - this ability to naturally protect you from dangerous rays, but yet still allow the encoding has been bred out over aeons by the Jehova - where did the Aryan (orion races come from)

Do consider and research unto yourselves, digital and analog waves/nature, pulsars/neutron stars and keep an eye out of supernovas.

WHO IS ELIJOVI
(SEE EXPLANATION IN ABOVE TEXT)

WHO IS ISHAEL

[Blue] you already know them as the Jehovan strain - in main they are pleiadian-reptilian - the two factions warring are of slightly different mixes - you have the pleaidian/orion mix which is your typical ultimate warlording faction which you label as Jehovah to this day and you have your plaeidain/sirius mix which is known as the Ishael faction.

Your Jehovah mix is what you know as your Jews.

The Ishael mix is what you know as your Arabs

Now this split is documented in your Christian bible - if you re-read carefully - Abraham had children thru many women, but the main two was his wife Sarah and his mistress Hagar. It is much more complicated than this, but your bible simplifies it by explaining it off as a bearing of children and right to inheritance.

Something you must understand - is these names are not actual people who existed - but likened unto titles just as Jehovah is a title and thus is Abram (Abraham) and also Isaac, and Ishmael/Ishael - these are titles for whole peoples/races and not just two people and wife so to speak.

The common denominator in all this is the Jehova/Reptilian stream and of course Abraham - you see Abraham stream was to some degree the human stream - who caught up in the genetic mixing - and power play of the Jehovah.

You see genetically both Jews (Jehovah/Abram/Sarah/Isaac) = Pleiadian/Orion mix.

And Arabs (Jehovah/Abram/Hagar/Ishmael) = Pleiadian/Sirius mix came from the same father so to speak.

Do you notice how it is both Jews and Muslim-Arabs who circumcise due to religion.

[Blue] We suggest you read your bible this will give you an idea - simply put the Hagar/Ishmael stream did not bow down to Jehovah and follow in his warring/warlord ways - whereas as the Sarah/Isaac stream did - and so Jehovah favored/empowered this strain/stream more so over the Ishmael stream - to the degree the Ishmael stream were thrown out of the house so to speak and downcast and at some point persecuted by the Jehovah stream - and it has been since this that the Ishael stream has come back to revenge for they feel they have been harshly done by the Jehovah who maintained power/control over them.

Originally the Ishael did not want power/control they were peaceful in nature and being mixed with the Sirius strain they were imbued with great knowledge for they went on to form Egypt and build the pyramids with the help of the Sirians - (this made Jehovah stream extremely jealous and more warring - you see Jehovah thought that they got the wrong end of the genetic make up of Abraham and that the Ishmael got the smart-genes.

~~~~~~~~~~~~~~~~~~~~~~

WHO IS RA?

From very early times Ra was a sun god. He took on many of the attributes and even the names of other gods as Egyptian myths evolved. A good example of this is the god Ra and Amun merging to become Amun-Ra or Ra and Horus combining to become Ra-Harakhte.

WHO IS ELOHIM?

The Catholic Version

Elohim is the common name for God. It is a plural form, but "The usage of the language gives no support to the supposition that we have in the plural form Elohim, applied to the God of Israel, the remains of an early polytheism, or at least a combination with the higher spiritual beings" (Kautzsch). Grammarians call it a plural of majesty or rank, or of abstraction, or of magnitude (Gesenius, Grammatik, 27th ed., nn. 124 g, 132 h). The Ethiopic plural amlak has become a proper name of God. Hoffmann has pointed out an analogous plural elim in the Phoenician inscriptions (Ueber einige phon. Inschr., 1889, p. 17 sqq.), and Barton has shown that in the tablets from El-Amarna the plural form ilani replaces the singular more than forty times (Proceedings of the American Oriental Society, 21-23 April, 1892, pp. cxcvi-cxcix).

Etymology

Elohim has been explained as a plural form of Eloah or as plural derivative of El. Those who adhere to the former explanation do not agree as to the derivation of Eloah. There is no such verbal stem as alah in Hebrew; but the Arabist Fleischer, Franz Delitzsch, and others appeal to the Arabic aliha, meaning "to be filled with dread", "anxiously to seek refuge", so that ilah (eloah) would mean in the first place "dread", then the object of dread. Gen., xxi, 42, 53, where God is called "the fear of Isaac", Is., viii, 13, and Ps. lxxv, 12, appear to support this view. But the fact that aliha is probably not an independent verbal stem but only a denominative from ilah, signifying originally "possessed of God" (cf. enthousiazein, daimonan) renders the explanation more than precarious. There is no more probability in the contention of Ewald, Dillmann, and others that the verbal stem, alah means "to be mighty": and is to regarded as a by-form of the stem alah; that, therefore, Eloah grows out of alah as El springs from alah. Baethgen (Beitrage, 297) has pointed out that of the fifty-seven occurrences of Eloah forty-one belong to the Book of Job, and the others to late texts or poetic passages. Hence he agrees with Buhl in maintaining that the singular form Eloah came into existence only after the plural form Elohim had been long in common use; in this case, a singular was supplied for its pre-existent plural. But even admitting Elohim to be the prior form, its etymology has not thus far been satisfactorily explained. The ancient Jewish and the early ecclesiastical writers agree with many modern scholars in deriving Elohim from El, but there is a great difference of opinion as to the method of derivation. Nestle (Theol. Stud. aus Würt., 1882, pp. 243 sqq.) supposes that the plural has arisen by the insertion of an artificial h, like the Hebrew amahoth (maidens) from amah. Buhl (Gesenius Hebraisches Handworterbuch, 12th ed., 1895, pp. 41 sq.) considers Elohim as a sort of augmentative form of El; but in spite of their disagreement as to the method of derivation, these writers are one in supposing that in early Hebrew the singular of the word signifying God was El, and its plural form

Elohim; and that only more recent times coined the singular form Eloah, thus giving Elohim a grammatically correct correspondent. Lagrange, however, maintains that Elohim and Eloah are derived collaterally and independently from El.

THE FUTURE OF DNA CHANGES

Researcher Donna Good Higbee, on a radio interview with Art Bell on May 23, 2002, talked about a change in DNA with an experiment on a meditator. Here is what she said:

"When the meditator entrains with the Schuman frequency, (which is rising) and then goes into a loving, compassionate state and becomes ONE with the spirit - (I think she means God) the DNA changes to a higher level of consciousness.

"An experiment was done with a man who had a sample of his DNA in a petri dish in a lab and when he raised his frequency of his consciousness to the level at which the Schuman frequency was at the time, the DNA in the petri dish unwound and rewound at a higher level and he reached a higher consciousness.

She said that many more people who entrain themselves with the Schuman frequency will evolve and have their DNA changed in this same way.

THE SCHUMAN FREQUENCY

Earth's Rising Base Frequency Earth's background base frequency, or "heartbeat," (called Schuman resonance, or SR) is rising dramatically. Though it varies among geographical regions, for decades the overall measurement was 7.8 cycles per second. This was once thought to be a constant; global military communications developed on this frequency. Recent reports set the rate at over 11 cycles, and climbing. Science doesn't know why, or what to make of it.

Our consciousness is accelerating exponentially!

Our brainwaves are at different frequencies depending on the state of mind that we are in.

1-4 Hz is delta and is associated with deep sleep
5-7 Hz is theta and is associated with meditation/dreams
8-12 Hz is alpha and is associated with being alert/aware/learning
13-30 Hz is beta and is very awake

Premonitions, remote viewing, misc. psychic phenomena, mind/body manipulations, etc. are commonly connected to the theta/alpha state at around 7-8 Hz. This is on the border of being in a deep meditative state and being alert and highly aware. It seems that normally, it takes some people years and years to be able to consciously enter this state at will by practicing different meditation techniques for years with much discipline. The only time it seems that the average everyday person can access these abilities is when they are sleeping.

We all go through several sleep cycles that bring us into the R.E.M state that we are all familiar with. We dream during this time even if we don't remember the dreams. Often, we have very revealing dreams of things that happen in the future, which do come true with great accuracy and some of the dreams are more symbolic and calls for interpretation.

During these dreams, we are usually unaware we are dreaming so we are like sleepwalking even in our dreams unless we become lucid. Lucid dreaming means that we are very awake inside our dreams and very aware of what is going on and can manipulate the dreams at will with some practice. We can tune in and have answers revealed to us in these dreams and these abilities seem to disappear when we wake up. If we could only bring our brain-waves down into these same frequencies while we are "awake," we would be able to have such different lives in this "normal waking reality." Many of us don't have time to practice, practice, and practice meditation on and on until we can do it by will. There is hope.

Our Earth has many different frequencies and pulses, but there is a very "main" pulse that is known as the Schuman Resonance. It was known to be at 7.83 Hz. (This is rising) This pulsing field that the Earth has is intimately connected to our own human consciousness and connects all consciousness. If we can tune into that field, we are tuned into everything connected to consciousness. Because we are innately synchronized to the nature of the universe and everything in it of course, we tune in to this field of 7.83 Hz when we go to sleep every night and dream. 7.83 Hz is that perfect frequency that is right in between the theta and alpha. 7-8 Hz. That is why we have this kind of access in our dreams and that is why we have this kind of access when we can will ourselves into that state by our own mind power or certain technologies known as binaural beats, which synchronize the hemispheres of our brain(s), stimulate new neural connection in the corpus collosum, and bring the brain-waves down to the theta/alpha state. Einstein had twice the amount of neural cells in parts of his brain than the average human being. It seems that the only way that we can access this state is by dreaming, meditation practices, binaural beat technology and a few other ways. Things are changing.

The Schuman Resonance is speeding up and is around 11 Hz or so. This means that we are tuned into this field just by being slightly relaxed. We don't have to go as "deep" to achieve the same affect. This obviously means that more and more people are going to have access to this "ability."

~~~~~~~~~~~~~~~~~~~~~~~~~~~~

Alvaro - A Conversation with the Elders

The Mayans also believed that humanity would be moving to a higher dimension around this time period. They called the end of this calendar cycle the end of time, stating that humanity would no longer need a calendar depicting linear time, for we would be moving to a higher dimension. The end of the Mayan Calendar has been calculated to be between December, 2011 and 2012, or 2013, but when it is correlated to our calendar, it may actually end around 2000, A.D. This correlates with the alignment of the Earth and Sun to the Galactic Core, which would be the definitive astronomical ending point of their calendar. The Mayan Calendar is the only calendar known to be based on Galactic Cycles. The Mayans claimed they created this calendar in order to monitor the light coming from the center of the Galaxy and how it affected our DNA. We now know through the work of Fritz Popp that DNA not only absorbs lights but also emits light. DNA also appears to be the bridge between our physical and etheric bodies. Modern science now realizes that our DNA directly reflects our consciousness, making it possible for us to willfully change our DNA.

As the Earth's frequency increases, every cell on the planet is attempting to raise its frequency in order to stay in step with the Earth. Therefore every cell and its energy field are attempting to cast off all negative frequencies and blockages preventing them from increasing their frequency and remain aligned with the Earth's frequency. This inner healing process is essential for us to stay connected and in harmony with the Earth and the Sacred Circuit. Currently it is believed that we are utilizing 22 of the 64 codons in our DNA, but with the activation occurring within the Sacred Circuit that we will be able to turn on and utilize more of our DNA's codons.

RECODING YOUR OWN DNA
By: Jelaila Starr

This is the opportunity of a lifetime! Increased earth energies are giving us the necessary framework and support so we can at last utilize the dormant 90% of the brain for which scientists have not found a purpose. We can have the best of both worlds- the joy of our physical bodies, and the psychic gifts of being fully conscious of our multidimensional place in the universe. How then can we seize this opportunity? We can do it by utilizing the increasing frequency to clear our emotional bodies and recode our DNA. Though all people collectively will feel the effects of the heightened earth energies, for those who wish to consciously work with the changes and accelerate their progress an accelerated process of DNA recoding, reconnecting and activation is now available. We call it the Accelerated DNA Recoding, Reconnection and Activation Process (RRAP).

DNA recoding, reconnecting and activation reunites our ten "unplugged" DNA strands back into our endocrine glands and reconnects us with our higher dimensional selves. Our endocrine glands, especially the hypothalamus and pineal, wake up from their atrophied state and begin to function as they were intended, giving our bodies rejuvenation and superior health and spiritually giving us multidimensional access. Our crown chakra crystals become activated allowing us to receive and interpret communications from other realms. What we have long awaited is here at last!

All the cleansing methods will be very important now. Fruits and vegetables for clearing are necessary. Copious amounts of purified water with a small amount of natural lemon juice and sea salt assist the body with detoxification and the anchoring of a higher frequency. During DNA Recoding, you will find fairly high levels of excreted proteins in body fluids such as urine. Your cerebrospinal fluid will be filled with discarded mineral deposits. You are literally sloughing off your body and you are rebuilding it while you still live in it!

The changes will be very intense and will be very challenging to you during the sloughing off process. You will in essence rearrange and rebuild your own DNA! An analogy of this would be living in your house while you are remodeling it. While living in your body, you will be rebuilding it.

Bodywork, liver cleanses and colonics are appropriate and useful. Counseling and/or regression work on stuck emotional patterns will provide great leaps in clearing and recoding the DNA by getting to the root of the imbalances and releasing them with compassion. The more quickly blocks and toxins are released from the emotional/physical bodies, the more easily your body can accept higher frequencies. As you clear you are incorporating higher dimensional frequencies into your physical/emotional reality and, therefore, your dietary requirements will change.

THE NEW JERUSALEM PLAN

Revelations 22-27

And the city had no need of the sun, neither of the moon to shine in it; for the glory of God did lighten it, and the Lamb is the light thereof. 24 And the nations of them which are saved shall walk in the light of it: and the kings of the earth do bring their glory and honour into it. 25 And the gates of it shall not be shu tat all by day; for there shall be no night there. 26 And they shall bring the glory and honour of the nations into it. 27 And there shall in no wise enter into it any thing that defileth, neither whatsoever worketh abomination, or maketh a lie; but they which are written in the Lamb's book of life.

By Joseph E. Mason

The great mysteries of life are quite elusive. We do not have the "hard facts" needed to feel sure that our theories about the mysteries are true. Sometimes we feel sure, but convincing others is not so easy. Alas, they want "facts," and we cannot produce them. Well, times are changing.

We will present many "facts" concerning some major mysteries of our world. These "facts" will show evidence that -

The ancient sites around the world are very precisely positioned on a global coordinate system in relation to the position of the Great Pyramid at Giza.

    * The positions of the sites are given in the geometry of their construction.

    * A very ancient system of numbers was used in the system, which we will call "Gematria."

    * "Gematrian" numbers are found in ancient myths and religions, including the Bible.

  * Gematrian numbers were used in systems of weights and measures by ancient peoples, including the Greeks, the Egyptians, the Persians, the Babylonians and the Romans.

  * The ancient Mayans used Gematrian numbers in their very accurate timekeeping.

  * The Code system uses mathematical constants, such as pi and the radian.

  * The system also uses conventions that are still in use, such as the 360-degree circle, 60-minute degree, 60-second minute, the base-ten numbering system, the 12-inch foot, and the 5280-foot mile.

  * The Nazca Line ground markings "locate themselves" on The Code Matrix system.

  * Crop circle formations suggest the same ancient numbers by way of their positions and measurements.

  * The very ancient "Monuments on Mars," including "The Face on Mars," were positioned in exact locations, just as the ancient sites on Earth.

The Code system is quite like the cartographic system we still use today . . . which was probably handed down to us from very ancient times. In both the old and new reckoning systems, the earth is divided into 360 degrees around the equator for longitude coordinates, and latitude coordinates are reckoned at 90 degrees, from the equator to either Pole. Each degree is further divided into 60 "minutes," and each minute is divided into 60 "seconds." Thus, by giving the degrees, minutes, and seconds of East or West longitude and same for the North or South latitude, we can "locate" any point on the earth, similar to the way we give two street addresses to locate a place in our cities and towns. The big difference between the two systems is that today we use Greenwich, England as the starting point (zero degrees), or "Prime Meridian," for the longitude coordinates, whereas the ancients used the Great Pyramid of Giza. The difference in longitude between the two Prime Meridians is 31 degrees, 08 minutes, 0.8 seconds, so this must be taken into account when calculating "The Code."

Following 'The Code Numbers'

It is not necessary to be a mathematical expert to learn The Code system. Some terms, such as Pi, the Radian (RAD), square root, 'e', and Tangent are mentioned as part of the decoding system, but a complete understanding of their meaning is not required to follow along. They are mostly various mathematical constants used in geometric calculations of circles and spheres. Brief explanations will be given in the articles that follow. To follow the calculations, it is most useful to have a **scientific calculator**. The Operating System Microsoft Windows has a calculator under "Accessories" in the Start Menu. After calling up the Calculator window, it can be changed to a scientific calculator on the Menu bar under "View." Recommended also is a pocket calculator with the needed functions on it, such as the TI-30Xa Solar, from Texas Instruments.

Some abbreviations will be used, such as:
W. = West
E. = East
deg = Degrees
min = Minutes
sec = Seconds
RAD = Radian
x = "times," multiply
/ = divided by
C. I. = Coordinate Intersect (explained below, as presented)

Carl Munck who calls himself an archeocryptographer is the pioneer in this field, having re-discovered an amazingly-advanced "geomath matrix" from very deep antiquity, encoded in the precise latitude/longitude positions of ancient pyramids, mounds, effigies, monuments, and stone circles.

Munck has been able to confirm the reality of this incredible discovery (or, re-discovery) by simply pointing-out what is *there* for all to observe, by way of modern satellite-accurate maps, simple math, and a hand-held calculator. Indeed; aerial photography, satellite imaging, and calculators (computers) have proven essential for the birth of archeocryptography.

In his 'decoding' of Stonehenge, Munck first determined that the original Sarsen Circle was constructed of 60 stones - 30 uprights and 30 cross-pieces. The Sarsen Circle, like any circle, has 360 degrees of arc on its circumference if we assume "our" circle/sphere math conventions. Here was a major key in this re-discovery process: the hypothesis that 360 degrees on a circumference was 'always' an integral part of this advanced 'matrix'!

Munck took the 60 original Sarsen Circle stones and multiplied them by 360 . . . 60 x 360 = 21600 - which "happens to be" the number of arc-minutes on any circumference, according to "our" math conventions. And, 21600 also "happens to be" the number of Nautical Miles on the polar circumference of Earth. Isn't it interesting that one Nautical Mile equals exactly one 'minute' of Earth latitude? Of course, we also "happen" to use the number 60 for "time circles" - minutes in an hour and seconds in a minute - as on the circumference of a clock face. We are finding out (re-discovering) that the numbers 60 and 360 are not *really* arbitrary, in terms of what we know as time and space.

The number 60 is very "geometric" because it is divisible by many whole numbers into many *other* whole numbers, and this is part of the inherent "nature" of our number system.

The distance, on a baseball field, from the pitcher's mound to home plate . . . 60 feet, 6 inches - is not really 'arbitrary', either. 60 x 6 = 360.

Using the most accurate maps available, Carl P. Munck looked to see if he could find some meaningful relationship between the precise location of Stonehenge, on Earth in terms of latitude and/or longitude, and the number 21600. He noted its latitude of approximately 51-deg 10 min North. Suppose he would, for instance, divide the number 21600 by 51, and then divide that result by 10 ? Yes, this is what he did:

21600 / 51 = 423.5294118
Then, 423.5294118 / 10 = 42.35294118

Amazingly, Stonehenge centers itself precisely at this latitude: 51-deg 10 min 42.3529 sec

Munck calls the product of a site's (centered) degrees x minutes x seconds . . . the 'Grid Latitude' (or 'Grid Longitude' for the site's centered longitude).

So; the Grid Latitude of Stonehenge is: 51-deg x 10 min x 42.35294118 sec North = 21600 North

Original Longitude of Stonehenge

One of Munck's major discoveries is his re-discovery of "our" (?) original prime meridian for longitude measurement. He determined that the prime meridian for this 'geomath matrix' passes directly through the center of The Great Pyramid at Giza in Egypt. So; we adjust our longitude (east or west, according to the site we are working with) by 31 deg 08 min 0.8 sec - the exact longitude distance between the current Greenwich, England prime meridian and the center of The Great Pyramid. In our current system, the longitude for Stonehenge is - 01 deg 49 min 28.0173748 sec W.Greenwich (West of Greenwich)

In the ancient "Code" system, the longitude for Stonehenge was - 32 deg x 57 min x 28.8173748 sec W.Giza = 52562.89164 W.Giza

To explain - using the best maps available, we know that Stonehenge is centered at W.Greenwich longitude 01 deg 49 min 28 sec. So; because Stonehenge is located not that far to the west of the Greenwich, England prime meridian, we *add* the (31 deg 08 min 0.8 sec) variance-distance onto the W.Greenwich longitude:

> 01 deg 49 min 28 sec W.Greenwich
> + 31 deg 08 min 0.8 sec (variance)
> --
> 32 deg 57 min 28.8 sec W.Giza

Now, if we multiply - 32 deg x 57 min x 28.8 sec -using the "numbers only" - we will be multiplying 32 x 57 x 28.8 -for a product of 52531.2. At this point, we look through the matrix to see if there is a figure "close to" 52531.2 -and we find such a figure in the number 52562.89164 - which turns out to encode the 'product' of certain math constants and a certain astronomical/geometric number, the multiplied product of: - RAD (deg) x Pi x 2Pi x Square Root of 2160 = 52562.89164

57.29577951 x 3.141592654 x 6.283185307 x 46.47580015 = 52562.89164

Now, to "check" this figure - we start with 52562.89164 - and divide, first by the number of degrees, and then divide that result by the number of minutes, like this . . .

52562.89164 / 32 / 57 = 28.8173748 sec

We can see, here, that this "very precise" number of longitude seconds is only 0.0173748 (28.8173748 - 28.8) longitude seconds away from our *approximation* of 28.8 longitude seconds. In terms of actual FEET, this would be a difference of approximately a Foot and a half. Yes, we now have figured out the W.Giza longitude of Stonehenge (the way Carl P. Munck did it)

32 deg 57 min 28.8173748 sec W.Giza

In dealing with circles and spheres, we run into the math constants of Pi and

RADIAN measure, and these constants are integral to this 'geomath matrix', along with the number 360. Pi is the ratio of circumference to diameter of any given circle or sphere. Radian (deg) is the arc-distance on the circumference that is equal to the radius of any given circle or sphere. In degrees of arc, the Radian is equal to 57.29577951 (deg) - to eight decimal places. It is an irrational number, like the Pi constant 3.141592654 - to nine decimal places.

[Note from Joe: The Radian can be figured by dividing 180 by Pi.]

The relationship between Pi, the Radian (deg), and 360 (deg) can be shown with this equation: RAD x 2Pi = 360

Now, back to the Grid Longitude of Stonehenge . . .

52562.89164 = RAD x Pi x 2Pi x Square Root of 2160 (46.47580015)

Here we have 4 terms, or quantities, multiplying to a number that encodes the precise original (Giza-based) longitude of Stonehenge. And, each of these 4 terms are important "entities" that are integral to both the design and the essence of this re-discovered 'matrix'.

Notice that the number 2160 is a "base-ten harmonic" of the number 21600, and vice-versa - the decimal point is simply moved one place, 'horizontally'.

Note also that 2160 refers to: diameter of The Moon in statute miles (regular miles), years in a Zodiac Age, and the total number of corner-angle degrees on the surface of a Cube.

Grid Point Value of Stonehenge

The intersection point of latitude/longitude is represented in this 'matrix', for any given site, by the ratio of the Grid Latitude to the Grid Longitude, always greater-than-one. This resulting number is the Grid Point Value:

52562.89164 / 21600 = 2.433467206

[Joe's note: The intersection point-Grid Point Value is also called the "Coordinate Intersect," or C. I.]

243

Munck has determined that the precise (matrix-valid) radius in Feet, of the Sarsen Circle at Stonehenge, is 48.66934411 - to eight decimal places. If we divide that radius in Feet by Stonehenge's Grid Point Value, we get . . .

48.66934411 / 2.433467206 = 20 - a base-10 harmonic of the 'binary' number 2.

Suppose we divide the Sarsen Circle radius in Feet into the RAD (deg) constant?

57.29577951 / 48.66934411 = 1.177245771

Munck found that this number is the TANGENT of the precise azimuth-of-orientation of the 'Avenue' at Stonehenge - 49.65408598 degrees.

He found further that 49.65408598 is equal to: (e / Pi) RAD - where 'e' is the base of the so-called "natural logarithms," observed in the 'growth patterns' of natural things such as conch shells - approximately the value 2.72

(2.72258992 / Pi) x RAD (deg) = 49.65408598

Stonehenge, of course, is a very important site in this re-discovered matrix. Next to only The Great Pyramid at Giza, it is apparently the most important site on Earth in the Geomath Matrix.

Introduction to Gematria and Code-Related Numbers

Some readers may be familiar with the Greek system of Gematria, or others, which have numbers such as 666, 777 and 888. Carl Munck first encountered the word "Gematria" around 1986. When he tried to find information about Gematria, he found that the word was not in the dictionary, and that the libraries and bookstores had nothing about it. Several years later he met a "genuine shaman of Gematria - code name HannaH," who virtually buried Carl with Gematrian materials.

The Gematria explained by HannaH's material is not the same system used by the Ancient Greeks, or other familiar systems. The Gematrian numbers all are divisible by nine and add to nine or a multiple. Carl noted that the basic numbers always end in 0, 2, 4, 6, or 8.

A Forgotten or Repressed Science?

Carl asked in his newsletter (Volume 3, Nr. 6, June 1994), "Is Gematria one of those fragmentary ancient sciences which the longer we probe, the less we understand?" He went on to say, "Academia would just as soon be rid of it for that very reason. Yet, we have an enormous body of evidence to indicate that the ancient Greeks, Egyptians, Persians, Babylonians and Romans were enormously involved with these very same numbers, many of which even found their way into their metrological systems thereby becoming units of weights and measures."

Carl asked HannaH to write an introduction to Gematria for 'The Code' newsletter.

Gematria by HannaH

The 5th Century B.C. trading empire of the Eastern Mediterranean Phoenicians saw the appearance of a writing mode in which alphabetical letters served as numbers. Even at this early date, however, its roots were lost in the mists of time. From this base evolved the Hebraic and later Greek systems of Gematria. Both had reached a high degree of development by the 3rd Century B.C.

These alpha-numeric alphabets exhibited qualities and inter-relationships for which there is no logical intention. Yet an entire symbolic teaching evolved around them which incorporated the principles of number, form, sound and astronomy. Only number combinations and figures could be utilized to express this knowledge. Today, we view numbers as merely an expression of quantity. To the ancients, every number had its own character and identity; a place in an arithmetic chain that leads from one dimension of understanding to another.

This extraordinary system of arithmetic, or concealed geometry, form the link between the languages of literature and mathematics. With this knowledge, ancient literature, metrology and Sacred Geometry can be viewed with new eyes. With numbers, alphabetical cryptography becomes the law. Biblical numbers and structure dimensions become alphabetical statements. The WORD (number) becomes FLESH (dimensional) for numbers are words.

(Example: 3168 = Lord Jesus Christ - - Kupios Inoors Xpioros)

Carl Munck Finds Gematrian Numbers Related to The Code

Among the material HannaH sent to Carl was some of the papers of the late Louis K. Bell, one of the foremost ancient metrologists of modern times. Carl found that some of the numbers were the same as the ones he had found in the Pyramid Codex. Carl gave examples in his newsletter -

In ancient Babylonia, a long unit of measure called the "Kasbu" was well known. It was 129600 "Susi" in length. 129600 is the square of 360, and in the global matrix, the same figure which was used to encode the West Giza Longitude of the Shark Mound on North Bimini Island.

Also in Babylonian metrology was the "Maneh," a unit for measuring volume. It was equivalent to 7776 cubic inches by modern reckoning, but to them, 21600 "Um." 21600 is the grid latitude of Stonehenge! Is this only coincidence? After all, at the time Babylonia was great, Stonehenge hadn't yet been built - at least where our dating of the site is concerned, a date which could be WAY off the mark.

A long unit of measure used by the ancient Egyptians was the "Schoenus," a unit of 216000 modern inches. The same figure finds the longitude of the Octagon at Newark, Ohio. Did they know that?

The Roman "Load" was 3000 Libra; 2160 pounds today. 2160, the grid latitude of Newark's Observatory Circle. More coincidence?

The earliest recorded bushel was equal to 2160 cubic inches.

Over time, the ancient Egyptians employed several "cubits" in their body of metrology. Among them was the so-called "Royal cubit" - 20.67 modern English inches. 20.67; the actual longitude of the Mycerinus Pyramid to the West of the Great Pyramid.

In ancient Persia, a "talent" of gold was equal to 388800 grains. 388800 is what happens - exactly what happens - when we multiply MY-2 (7.396853329) by 52,562.89164, the grid longitude of Stonehenge. Who told them about that?

[Joe's note - 7.396853329 is a master Giza longitude]

Carl suspected that formal ancient metrology was rooted in the even more ancient pyramid codex. He went on to read into the subject, including the works of Charles Warren, and A. E. Berriman. Most of the authorities agreed that no one knew where ancient metrology came from - it was already in use when men first began writing. "Obviously," Carl said, "it is incredibly ancient."

Carl's Breakthrough in Gematria

Carl listed some of the Gematrian numbers with their "Alpha" or "Word" meanings in the newsletter -

- 144 = Light
- 288 = Double light, the Kingdom of Heaven.
- 432 = Consecration (also the square root of the classical speed of light, 186624 miles per second). Several Biblical references are also tied to it; Luke 8:15, Revelation 2:17, etc.
- 396 = Classical earth radius (3960 miles).
- 576 = Prophecy and Gospel.
- 864 = Time (2) the source of light and life, (3) Most Holy.
- 1152 = Witness (576 x 2). Biblical references include Luke 14:26, Revelation 3:12, 12:11 and 19:9.
- 1296 = Circle of space (360 x 60 x 60). 1296 was also Plato's favorite number.
- 1548 = Priest of God.
- 1728 = A-flat in music.
- 2304 = False Christ's and False prophets (1 Cor. 14:22, Mark 13:12).
- 3168 = Lord Jesus Christ.
- 3888 = New Jerusalem (Rev. 21:2, 1 Cor. 12:27, Luke 8:21, etc.).
- 5184 = Victory over the beast (Rev. 15:2).

Carl explained that although this is quite confusing to the layman, even when the Biblical references are consulted, "the shaman of these sacred numbers are convinced that certain passages in Holy Scripture actually represent a codex in their own right. It was said that certain communications from ancient men of wisdom were very carefully positioned in the Bible in order to secretly transmit vital information across time itself - not unlike what we are seeing in the pyramid codex."

Carl listed some units of weights used by the ancient Romans, marking the Gematrian numbers with an asterisk (*):

*432 grains = 1 Uncia	3024 grains = 7 Septunx
648 grains = 1.5 Sescuncia	3456 grains = 8 Bessis
*864 grains = 2 Sextans	*3888 grains = 9 Dodrans
*1296 grains = 3 Quadrans	4320 grains = 10 Dextans
*1728 grains = 4 Triens	4752 grains = 11 Deunx
2160 grains = 5 Quintux	*5184 grains = 12 Libra
2592 grains = 6 Semis	

Another Roman system of weights was also listed

36 grains = 12 Semisextula	216 grains = 72 Semuncia
72 grains = 24 Sextula	*432 grains = 144 Unica*
108 grains = 36 Sicilicus	*5184 grains = 1728 Libra*
*144 grains = 48 Duella	

Surprisingly, many of the Roman numbers are the same as those used in the Gematrian system. Since metrology came before written records, and was likely handed down to the Romans, the number system came long before the Bible.

Even more amazing is the fact that the same system of numbers was used by the ancient Mayans in the West in their very precise time-keeping! The Mayans used a 20-day month in their calendar. Carl showed the arrangement in the newsletter, again marking the Gematrian numbers with an asterisk (*):

20 days = 18 kin	*288 days = 20 bactun
36 days = 20 uinals	*576 days = 20 pictun
72 days = 20 tuns	*1152 days = 20 calabtun
*144 days = 20 katun	*2304 days = 20 kinchilton

The Mayans also broke down their hours into specific groups of minutes:

24 hours = 144 minutes*	6912 hours = 41472 minutes
48 hours = 288 minutes*	13824 hours = 82944 minutes
864 hours = 5184 minutes	27648 hours = 165888 minutes
*1728 hours = 10368 minutes	55296 hours = 331776 minutes

Some give other figures for the various Mayan time periods, but the numbers are also Gematrian or Gematrian-related.

The Mayan Calendar Numbers,
Illustrating the Gematrian Number Relationship

1 KIN = 1 Day or 24 hours = 144 "Mayan Minutes"

20 KIN = 1 UINAL = 1 Haab Calendar Month of 20 Days = 2880 "Mayan Minutes"

18 UINAL = 1 TUN = 1 Haab Calendar Year of 360 Days = 51840 "Mayan Minutes"

On The Tzolkin Calendar, the cycle is 260 KIN (days), composed of 20 'wavespells' (see Jose Arguelles, et al) of 13 KIN (days) each. So; there are 13 'tones of creation' . . . 13 KIN . . . in each of the 20 'wavespells'. Each 'wavespell' is represented by a Mayan Glyph symbol.

A half-day, or one-half KIN, is 12 hours. We could think of this as "daytime" and "nighttime". Then, each 'daytime' and each 'nighttime' can be split into two 6-hour intervals. Each 6-hour interval is equal to 36 "Mayan Minutes", which gives us a basic "gematrian" unit of 36 "Mayan Minutes". As Carl P. Munck shows in his work, these 'intervals of 36' can be plotted as two separate sine waves according to the two common tangents (plus and minus) of gematrian numbers.

Here is a table of some Mayan Calendar units and their equivalent numbers of gematrian "Mayan Minutes" :

Kins		Days		Hours		"Mayan Minutes"
1/4	=	1/4	=	6	=	36
1/2	=	1/2	=	12	=	72
1	=	1	=	24	=	144
2	=	2	=	48	=	288
3	=	3	=	72	=	432
3.5	=	3.5	=	84	=	504
4	=	4	=	96	=	576
5	=	5	=	120	=	720
6	=	6	=	144	=	864
7	=	7	=	168	=	1008
8	=	8	=	192	=	1152
9	=	9	=	216	=	1296
10	=	10	=	240	=	1440
11	=	11	=	264	=	1584
12	=	12	=	288	=	1728
13	=	13	=	312	=	1872
14	=	14	=	336	=	2016
15	=	15	=	360	=	2160
16	=	16	=	384	=	2304
17	=	17	=	408	=	2448
18	=	18	=	432	=	2592
19	=	19	=	456	=	2736
20	=	20	=	480	=	2880

20 KIN = 1 UINAL = 1 Haab Calendar Month of 20 Days]

Since these number systems were in place long before the arrival of Columbus in the West, the mystery thickens. Carl suggests that the ancient people held the numbers to be of vital importance, and thus placed them in their metrology and calendars in order to preserve them in the best way they could. The numbers were there, before the beginning of writing. The people who recorded the numbers via their special systems, probably did not know what the numbers really meant.

Carl checked the tangents of the numbers, and realized there were just four, and only two if the plus/minus signs are ignored. He organized the numbers by their Tangents, and noted which number systems used them:

Common Tangent of + 0.726542528   Common Tangent of - 0.726542528

Number	Gematria	Mayan	Roman	Number	Gematria	Mayan	Roman
36		*	*	144	*	*	*
216			*	864	*	*	
396	*			2304	*	*	
576	*	*		3024		*	
1296	*		*	5184	*	*	*
3456		*	*	13824		*	
20736		*		82944		*	
55296		*					
331776		*					

251

Common Tangent of + 3.077683537   Common Tangent of - 3.077683537

Number	Gematria	Mayan	Roman	Number	Gematria	Mayan	Roman
72		*	*	108			*
252	*			288	*	*	
432	*		*	648			*
1152	*	*		1548	*		
2592	*		*	1728	*	*	*
4752			*	3168	*		
6912		*		3888	*		*
41472		*		10368		*	
				27648		*	
				165888		*	

Sine Waves

Carl figured a certain logic was demanded by these numbers, so he arranged them into two separate scales, organizing them by their tangents, and marking the numbers that came from the ancient systems with asterisks (*), and filling in the "blanks," with appropriate numbers, something like this:

252

+ 3.077683537	72*	252*	432*	612	792
- 3.077683537	108*	288*	468	648*	828

+ 0.726542528	36*	216*	396*	576*	756*
- 0.726542528	144*	324	504	684	864*

In the newsletter, Carl had a longer list of these numbers in vertical columns. He also drew in sine waves connecting the numbers, which seemed to be suggested by their logic. He noted the consistent differences between the various numbers in the top two rows of 36 and 144, such as 108 - 72 = 36 and 252 - 108 = 144. The differences between the bottom rows are 108 and 72, such as 144 - 36 = 108; and 216 - 144 = 72.

The suggestion of sine waves, Carl said, is very, very obvious. Did the ancients know about sine waves? Did they have oscilloscopes? Were they suggesting a certain frequency?

A Frequency of Light

Carl was shocked when he multiplied the two Gematrian tangents:

3.077683537 x 0.726542528 = 2.236067977

He knew that 2.236067977 is THE SQUARE ROOT OF FIVE!!!

That's the pyramid codex talking!", Carl says.

He asks, "Why does the square root of five answer the sine waves of the Sacred Numbers? What was the reasoning behind it?"

"Because the square root of five is itself a Tangent; the Tangent of 186234.09485."

Which is the 'SPEED OF LIGHT IN AIR'!!!

Carl points out that the speed of light in a vacuum is 186282.5894 miles per second, but when light travels through air, it is slowed down to 186234.09485 miles per second. Enter this speed-of-light-in-air number into your calculator, and then press the tangent key, to see that it is very close to the number arrived at by multiplying the two Gematrian tangents.

My computer calculator gives these figures:

Tangent of 36 = 0.7265425280054

Tangent of 108 = -3.077683537175

0.7265425280054 x -3.077683537175 = -2.2360679775

Tangent of 186234.09485 = -2.236067197552

The difference is:
-2.2360679775 - -2.236067197552 = 0.0000007799473440429

Carl concludes -

"And there we have it, the reasoning behind the Sacred Numbers of Gematria, the same ones preserved in eastern metrology and western calendrical computing; square roots and tangents - all keyed to the terrestrial speed of light - and delivered through the pyramid codex in nearly the exact methodology they used in keying the earth's equatorial circumference to the cube root of double-Pi when they built the Great Pyramid at Giza."

"No communications across ancient oceans? No prehistoric writing that makes any sense? Ignorant stone age progenitors? I'm not buying into that kind of thinking anymore, not when I can so easily find this kind of mathematical evidence to the contrary."

"Someone back there had it all; maps of enviable accuracy, a complete knowledge of every inch of our planet, a thorough understanding of mathematics and, yes, even calculators and computers we take for granted today - because without such tools, they could never have put it all together. Why do I say that? Because the U.S. Geological Survey advises me that they have the only computer in the United States which is programmed to calculate accurate distances between widely separated points anywhere on the planet - which means - that before the ancients could have marked out the pyramid grid system, they required a computer of the same caliber!!"

An Example Calculation

In order to make this more clear, I'll give an example calculation (follow along with your scientific calculator, if you wish). This follows Carl's writings above concerning -

* Enter the number 36 into your calculator and press the tangent key. The result should be 0.726542528
* Press the "Memory Store" key to store this number.
* Enter the number 72 into your calculator and press the tangent key. The result should be 3.077683537
* Press the "x" (multiply) key, then press the Memory Restore key, then the "=" (Equals) key. The result should be 2.236067978 (the result of 0.726542528 x 3.077683537).
* Now, press the "C" (Clear) key, then enter the number 5.
* Press the Square Root key, to display the square root of five, which should be 2.236067978, the same number you arrived at by multiplying the tangents of 36 and 72.

Again, there are only four tangents, and just two tangents when the plus (+) and minus (-) signs are ignored. Since it is unlikely that the ancients had modern calculators or computers, Carl wondered just how they were able to consistently use numbers that had only the two tangents.

Joe Mason's Gematria System

Reading Carl's work was staggering to me - it felt like my head was reeling! I'm sure this would have been the case even if I had not experienced all the "coincidences" about such numbers - but read on, to grasp how all this fit in with my own findings.

I'll give a few examples. In September 1991, I read John Michell's article in The Cerealogist, #4, about the great triangular crop formation that appeared near Barbury

Castle. A diagram with dimensions was illustrated. John pointed out that the sum of all the four circular areas in the formation was 31680 square feet. He went on -

"The significance of this number, in arithmetic, cosmology, ancient theology and temple architecture was first explored in City of Revelation (1972) and is summed up in a section of The Dimensions of Paradise (Thames & Hudson, 1988). In traditional cosmology, 31680 miles was taken to be the measure around the sub-lunary world, and the early Christian scholars calculated the number 3168 as emblematic of Lord Jesus Christ. The same number was previously applied to the name of a leading principle in the pagan religion."

I tried some calculations in an attempt to figure out "31680." I tried assigning the number 8 to the North sun symbol, and 9 to the moon symbol at the southwest corner of the triangle, and multiplied to get 72, which are the number of Divine Names used as codes in Creation according to Dr. J. J. Hurtak, author of 'The Book of Knowledge, The Keys of Enoch'. To arrive at the number 31680, I needed to assign the number 440 to the ratchet (Mercury) spiral glyph on the southeast corner of the crop formation (8 x 9 = 72 x 440 = 31680). It struck me that 440 yards is a quarter mile, so I tried dividing 31680 by 5280, feet in a mile, to find it was exactly 6 miles. At the time, I wondered how ancient people could use one of our "modern" measurement numbers. Little did I know! Interestingly, a relative informed me later that 440 is the cycles per second of the musical note of "A."

Back around 1992, a strange thing happened. One night at work the numbers 72 and 360 kept coming into my mind over and over. I knew about the 72 Divine Names, and I had read that 360 was called a "Prophetic Year," by certain proponents of the Bible. It is part of an interpretation concerning the dream of Nebuchadnezzar in the Book of Daniel. He dreamed that a great tree was cut and banded, which caused a period of insanity for seven years. This is calculated as Prophetic Years, giving 7 x 360 = 2520 years. From the fall of the Temple at Jerusalem, this is said to give the year 1914 as the beginning of the Apocalypse. I finally stopped and multiplied the numbers coming into my head. 72 x 360 = 25920. I was startled, because I knew this was the number of years of the precession, caused by the "wobble" of the earth's axis, giving us our 12 Zodiac Ages of 2160 years each.

I had read about the precession number in Joseph Campbell's, The Inner Reaches of Outer Space back in 1990. It was mentioned that when the precession number is divided by the ancient number 60, called "Soss," the result is 432, which is a cycle of time number (Consecration in Gematrian). Apparently the ancients knew about the precession long ago.

In 1992 and 1993, I had some strange dream-coincidences which eventually became centered on Revelation 11:11. The verse includes the words, "three and a half days." At one point, I re-read some dreams I had received, and two of them made a connection. In one of them a voice said, "The children were born in the sign of 42." In the other dream, I saw "Trinity 11:2." I looked up Revelation 11:2, and found that it speaks of the holy city being trampled over for 42 months. I then realized 42 months is 3 1/2 years, perhaps connecting with the 3 1/2 days in Rev. 11:11. I then read the next verse, Rev. 11:3, which speaks of 1260 days. This was not quite 3 1/2 years, but dividing 1260 by 3.5 gives 360. It's like 3 1/2 times around a circle, again matching the 3 1/2 in the other verses. At the time, I did not know that the Hebrew calendar had 30-day months, but I now see that 1260 days is another way of indicating 3 1/2 years.

In Joseph Campbell's book, he gave the number of years from Adam's creation to the time Noah's Ark landed on the mountain, as 1656. The number of weeks in that period of years is 86400, it is figured. A human heart, beating once a second, gives the same number, 86400, in one day (60 x 60 x 24). Dividing the number in half gives 43200, strongly suggesting the ancient cycle of time number. The number 108 is the number of names of the Mother Goddess in India, and figures in the time cycle number as 108 x 4 = 432.

I had written about these subjects in a letter to Madelon Rose Lodge, which she passed on to Carl. As you can see, many of the numbers are the same or similar to those in Carl's work. I noticed that Carl had the number 1656 listed in his "sine wave" type illustration (I stopped short of it in my rendition above). But it was apparently a "fill in the blank" type number, as it had no asterisk indicating that it was used by the ancients. The number 1260 was not listed anywhere, yet it seemed to me that it should fit somehow.

Joe's Dream of the Gematrian Wheel

Some months after learning of Carl's work, I had a dream of a circle divided into parts, and I knew it was about the Gematrian system. It came out to a 360 degree circle, or "Wheel," divided into 10 parts of 36 degrees each, giving the sequence - 36, 72, 108, 144, etc. Full revolutions produce the same numbers with factors of ten - 360, 720, 1080, 1440, etc. The pattern keeps repeating on a base-ten system, so, for example, 144,000 is 400 times around the "Wheel." Each section is divided into 6 parts, for a total of 60 marks. The top and bottom points of the "Wheel" have a zero tangent. The other eight points have the same four tangents listed by Carl, two if you do not consider plus and minus signs

The Gematrian Wheel

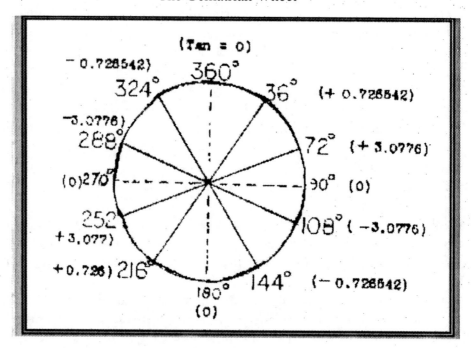

The Bythorn Mandala crop formation of 1993 had a ten petal lotus with a five-pointed star inside. It may hint at the Gematrian system by the ten petals, and the star, which has 36 degrees in each point, and 72 degrees between points. The design is very similar to a yantra to the Goddess, Kali (one of 108 aspects of Sakti) of the eastern religions. Two of the points of the star were facing toward the North. In esoteric traditions, such a star with two points (or horns) up, signify the Kali-Yuga time cycle, called the Age of Iron, which we are now in. This is said by some to be 432,000 years.

Interestingly, Daniel's interpretation of Nebuchadnezzar's dream of the frightening image, was that it represented the Ages, symbolized by the metals, gold, silver, bronze, and iron, followed by the iron and clay mix in the feet of the image. The Hindu chronology has the same four metals in the same order.

Twenty-Part ("666" Tangent) Wheel

Some other significant numbers are located at "in-between" points on the "Gematrian Wheel." It could be considered a 20-part Wheel. Each of these points are 18 degrees between the Gematrian numbers, such as 18, 54, 90, 126, 162, 198, and 234. Notice that 54, 126, and 234 all have the same tangent (again, ignoring plus/minus). Check this against the number 666, to see it has the same tangent. 666 is one of the '"in-between" points, being between 648 and 684 on the "Gematrian Wheel." Notice too, that some of these numbers rearranged, and with various zeros, form regular Gematrian numbers. For example, add a zero to 126 to get 1260, or insert a zero into 234 for 2304. Notice also that the "in-between" numbers also add to nine or a multiple of nine, and are divisible by nine. The numbers often show a repositioning, such as 432 and the reverse, 234 (an in-between point), and 324. Such is the odd nature of Gematrian and Gematrian-related numbers.

Six-Part Wheel

Other related numbers can be put on a six-part wheel, of 60 degrees per segment, giving the sequence 60, 120, 180, 240, 300, etc. Various designs, such as the Star of David, fit with this "Wheel." Remember that Joseph Campbell pointed out that 60 was an important number called, "Soss," by the ancients, who used it in various calculations, as we do today with our time-keeping and coordinate system.

Remember too, that 31680 divided by 6 results in 5280, feet in a mile. Carl points out that these numbers were also used by the ancients, and the tangents are the square root of three (again, excluding the top and bottom marks). The number 88, which sometimes appears in dreams, may be something of a "connecting" number between the two "Wheels," as 88 x 60 = 5280 and 88 x 360 = 31680.

I will speak of the various numbers in terms of the "Wheels," explained above. If a number fits on the ten-part "Gematrian Wheel," meaning it is evenly divisible by 36, I will term it a Gematrian number. Keep in mind that this is my personal convention. Others may not consider certain numbers, such as 1260, as being Gematrian. If a number, such as 666, fits on the 20-Part Wheel, but not on the 10-Part Gematrian Wheel, I consider it Gematria-related, as being an "in-between point" on the Gematrian Wheel. If an established convention existed, I would use it instead of my personal system, but such a convention is not available at this point.

Following Along - Checking for Gematrian Numbers

Keep in mind, as you read on, that when a number is listed that ends with an even number, and adds to nine or a multiple of nine, it may be a Gematrian number. If it divides evenly by 36, then it is one of the Gematrian numbers in my system.

You can also verify it by entering the number on your calculator, and checking to see that the tangent is equal to 0.726542528 or 3.077683537. The tangents are both positive and negative numbers, but we will ignore that, for the most part, in our study of The Code.

The above is true when the ending number is 2, 4, 6, or 8. Some Gematrian numbers end in a zero, such as 1260. Larger Gematrian numbers that end in zero, such as 1080, also have a zero tangent, but you can still check it by removing the final zero or zeros, and checking the tangent. For the number 1080, remove the zero and check the tangent of 108 to see it is -3.077683537.

Taking the Stonehenge latitude number, 21600, as another example - take off the ending zeros and check the tangent of 216, to see that it is 0.726542528. Some Gematrian numbers have other special attributes to them, which we will point out on these pages. An example is 216, which is 6 cubed, or 6 x 6 x 6. As mentioned, 2160 is the diameter in miles of the Moon, and 2160 is the number of years in one Zodiac Age. Another example is 1296. It is six to the fourth power (6 x 6 x 6 x 6). Its base-ten harmonic, 12960, is the number of years in half the precession (25920 / 2). As you see, the numbers are related. The twelve Zodiac Ages of 2160 years each, total 25920 years, for one grand circuit of 360 degrees.

A Few Theories

Finding such mysteries throughout the 'The Code/Gematria' system leads one to suspect that it is not just an arbitrary system, but rather that it was fashioned by a very high intelligence in the far distant past. No one knows the source, but there are a number of theories, such as the existence of a high culture like Atlantis in pre-history, or that extraterrestrials interacted with humans long ago and taught them the system. Some believe the system to be simply Creation Numbers used by God or the gods. If that seems farfetched, well - read on.

The great accuracy of The Code holds true only with the latest satellite mapping coordinates. Carl says the plates of the earth have shifted a bit since some of the sites were built. Since, "The Code" shows accuracy within yards, the question is, "How did the ancients know how to do this." He thinks it is like a time-capsule, because it could have never been figured it out until now. Many years ago, the ancient sites were not located at the same coordinates where we find them today; so, whoever devised 'The Code" must have known where the sites would be located in the future.

I have some evidence, which I will share later, that dreams impart some of the same numbers to people in their sleep. So, my theory is that the numbers and other information came through dreams and/or visions in the past, and that is why there is consistency over time and distances. The ancients may have built the pyramids and other sites based on their dreams and visions, while perhaps not really understanding the overall system to any great extent.

Another plausible theory that I favor is that a crop circle phenomena occurred in the distant past, and that the ancient peoples built the structures upon the crop formations. Crop circle researchers have pointed out that most of the crop circles in England appear near ancient sites, sometimes right next to them, such as the Spider Web formation near Avebury in 1994, the Julia Set formation next to Stonehenge in 1996, and Koch Snowflake near Silbury Hill in 1997.

The researchers also say that the ancient sites are located at crossing points of dowsable 'ley lines' and that the crop formations also appear on these points. Experienced dowsers have found that earth-energy within various crop formations form geometric patterns, such as stars and cross-like shapes. In one case, a pattern similar to The New Jerusalem Plan, based on the vision of Saint John in Revelation 21, was detected in a crop formation. The same pattern has been "dowsed" within certain ancient sites, such as Stonehenge and Avebury.

Crop Circles Mystery:
Are Dream & Mythological Symbols Related to the Crop Pattern Phenomenon?

An article about patterns found by dowsing in crop circles and megalithic sites shows one with 12 circles in a ring with a 12-pointed star inside, formed by four overlapping triangles. It is called The New Jerusalem Plan and it is based on the vision of St. John in Revelation 21. It is said to represent the order of the Heavens made apparent on Earth. As I am not a conventional Christian, I was quite surprised, because it seemed to match my dream experience.

Hazel Eddleston, "Geometric and Symbolic References in Crop Markings," in The Cereologist, No. 3 (Spring, 1991) The Journal for Crop Circle Studies, London

After seeing that a Teutonic Cross was found by dowsing in a crop circle, I realized that the New Jerusalem Star could be derived from the quintuplet set by sliding the triangles of the overhead pyramid to overlap. A coincidence soon followed when I read a little pamphlet from a group called Solara 11:11. They teach that the Key to the great change is to form star mandalas of overlapping triangles.

Using four Barbury triangular shapes in my sliding triangle idea reveals the New Jerusalem Plan from the quintuplet set (Q, R, S).

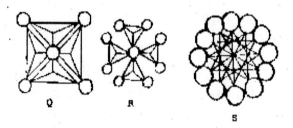

Q   R   S

Postscript

Since writing the above article in about 1992, much has happened. In some ways the article was predictive of crop formations yet to appear. For example, the Bythorn Mandala formation appeared in August, 1993. It was flower-like with a star inside and was based on interlocking circles in a ring. Many other interlocking ring type formations have appeared, including six-fold and twelve-fold types. One theory is that many formations of this type are related to the chakra system.

In 1997 I met Dee Finney and we began creating the 'greatdreams.com' web site, Dreams of the Great Earth Changes. One section of the site is about crop circles and their connection to dreams.

Dee created a page that compares dreams and visions to crop circle formations:

CROP CIRCLE TO DREAM/VISION COMPARISONS
http://www.greatdreams.com/ccdrm.htm

In the months after I wrote the article, some of the dreams and symbols became somewhat like puzzle-pieces that fit together into a larger picture. Again, "coincidence" was part of the process. The primary elements are now in this series of articles:

Humanity On The Pollen Path
http://www.greatdreams.com/plpath1.htm

The "11:11" coincidence mentioned in the article led eventually to Revelation 11:11. The meaning became clear - humanity has been on a time cycle path that corresponds to the chakra levels. We are near the 3 1/2 mid-point and a leap to the fourth-heart chakra level of consciousness evolution. Many other people are reporting strange coincidences involving 11:11.

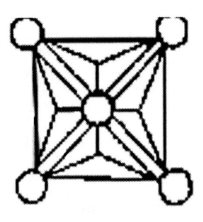

DIAGRAM Q

Diagram Q evolved, as I found that it matches the Four Living Creatures of Ezekiel and Revelation when the four "wheels" are drawn in. In diagram Q, I left out the wheels, which are patterned after the central circle and rings in the Barbury Castle formation (1991).

The same four triangles, remember, can be arranged like The New Jerusalem Plan. It is similar to diagrams of the Zodiac and to the symbol of the heart chakra. The Four Living Creatures, I found, trace back to the camp positions of the twelve Tribes in Numbers 2 of the Bible. The four major Tribes correspond to the Living Creatures, and to the Zodiac signs of the solstices and equinoxes during the Age of Taurus. In each quarter is a major Tribe and two other Tribes, for a total of twelve Tribes. In the center of the encampment is the Tabernacle. The camp arrangement is a reflection of "heaven," that is, the circle of Zodiac signs in the sky above.

It is probably not a meaningless coincidence that The Tree of Life appeared as a crop circle formation in 1997, or that the Menorah appeared as a formation in 1999. The Tree of Life stands in the center of The New Jerusalem in Revelation 22:2. The Menorah, the lampstand with seven lamps, is in the Tabernacle. The son of man stands in the midst of the seven lampstands in Revelation 1:12, 13. The two olive trees, the two anointed, stand on each side of the Menorah in Zechariah 4, and stand up after 3 1/2 days of being dead in Revelation 11:11.

(See the Tree of Life formation in the Tree of Life Section. See the Menorah formation in the Menorah Section)

The crop circle formation mentioned in the Cereologist article noted above, the one in which the basic pattern of The New Jerusalem Plan was found by dowsing, appeared in 1989 at Winterbourne Stoke. The wheatstalks were laid down at right angles in a quadrant pattern. There was a circular swirl in the center and a one-meter-wide clockwise band around the circumference. This was said to be a Swastika-circle.

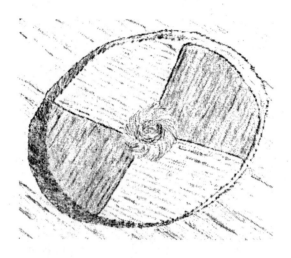

WINTERBOURNE STOKE - 1989

I received a letter from Carolyn North in December 1992. She had read my article in the Dream Network Journal. She also sent her little booklet, "Crop Circles, Hoax or Happening?" On page 12 of the book is a photograph of the 1989 Swastika-circle at Winterbourne Stoke.

Concerning this formation, Carolyn wrote:

"When the whirlwind theory was in its heyday, a magnificent circle appeared with four quadrants and an intricately woven hub, the wheat in each quadrant laying neatly in different orientations, creating in textured pattern, an ancient Celtic symbol indicating the coming of great changes.

Four days later the Berlin Wall came down."

Over the years, I realized that certain events of 1989 seemed to carry symbolism. The "World Series Earthquake" took place that year on October 17 in San Francisco. The highly spiritual baseball film, "Field of Dreams" also came out that year. A voice spoke to the farmer in his cornfield, saying, "If you build it, they will come." He built a baseball diamond in his cornfield, and then spiritual beings, including his own father, came to play.

I doubt that it is a coincidence that 13 x 153 = 1989. In the Bible, Jesus made his last appearance to the disciple fishermen and spoke of the 153 Fish in the Net.

A related coincidence is that the number 1224 (8 x 153) is common to the Fish in the Net story and to the New Jerusalem Plan.

David Fideler relates the 153 Fish in the Net story in his book, "Jesus Christ, Sun of God." He credits John Michell's "City of Revelation" for some of the information. The story has an underlying geometrical design, starting with a Flower of Life type pattern, signifying the six fishermen disciples surrounding Simon Peter. The Greek word for "FISHES" and "THE NET" were both equivalent to 1224, and 153 is 1/8 that amount. The circle turns out to have a diameter of 1224 units.

The net, 1224, with fishes, 1224, together number 2448 and 2448 is the measure round the perimeter of the "fish" in the net.

An on-line writing of Daniel Gleason shows how the verses of John 21 illustrate that the diameter of the Sea of Tiberias (where the Fish in the Net story takes place) by computation has a diameter of 2448 units, which is exactly sixteen times 153.

The New Jerusalem Plan has a large circle in the center to represent the planet Earth, with a diameter of 7920 miles. There are twelve circles representing the Moon drawn around the Earth circle. The Moon circles have diameters of 2160 miles. The diameter across the entire New Jerusalem Plan, therefore, includes one Earth diameter and two Moon diameters, thus:

$$2160 + 7920 + 2160 = 12240 \text{ miles.}$$

The diameter "coincidentally" is equal to 153 x 80.

Crop Circles and The New Jerusalem Plan

There was a very interesting article in The Cerealogist #3, the Spring 1991 issue, on page 15. It was written by Hazel Eddleston. There were seven diagrams with the article. One of the diagrams was a drawing of the Winterbourne Stoke formation.

Another drawing showed marks representing energy points found by dowsing within the crop formation. In a third drawing, the same energy points were superimposed on another diagram called, "The New Jerusalem Plan." The energy points from the crop formation fell exactly within the various parts of "The New Jerusalem Plan" diagram. This is the text of the article -

Geometric and symbolic references in crop markings

On Easter Sunday 1990 it occurred to me that there might be connections between crop circles, sacred geometry and ancient religious symbols. Tracing various forms of the New Jerusalem diagram into plans of the 1989 circle at Winterbourne Stoke, I was amazed to see how well they fitted together.

The New Jerusalem was seen in a vision by St. John (Revelation 21) near the beginning of the Age of Pisces about 2,000 years ago. It represents the divine order of the heavens made apparent on earth. The diagram was first published in John Michell's "City of Revelation" and is further examined in books such as "The New View over Atlantis" and "The Dimensions of Paradise." It is the underlying plan of Stonehenge, built almost 4,000 years ago near the beginning of the Age of Aries, and versions of it appear in eastern mandalas, Gothic cathedral rose windows and other symbols of the universe worldwide.

Dowsing has revealed a definite connection between the physical dimensions and the patterns of energy at certain crop circles, as well as of Stonehenge, Avebury and other ancient sites. I found that the three similar circles at Corhampton in 1988 fitted the plan of Stonehenge exactly.

We are now at the beginning of the Age of Aquarius so perhaps we should not be surprised at the strange occurrences of today.

Symbols, which have appeared in cornfields include the equilateral (at Cullompton) and the isosceles triangle. The triangle is the first geometric form to contain space and as such expresses the womb and the feminine among its meanings. The circle represents harmony, the eternal, spirit, the heavenly. Pictograms have become increasingly complex and stunning, but no pentagons, hexagons etc. have yet occurred. One wonders whether the labyrinth and other archetypal symbols might yet appear.

Archetypal symbols are primordial and trans-cultural. I believe that the circles and pictograms touch us deeply, even if we are not consciously aware of it.

Arabesques and an eight-ringed spiral were seen near Avebury last year. In Sufism both express spiritual states, time and music in their variable, rhythmical forms. The similar Catherine wheel swirls, clockwise or anti-clockwise, are central to many crop circles. The importance of spiral forms is returning into our consciousness with knowledge of the vital forces in living water, its movements, waves, falls and swirls, which cleanse and revitalize it, with similar processes acting on our bodies and spirits. The spiral is also an ancient Celtic symbol of Divinity. A Sufi garden or courtyard, designed as a mandala, contains a centrifugal movement, outward into nature, or a centripetal movement inwards to Spirit, represented by water.

Concentric rings depict the water, the spiritual centre of the garden. Many crop circles involve concentric rings, as does the complete New Jerusalem plan. When the dumb-bell shapes began to appear, I was reminded of an incident about 25 years ago at school, when our biology class was interrupted by the appearance of a UFO floating slowly over a nearby hill towards us. We all crowded to the third-floor window and watched as this black dumb-bell shape, about two feet long, hovered outside the glass about a yard away from us. Then it gently floated away at about 45 degrees to the direction from which it had come, skimming low over trees and roof tops.

Not all crop configurations appear to comprise sacred or symbolic figures, but the fact that the ancient New Jerusalem plan, mandalas and other archetypal forms are present in at least some circles and pictograms suggest that they have a spiritual content; also that there is an involvement with a higher intelligence and, more importantly, a higher spirituality. Perhaps their appearance is timely at this stage of the world's crises. People are experiencing a changing perception of earth and all its life forms. The crop formations may contain or presage essential knowledge, which will be revealed when the time is right.

[end of quote]

I was quite amazed when I read the story and saw the diagram of "The New Jerusalem Plan." In my dream on October 18, 1990, there were twelve circles in a ring. One of the stars that I drew, based on my splice box dream and the Navaho sand painting, had twelve points, and formed four overlapping triangles, much like the depiction above. The "coincidence" of seeing the two depictions side-by-side in the Myth book of the Buddhist Mandala and the Navaho sand painting seemed to connect the two types of symbols together - one with circles in a ring, and the other, star shapes. My own dreams and coincidences seemed to focus on the same type of symbols.

With a lump in my throat, I found a Bible and read Revelation 21. I had never been a professing Christian, but I now felt that my experiences were leading me to the Bible. My dreams and "coincidental" experiences continued, and began to include various passages in the Bible.

The Four Living Creatures Or Merkabah
by Joseph E. Mason

After I learned about The New Jerusalem Plan, I thought about the similar patterns that came to me. The twelve-pointed star is formed by four overlapping triangles. The diagram of the pyramid, as viewed from above, and corresponding to the quintuplet set of crop circles, also had four triangles - the four faces of the pyramid. By changing the shape of the triangles, based on the perspective of the viewer, the four triangles could also be put into a Teutonic Cross. I remembered that a twelve-pointed star and a Teutonic Cross had been found by dowsing within crop circle formations. The basic pattern of The New Jerusalem Plan had also been found within a crop circle formation.

A breakthrough came for me when I read a letter to the editor in a crop circle journal. The writer stated that the Barbury Castle crop circle formation (1991) fit exactly within the New Jerusalem Plan. By comparing the two symbols, I could see how it fits -

I drew three shapes, based on the idea -

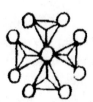

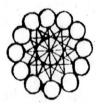

The four simplified triangles are patterned after the crop formation, with circles at each of the three corners. The left illustration forms a Teutonic Cross by overlapping four of the circles in the center. The middle illustration indicates a pyramid as viewed from above, formed by "lowering the bases" of the four triangles in the Teutonic Cross design. Each triangle in the middle illustration is changed (foreshortened) in shape, indicating the angle of perception. The illustration on the right is similar to The New Jerusalem Plan, and is formed by the same four triangles overlapped on center.

I felt that it was significant that The New Jerusalem Plan is quite similar to Zodiac designs, where four overlapping triangles touch the various signs. The triangles are designated - fire, air, water and earth.

Ezekiel's Four Living Creatures

Another breakthrough came to me many months later, in 1992. I read several references to Ezekiel's vision of the Four Living Creatures, including the idea that the four creatures represent the Zodiac signs corresponding to the positions of the solstices and equinoxes during the Age of Taurus. I opened my Bible, and read the verses. I felt that coincidence was at work again, as the description seemed to fit with my drawing of the pyramid formed by the four triangles based on the Barbury Castle crop formation. But, in my illustration, I had not drawn in the central circle with rings within the triangles. These seemed to correspond to the "four wheels" described by Ezekiel. I then drew in the circles with rings inside each of the four triangles -

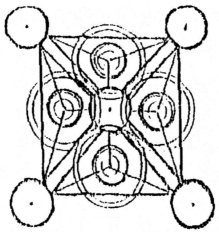

DIAGRAM OF THE 4 LIVING CREATURES

By reading the first page of Ezekiel, and comparing it to the illustration, one can see the connections.

Comparison: As I mentioned, the four living creatures are thought to represent Zodiac signs. I first read about the idea in 1990, in Joseph Campbell's, 'The Inner Reaches Of Outer Space.' A photograph is shown on page 77 of a "chimeral cherub," a large limestone carving. It is a portal guardian from the palace of Ashurnasirpal II at Nimrud, Assyria, 833-859 BC. The chimeral cherub combines the body of a bull, feet of a lion, wings and breast of an eagle, and a human head wearing a miter with six horns. Ezekiel lived during the late 6th century BC, and was located in the area of Babylon, so it is likely that he was familiar with this symbolism. The four living creatures correspond to the Zodiac signs during the Age of Taurus in this way - Lion = Leo - summer solstice Ox = Taurus - spring equinox Eagle (which later became Scorpio) = autumnal equinox Man = Aquarius, the Water Bearer - winter solstice The same four triangles in The New Jerusalem Plan design, when viewed as a Zodiac, represent three Zodiac signs each, with the same "four living creatures" above included in each, that is, one tip of each triangle touches the corresponding Zodiac signs - which are represented by the circles in my three illustrations.

The Woman With Child in Revelation 12 also seems to symbolize the Goddess. In Part One of this series of articles, I pointed out that the "three and a half" time cycle is indicated in two verses of Revelation 12. The Woman is taken to a place during the cycle. Joseph Campbell said that the virgin birth symbolizes the birth of the Spiritual Man out of the animal man, and is achieved at the Heart chakra. The Woman With Child has a crown of twelve stars, perhaps suggesting The New Jerusalem and the Heart Chakra, which is symbolized by a Lotus flower with twelve petals, with a Star of David inside.

Coincidental Crop Circle Comparisons to
the Heart Chakra and The New Jerusalem Plan

In April 1992, I made a somewhat incorrect drawing, based on the tiny illustration in the Cerealogist article -

THE NEW JERUSALEM PLAN

(my own drawing)
Two days prior, I had made this drawing:

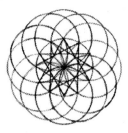

HOPI NEW JERUSALEM FLOWER

I wrote a caption at the bottom: "Comparison of the twelve petal flower to The New Jerusalem Pattern." The idea came from an illustration depicting the Hopi creation myth of Spider Grandmother -

SPIDER GRANDMOTHER - HOPI CREATION STORY

There is a twelve-petal sunflower on the left side. In my drawing, I extended the petals into full circles to make the design, then colored the petals of the flower yellow. The myth tells how Spider Grandmother teaches the humans how to weave after the fourth and final stage of an evolutionary process. I felt that the sunflower may be a hint about this weaving. The idea is that this fists with the fourth chakra, the heart chakra, which seems to be related to The New Jerusalem, with its twelve pearls, gates, angels, and gemstones.

In June 1992 I sent photocopies of these and other diagrams, along with an essay, to crop circle researchers in England.

In the following years, various crop circle formations seemed to fit well with some of the diagrams that I had done. The first one came in 1993 and was a ten petal formation known as the -

BYTHORN MANDALA CROP CIRCLE FORMATION

I believe this was the first crop formation suggesting circles in a ring. The following year another ten-fold pattern appeared next to Avebury stone circle. Interestingly, as regarding the Hopi Spider Grandmother myth, the formation looked like a spider's web:

THE SPIDER WEB CROP CIRCLE FORMATION OF 1994, AVEBURY

In 1997 a formation appeared that was similar to my drawing based on the Hopi myth -

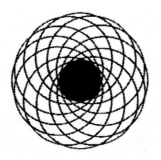

12 FOLD TORUS - ALTON BARNES nr AVEBURY, WILTSHIRE - JULY 1997

Also in 1997 a formation with a twelve pointed star appeared -
12 POINT STAR with 36 LINES

CLEY HILL, Nr WARMINSTER, WILTSHIRE, JULY 1997

A formation appeared in July 2000 that had twelve circles in a ring with a cross type shape inside:

CROSS IN 12 CIRCLES
STEPHEN'S CASTLE DOWN, HAMPSHIRE - JULY 2000

In August 2000 a formation appeared that came to be known as the Sunflower:

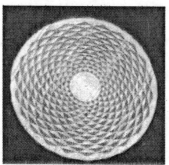

SUNFLOWER - 308 TRIANGLES
WOODBOROUGH, WILTSHIRE, AUGUST 2000

From this point on, I will list only the formations that have geometric similarities to the New Jerusalem Plan and the symbol of the heart chakra. Keep in mind that the major symbol for the heart chakra is a twelve-petal lotus flower with a Star of David inside. The New Jerusalem Plan is similar, with a double Star of David inside a ring of twelve circles. Many related crop formations have appeared, starting in 1991, such as Star of David types, Flower of Life types, and hexagon-cube types.

In June 2002 a twelve-petal Sunflower type formation appeared that had an uncanny similarity to my 1992 drawing based on the Hopi Myth

12 PETAL SUNFLOWER
TELEGRAPH HILL, LILLEY nr LUTON HERTFORDSHIRE, JUNE 2002

Many more formations have appeared since these. They fit well with the idea of the opening of the heart chakra. The six-fold design suggests the Star of David.

Another formation appeared in 2003 with twelve circles around a six-petal design, forming a cube like hexagon:

SCROPE WOOD nr MARLBOROUGH, WILTSHIRE - JULY 2003

Teachers of the Flower of Life explain how the cube shape, known as Metatron's Cube, comes from the basic pattern. The New Jerusalem is also said to be related to the cube.

On page CXLVII from Manly Hall's, "The Secret Teachings of All Ages." Table X shows a cube. The associated text reads, "TABLE X, Figures 10-15. Figure 10 shows the New Jerusalem in form of a cube, with the names of the twelve tribes of Israel written on the twelve lines of the cube. In the center is the eye of God."

(see next page)

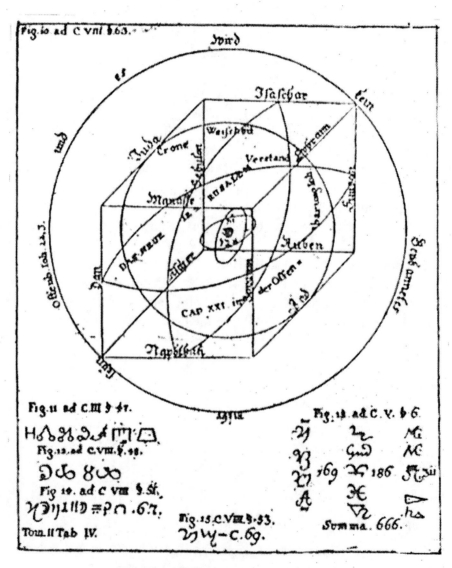

TABLE X, Figures 10-15.

WHERE IS THE NEW JERSALEM?

(MEANING- 'PLACE OF PEACE')

Revelation 21: "And I saw a new heaven and a new earth: for the first heaven and the first earth were passed away; and there was no more sea, And I John saw the holy city, new Jerusalem, coming down from God out of heaven prepared as a pride beautifully dressed for her husband."

THE NEW JERUSALEM ACCORDING TO THE BOOK OF REVELATIONS

Revelation 3:

Rev. 3:10 - Because thou hast kept the word of my patience, I also will keep thee from the hour of temptation, which shall come upon all the world, to try them that dwell upon the earth. 11 - Behold, O come quickly; hold that fast which thou hast, that no man take thy crown. 12 - Him that overcometh will I make a pillar in the temple of my god, and he shall go no more out: and I will write upon him the name of my god, and the name of the city of my God, which is new Jerusalem, which cometh down out of heaven from my god: and I will write upon him my new name. 13 - He that hath an ear, let him hear what the Spirit saith unto the churches. 14 - And unto the angel of the church of the Laodiceans write; These things saith the Amen, the faithful and true witness, the beginning of the creation of God: 15 - I know thy works, that thou art, neither cold nor hot ; I would thou wert cold or hot. 16 - So then because thou art lukewarm, and neither cold, not hot, I will spue thee out of my mouth.

17 - Because thou sayest, I am rich, and increased with goods, and have need of nothing; and knowest not that thou art wretched, and miserable, and poor, and blind, and naked: 18 - I counsel thee to buy of me gold tried in the fire, that thou mayest be rich; and white raiment, that thou mayest be clothed and that the shame of thy nakedness do not appear; and anoint thine eyes with eyesalve, that thou mayest see. 19 - As many as I love, I rebuke and chasten: be zealous therefore, and repent. 20 - Behold, I stand at the door, and knock; if any man hear my voice, and open the door, I will come in to him, and will sup with him, and he with me. 21 - To him that overcometh will I grant to sit with me in my throne, even as I also overcame, and am set down with my Father in his throne.

Revelation 21:

Rev 21:1 And I saw a new heaven and a new earth: for the first heaven and the first earth were passed away; and there was no more sea. 2 And I John saw the holy city, new Jerusalem, coming down from God out of heaven, prepared as a bride adorned for her husband. 3 And I heard a great voice out of heaven saying, Behold, the tabernacle of God is with men, and he will dwell with them, and they shall be his people, and God himself shall be with them, and be their God. 4 And God shall wipe away all tears from their eyes; and there shall be no more death, neither sorrow, nor crying, neither shall there be any more pain: for the former things are passed away. 5 And he that sat upon the throne said, Behold, I make all things new. And he said unto me, Write: for these words are true and faithful. 6 And he said unto me, It is done. I am Alpha and Omega, the beginning and the end. I will give unto him that is athirst of the fountain of the water of life freely. 7 He that overcometh shall inherit all things; and I will be his God, and he shall be my son. 8 But the fearful, and unbelieving, and the abominable, and murderers, and whoremongers, and sorcerers, and idolaters, and all liars, shall have their part in the lake which burneth with fire and brimstone: which is the second death. 9 And there came unto me one of the seven angels which had the seven vials full of the seven last plagues, and talked with me, saying, Come hither, I will shew thee the bride, the Lamb's wife. 10 And he carried me away in the spirit to a great and high mountain, and shewed me that great city, the holy Jerusalem, descending out of heaven from God, 11 Having the glory of God: and her light was like unto a stone most precious, even like a jasper stone, clear as crystal; 12 And had a wall great and high, and had twelve gates, and at the gates twelve angels, and names written thereon, which are the names of the twelve tribes of the children of Israel: 13 On the east three gates; on the north three gates; on the south three gates; and on the west three gates. 14 And the wall of the city had twelve foundations, and in them the names of the twelve apostles of the Lamb.

And he that talked with me had a golden reed to measure the city, and the gates thereof, and the wall thereof. 16 And the city lieth foursquare, and the length is as large as the breadth: and he measured the city with the reed, twelve thousand furlongs. The length and the breadth and the height of it are equal. 17 And he measured the wall thereof, an hundred and forty and four cubits, according to the measure of a man, that is, of the angel.

18 And the building of the wall of it was of jasper: and the city was pure gold, like unto clear glass. 19 And the foundations of the wall of the city were garnished with all manner of precious stones. The first foundation was jasper; the second, sapphire; the third, a chalcedony; the fourth, an emerald;

20 The fifth, sardonyx; the sixth, sardius; the seventh, chrysolyte; the eighth, beryl; the ninth, a topaz; the tenth, a chrysoprasus; the eleventh, a jacinth; the twelfth, an amethyst. 21 And the twelve gates were twelve pearls: every several gate was of one pearl: and the street of the city was pure gold, as it were transparent glass. 22 And I saw no temple therein: for the Lord God Almighty and the Lamb are the temple of it. 23 And the city had no need of the sun, neither of the moon, to shine in it: for the glory of God did lighten it, and the Lamb is the light thereof. 24 And the nations of them which are saved shall walk in the light of it: and the kings of the earth do bring their glory and honour into it. 25 And the gates of it shall not be shut at all by day: for there shall be no night there. 26 And they shall bring the glory and honour of the nations into it. 27 And there shall in no wise enter into it any thing that defileth, neither whatsoever worketh abomination, or maketh a lie: but they which are written in the Lamb's book of life.

Rev 22:1 And he shewed me a pure river of water of life, clear as crystal, proceeding out of the throne of God and of the Lamb. 2 In the midst of the street of it, and on either side of the river, was there the tree of life, which bare twelve manner of fruits, and yielded her fruit every month: and the leaves of the tree were for the healing of the nations. 3 And there shall be no more curse: but the throne of God and of the Lamb shall be in it; and his servants shall serve him: 4 And they shall see his face; and his name shall be in their foreheads. 5 And there shall be no night there; and they need no candle, neither light of the sun; for the Lord God giveth them light: and they shall reign for ever and ever. 6 And he said unto me, These sayings are faithful and true: and the Lord God of the holy prophets sent his angel to shew unto his servants the things which must shortly be done. 7 Behold, I come quickly: blessed is he that keepeth the sayings of the prophecy of this book. 8 And I John saw these things, and heard them. And when I had heard and seen, I fell down to worship before the feet of the angel which shewed me these things. 9 Then saith he unto me, See thou do it not: for I am thy fellowservant, and of thy brethren the prophets, and of them which keep the sayings of this book: worship God. 10 And he saith unto me, Seal not the sayings of the prophecy of this book: for the time is at hand. 11 He that is unjust, let him be unjust still: and he which is filthy, let him be filthy still: and he that is righteous, let him be righteous still: and he that is holy, let him be holy still. 12 And, behold, I come quickly; and my reward is with me, to give every man according as his work shall be. 13 I am Alpha and Omega, the beginning and the end, the first and the last. 14 Blessed are they that do his commandments, that they may have right to the tree of life, and may enter in through the gates into the city. 15 For without are dogs, and sorcerers, and whoremongers, and murderers, and idolaters, and whosoever loveth and maketh a lie. 16 I Jesus have sent mine angel to testify unto you these things in the churches. I am the root and the offspring of David, and the bright and morning star. 17 And the Spirit and the bride say, Come. And let him that heareth say, Come. And let him that is athirst come. And whosoever will, let him take the water of life freely. 18 For I testify unto every man that heareth the words of the prophecy of this book, If any man shall add unto these things, God shall add unto him the plagues that are written in this book: 19 And if any man shall take away from the words of the book of this prophecy, God shall take away his part out of the book of life, and out of the holy city, and from the things which are written in this book. 20 He which testifieth these things saith, Surely I come quickly. Amen. Even so, come, Lord Jesus. 21 The grace of our Lord Jesus Christ be with you all. Amen.

CROP CIRCLES AND THE NEW JERUSALEM

At least three Christian symbols have appeared in crop formations, two of them indirectly. In 1992, the Christian "Fish" symbol appeared as part of a crop formation.

Dowsing within the Winterbourne Stoke Swastika Circle of 1989, reveals the basic design of The New Jerusalem Plan, based on Saint John's vision in Revelation.

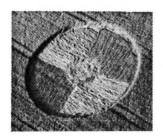

The total of the square footage of the circles in the Barbury Castle formation of 1991 was 31,680, a number associated with a distance around The New Jerusalem. One tenth of that number, 3,168, was associated with "Lord Jesus Christ" by the early Christians, and previously to a figure in the Pagan religion. A "666" type crop formation appeared in 1993. The sixes were arranged in a triangle.

The Greek Gematrian number is:

3888 = New Jerusalem (Rev. 21:2, 1 Cor. 12:27, Luke 8:21, etc.).
144Pi x 8.594366927 = 3888

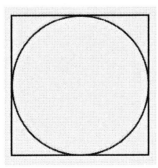

SQUARED CIRCLE

There are some amazing coincidental connections with various concepts and symbols in the Tantra book. One of these concerned the goddess Kali. She fits exactly with the meaning of the harlot of Revelation 17. From previous dreams, some from other people, the concept had come that the harlot represents the energy in our karmic cycle of time, which is nearing its end.

The energy of the new cycle seems to be represented by 'The Woman With Child' in Revelation 12. She wears a crown of 12 stars. The New Jerusalem, described in Revelation 21, also has 12 gates, pearls, jewels, and angels. This fits with the idea of the leap to the Heart chakra, because it is symbolized as a 12-petal lotus flower with a Star of David inside.

In the Eastern religions we are said to be in the Kali Yuga time cycle, the Age of Iron. The metals corresponding to the four Yugas, or ages, in the Hindu chronology are gold, silver, bronze, and iron. We rid ourselves of Kali at the end of the time cycle, and reach "Moksha," or Nirvana, the abode of blessed Peace and Spirit. (see Isis Unveiled, vol. 2, page 275, by H. P. Blavatsky).

I theorized that we are nearing the end of the Kali Yuga, and that Revelation has the same meaning.

These same four metals, and their meanings are quite similar to the dream of Nebuchadnezzar in Daniel 2:31-45. Daniel 12:7, which is repeated in Revelation 12:14, suggests the 3 1/2, by "a time, two times, and half a time." .(1 + 2 + 1/2 = 3 1/2). Further, Daniel 9:27 suggests the mid-point of the seven chakras as, ". . . a strong covenant with many for one week; and for half of the week . . ."

In H. P. Blavatsky's, 'The Secret Doctrine", on pages 4 and 5, a number of ancient symbols are depicted. Every one of them has appeared as a crop formation in some form. One of them is a five-pointed star reversed, with two points (horns) turned heavenward, that is, pointing up. This, she says, is the esoteric symbol of the Kali Yuga. The star in the crop formation had two points to the north, and one to the south.

Another symbol of Kali is the swastika. Several swastikas or swastika-circles have appeared. The swastika circle of 1989 and the swastika of 1997 appear below. Unfortunately, some of the swastika crop formations were mowed off by the farmers as soon as they appeared.

In January 1994, in "The Circular," Volume 4, Number 3, on page 8 is an article by Lucy Pringle, titled, "The Symbolism of The Bythorn Wonder."

Lucy wrote that the symbol powerfully denotes spiritual rebirth and enlightenment, and that the star is the Star of Shiva, the Destroyer and Creator. He is androgynous, and is part of the Brahman Triad or Trimurti, together with Brahma (the Creator) and Vishnu (the Preserver).

The Triad is similar to the Holy Trinity, and indicates aspects of God. They are conceived of as both Gods and Goddesses, to achieve balance, consistent with the Yin/Yang concept of balance and harmony.

Death, the Destroyer, holds the seed of rebirth. Out of the seed of death bursts the flower of birth, like the Phoenix.

Lucy also said that the formation also relates to the planetary and cosmic cycle, perhaps suggesting a planetary "shift."

Quoting Lucy:

"In the Eastern tradition, the Lotus flower suggested by the petals in the formation depicts Spiritual Enlightenment, paralleled in the West by the Rosicrucian Rose, which normally has five or ten petals. The lotus flower traditionally represents spinning vortices of cosmic energy at the various chakra points of the body, different number of petals corresponding to different chakras, for example the four petalled lotus corresponds to the base chakra, six petals to the sacrum, and twelve petals to the heart and so on, therefore the fact that the Lotus has ten petals is significant. It is widely thought that the solar plexus chakra (ten petalled) relates to the emotional aspect of our being, the energies of which flow into the heart."

Such a Rose formation did appear after Lucy's article was written. It also had ten petals on the outside. A five-petal design was on the inside. Thus, it has a similarity to the Bythorn Mandala, and may also represent the third chakra:

In 1998 Dee had a dream that pointed towards Peace at the end of Revelations:

THE GREATEST PROPHECY
3-21-98 DREAM:

I was at my 16th St. house. In the backyard were a lot of foreign religious leaders in army uniforms and every one had a gun. I saw some Christian ministers coming from the south. None of them had guns, but they all had silver bullets. The Christian ministers threw the silver bullets to the foreign religious leaders so they would have something to shoot with but by the time they came together, there was no one to shoot at.

I went out into the yard where some cats had been fighting over some scrambled eggs on the ground, and I cracked open an egg onto a white plate on the ground and it became a perfect white circle with a perfect central golden globe in the center.

I then went to 15th and Garfield, a black neighborhood. I entered a church there where they were having a jazz concert. I was observing them from the balcony. There was an equal number of black and white people there and they were in perfect harmony.

I then went downtown where heaters and air conditioners were being sold. Finally, the last one of each kind was sold. The husband of the business owner asked the female business owner if she was going to stockpile more as the warehouse was now empty. She said, "No! Not until there is a need and there isn't now, there's a perfect balance of heat and cold.

End Of Dream

(Interpretation) This dream seems to imply that there will be an end to all religious wars when we realize there is but one perfect God, and all things are brought into harmony and balance.

3-21-98 - DREAM - I was working at the courthouse. The last letter I had written was by hand 15 years earlier, so when I sat down to type the new letter on the word processor, it was new to me. I was going to write about the heat, but there wasn't any word for that. I was going to write about the cold, but there wasn't any word for that.

I then went over to a huge shiny brown table. There was a little three year old boy sitting there, dressed in a black and white suit, all by himself. He looked very sad because there were charges brought up against him.

The attorney came in then. It was a Jewish female attorney, dressed in a beautiful bright blue suit. She looked over the charges against the boy and then left.

The little boy's mother came in then and asked about the little boy's case. I said, "You can take him home. His attorney is the best in the world, and there will be no trial."

I went home then and was going to go to the library to get some books, but I had forgotten to put on my beige slacks. (I was dressed all in beige clothing, including beige high-heeled shoes). By the time I got my slacks on, the books I wanted had already been delivered to me.

I was also going to stop in at the dry cleaners to pick up the little boy's suits for the trial and when I turned around, his three little brown suits were handed to me. They had already been cleaned and were stain free.

End Of Dream

(Interpretation): There will no longer be extremes of any kind, thus no word is necessary to explain them.

The child could represent the 3 years of Jesus Christ's teachings. The Jewish attorney could find no error in them, she was wearing a suit the color of truth, thus the charges against him were dropped, and there was no trial necessary.

The knowledge I wanted and needed was already at hand, in my dreams and visions, all within, available from spirit and my higher self.

The stain free suits also show that no sin was committed during the three years and thus no trial was necessary.

~~~~~~~~~~~~~~~~

Interpretation by Joe Mason
3-21-98

Dear Dee,

As you said, it seems obvious that the dreams are speaking about changing religious concepts. The "duality" symbolism is very strong in the dreams.

The "silver bullets" may be related to the duality symbolism of gold/silver, sun/moon, male/female, which are very big symbols now, including various crop formations. (1) For example, the 1991 Barbury Castle crop formation had glyphs at the corners that correspond to sun, moon, and Mercury, which are alchemical symbols. (2)

Guns and bullets have appeared in other dreams. Some say they are "phallic" symbols, which seems right for obvious reasons. And, of course, the phallus, or lingam, is a very ancient male symbol. In terms of the human brain, the left side seems to be symbolically "male," and related to rational, analytical thinking.

Bullets usually travel through the air to reach the target, which could be related to Jung's four psychological functions, symbolized by fire, air, water, and earth. In his theory, these correspond, in order of descent, to inspiration, thinking, emotions, and sensations. So, perhaps, bullets sent through the "air," indicate that they symbolize "thinking," or ideas and beliefs. We all know this, of course, as we use expressions like "The smoking gun."

In late August, 1990, my coworker, Jeff, told me that he had a dream:

"I was with Joe (Mason) and Glen (another coworker) working on a machine that handled metal rods. (in reality, we had such a machine at work for cutting rods to make mortar shells in our ammunition plant) We were in the parking lot of Candlestick Park, where the San Francisco Giants baseball team plays. Some bullets landed around us, but they fell spent, as if they had no power. I looked up and saw a soldier dressed in a white uniform, parachuting down in the sky. He had a very modern rifle, with scopes and a laser on it. But it was not him shooting. Some other soldiers, in regular uniforms, were parachuting down above and behind him, and they were shooting at the white paratrooper with regular rifles. I knew that the white paratrooper was going to take me hostage. I was very frightened, so I lay down on the ground, with my feet pointing toward him. He landed on the ground, came to me, and made me stand up, taking me hostage."

I speculated that the dream might be related to the events in the Persian Gulf at the time. Iraq had invaded Kuwait about three-weeks prior. The U.S. forces were outnumbered, but had more modern weapons, such as laser-guided bombs. Jeff pointed to his chest and said, "Yeah, the white soldier had a new weapon that could put a laser light on you." An air war seemed to be likely. And there were thousands of hostages being held in Iraq.

But, the dream could be interpreted in another way. White represents purity and truth. Things from the sky are from "heaven," or higher levels, representing messages from the Divine. The soldiers could represent the battle of new and old ideas and beliefs. The new ones are outnumbered in terms of earthly believers, but they are of a more pure "light," and relatively invulnerable to old beliefs. The light forms a red cross over your heart, indicating emotions. Jeff is taken hostage, meaning that he is captivated by the new ideas. This forces him to stand up, or support the new ideas.

In the following months, as the Gulf War unfolded, I found it very interesting that the Iraqi weapons, such as the scuds, were ineffective, they fell down spent.

End Of Dream

Interpretation

The cats fighting over the scrambled eggs may be related to ancient symbols. The Egyptians regarded cats highly, even mummifying them. The feline species, such as lions and tigers, are major symbols from the past. The Sphinx, of course, is the man/cat. One possible meaning is the idea of "hunting," as a metaphor of the quest for spiritual knowledge. Interesting too, "Garfield" is another kind of cat.

As you well know, you and others have dreamed about eggs in various forms before. Considering the overall context of the dreams, I would think the perfect egg you displayed represents the new views about creation and spirituality that will come into being, as the old views fall apart. The geometry of your egg is much like depictions I saw in "The Sacred symbols of Mu," which are said to represent the Monotheistic Deity. The design has often appeared as a crop formation, or a part of a crop formation. This part of the dream may mean that people will come to realize that there is only One God, even though we have "scrambled" the idea.

Eggs, I think, are similar in symbolism to birthing a child. Such symbols can represent the birth of new ideas and ways. The cats fighting over the scrambled eggs seems similar to the South American myth of Yaheh Woman, which I read about in "Shamanic Voices," by Joan Halifax. Yaheh Woman gives birth to a baby, then goes into the hut where the men are gathered, and asks, "Who is the father of this child?" The men all claim to be the father, and start pulling at the baby, tearing it into pieces.

The black and white people seem to represent another duality, among other things. Sometimes "black" or black people seem to indicate "invisible," indicating the spiritual realm or beings, rather than anything negative. This may also suggest tolerance and unity of the races in the future, or perhaps tolerance of all those who are "different" from us in appearance or viewpoint. I believe this is expressed in Revelation, as Babylon being thrown down by violence.

I believe most Christian people want this balance and harmony too, but perhaps they need to be more tolerant of other views. I found a part of the Bible that may suggest this also, in:

Isaiah 65:17-25:

17 For, behold, I create new heavens and a new earth: and the former shall not be remembered, nor come into mind. 18 But be ye glad and rejoice for ever in that which I create: for, behold, I create Jerusalem a rejoicing, and her people a joy. 19 And I will rejoice in Jerusalem, and joy in my people: and the voice of weeping shall be no more heard in her, nor the voice of crying.

20 There shall be no more thence an infant of days, nor an old man that hath not filled his days: for the child shall die an hundred years old; but the sinner being an hundred years old shall be accursed. 21 And they shall build houses, and inhabit them; and they shall plant vineyards, and eat the fruit of them.

22 They shall not build, and another inhabit; they shall not plant, and another eat: for as the days of a tree are the days of my people, and mine elect shall long enjoy the work of their hands. 23 They shall not labour in vain, nor bring forth for trouble; for they are the seed of the blessed of the LORD, and their offspring with them. 24 And it shall come to pass, that before they call, I will answer; and while they are yet speaking, I will hear. 25 The wolf and the lamb shall feed together, and the lion shall eat straw like the bullock: and dust shall be the serpent's meat. They shall not hurt nor destroy in all my holy mountain, saith the LORD.

Since it was a "jazz" concert, it may refer more specifically to the United States, because jazz was born here from the black race.

My dreams and experiences have suggested that America has a special role to play in the changes. We are like the "baby" nation birthed by the rest of the world. We came here to live as one, and lead the world to unity. We are the new Babylon, but will become The New JerUSAlem.

I spell the word with the capital "USA," because it is that way in "The Book of Knowledge:The Keys of Enoch." (4) Dr. Hurtak was told in his vision that America will become The New JerUSAlem.

Our "Babylon" condition has been a theme in our history, perhaps reaching a key point in the Civil War, with freedom from slavery of the black race, and unity of the North and South, another duality symbol. Of course, we are not there yet, but I do think it will continue in that direction, and "we shall overcome some day," as we sing.

The heaters and air conditioners and the perfect balance of heat and cold (more duality symbolism) may be related to an idea I got from Pablo's dreams in January 1992. He had them all recorded on a single page. In the first dream, Gorbechev spoke to the inmates at a prison (Pablo was a Cuban prisoner at Fort Levenworth). Gorbechev spoke of capitalism and communism (another duality). I felt this was related to "The Cold War." In another dream, a big bird came down, whose eyes were turned to the infrared, to help a sick man. They hugged one another, loved one another. Infrared is an indication of the amount of heat. He also dreamed of a Russian woman discussing whether the winters were more severe in Russia or the U.S. He dreamed of children riding on a tractor driven by a farmer. A little child asked for ice cream. The farmer said, "No more ice cream today."

I felt that the cold/warm symbols were being used as metaphors about the relative amount of love, or lack thereof. I later found myths, such as the story of

Persephone, that may carry this symbolism. She was the daughter of Demeter (or Ceres), the Goddess of the Harvest. She was very beautiful, and the gods we attracted to her. Wherever she danced on her light feet, flowers sprang up. Hades (or Pluto) opened up a hole in the ground and took Persephone down into Hades. It was dark and she was very unhappy there. She ate nothing, except a few seeds of the pomegranate, which is The Food of the Dead. Later, Demeter bargained with Zeus for the return of her daughter. Zeus ruled that she could return, but she had to go back down to Hades for a period of months each year, one month for each of the seeds she had eaten. This is what causes the winter season.

The pomegranate is also mentioned in the Bible a number of times. My friend, John, came up with a brilliant interpretation a few years ago - "seeds divided by partitions." To me, this fit with part of my theories concerning Revelation 11:11. The two olive trees in the Rev. 11 verses seem to be related to Zechariah 3 and 4. In verse 4, right in the middle of the part about the two olive trees, it speaks of Zerubbabel making the great mountain into a plain and bringing the top stone forward. I had a dream where a great mountain was the "beasts" of fears. Later, I happened to watch a TV program about ancient times, which gave me an important clue. The name "Zerubabbel" was a name taken by the Jews when they returned from Babylon, and means "seed of Babylon." After hearing John's interpretation of the pomegranate, I felt it fit well with Zerubbabel.

In Haggai 2:5, Joshua and Zerubbabel are told to "fear not." In Haggai 2:19, the seed, the pomegranate, and the olive tree are mentioned. Then, in verse 2:20-23, it tells of when the Lord will shake the heavens and the earth. The final verse, 2:23, says that Zerubbabel will be made like the Lord's signet ring on that day.

When I was reading this several years ago, I had some related synchronicities with Blavatsky's, "Isis Unveiled." I happened to open the book to a page that spoke of God's Signet Ring. She said it was a Tetragrammaton, the four letters of the Divine Name, and symbolized by the Tau Cross. It is the mark on the forehead given to the 144,000 thousand in Revelation 7. Rev. 14:1 says they have "his FATHER'S NAME written on their foreheads."

From this and other hints, I believe that mankind is not guilty or condemned, as they say, and will be the hero when the truth finally comes. Babylon, or the seed of Babylon, seems quite negative, suggesting intolerance, division, conflict, and violence, yet these verses suggest the seed of Babylon leads to a very positive outcome.

The "cold" or "winter" season and a change in it are also suggested in the Song of Solomon, verses 2:11, 12 - "for lo, the winter is past, the rain is over and gone. The flowers appear on the earth, the time of singing has come, and the voice of the turtledove is heard in our land."

Your dream suggests that it can also be "too hot." I doubt that this means "too much love," as in my interpretation above. My guess is that it refers to too much "passion," in the sense of feeling so strongly about something you would kill for it. I see a similar symbolism and meaning in many ways. Human beings tend to have a strong desire for justice and righteousness on the one hand, and a loving, forgiving side on the other. I see it in such things as - Old Testament/New Testament, Conservative/Liberal, Republican/Democrat, prosecuting attorney/defense attorney, Capitalism/Communism, etc. It is also part of the meaning of The Tree of Life, in regard to the left and right columns. (5) The middle column shows a balanced condition.

There are many indications that mankind has been out of balance, and that the "male-rational" side has been dominant in the time cycle. There are many signs that the "feminine-intuitive" side will increase, so that mankind will become "balanced." One example is the crop formation that appeared at Tweksbury in 1992. It had the male/female signs of Mars and Venus joined together.

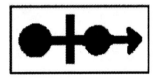

The little boy in the courthouse, I would say, represents mankind at this point in time. He is three years old, perhaps suggestive of the first three chakra levels, in our evolutionary childhood. I have written about the crop circles as chakras and the leap to the heart chakra, indicated in Revelation 11:11. (6) You have told me that the color brown in your symbols represents the earth plane, so this may fit.

The black and white suit worn by the boy, is again the black/white duality symbolism. The courthouse, I think, may be related to the "final judgment" symbolism at the end of the cycle of time. In the Egyptian myths, the heart is weighed against the feather (truth) in the Judgment Hall. If one has not reached the fourth (heart) level, he or she does not advance, but rather, returns in another earth incarnation.

The hand-written letter of 15 years earlier seems to suggest something from the past, perhaps old ideas and beliefs that will be changing, as indicated by the "new letter on the word processor." The Hopi say that the Sacred Symbols will be newly understood as the time of Purification comes. I believe that process is already underway, and it could be suggested by this part of your dream.

The part of the dream where the boy looks very sad because charges were brought up against him, could refer to how we have been taught to feel. We have been taught in the western world that we are tainted by original sin, and other such teachings.

The Jewish female attorney fits very well into my feelings about the dream. The Christian beliefs, of course, include the old Jewish ones. Some of the early Christians wanted to have a Bible with only a New Testament with the teachings of Jesus. The old way was "The Law," the new way would be "Love." The circles on The Tree of Life, have the female symbols on the left when viewing it. It is said to reverse, when one pictures being inside the Tree. The female circles symbolize severity and judgment in this case.

Also, in the Egyptian beliefs, the Goddess Maat, has the feather (truth) as her symbol. She governs over the moral order of the universe.

The charges against the boy being dropped, seems to fit with my idea about Zerubbabel above. Mankind is not "guilty" of original sin, or whatever. The beliefs in this were just part of the "script" in this stage play of life.

The "library," I have speculated, can be a symbol of the collective unconscious, or information in the spiritual realm, such as the Akashic Records. The information can be accessed in dreams, visions, inspirations, or meditations. This may be hinted in your dream, by the books you wanted being delivered.

The boy's three little brown suits being clean and stain free, may hint at the Trinity and seem to reinforce the idea that he is "not guilty" or sinful. As I was composing the above part of this writing, I realized that Zechariah 3 fits well with this last part of the second dream.

In that verse, Joshua is accused by Satan, who is standing next to the Angel. Joshua is clothed in filthy garments. The Angel commands that the filthy garments be removed. His "iniquity" is taken away, and he is then clothed in clean apparel. He is called, "a brand plucked from the fire."

According to Blavatsky, the concept of Satan was taken from the Egyptian story of Typhon-Set, who killed his brother, Osiris. To the Egyptians, this was not evil, but represented the "opponent" force. The ancient word, "satin," meant "opponent." This is suggested in Zechariah 3, I do think, and it seems to be a purification process.

Revelation 3:4 speaks about those who have not soiled their garments, so this symbolism is quite important. Joshua and Zerubbabel, I feel, are related to the two olive trees of Revelation 11. My guess is that this is yet another duality symbolism. Joshua is the priest, and Zerubbabel is the governor. This can refer to church/state, or inside/outside or dreaming-spiritual self/waking self symbolism.

The two olive trees could also be related to the left and right columns of The Tree of Life. I believe we are headed toward a balanced condition when the two trees stand up.

Turning my eyes to the infrared,

Joe

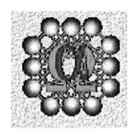

SWEDENBORG'S NEW JERUSALEM

Emanuel Swedenborg (1688-1772)
New Church - New Jerusalem

The New Sky and the New Land and What "The New Jerusalem" Means

It says in the book of Revelation:

I saw a new sky and a new land. The first sky and the first land had disappeared. - Then I saw the holy city, New Jerusalem, coming down from God out of the sky like a bride ready for her husband. . . .

The city had a huge, high wall with twelve gates, and twelve angels at the gates. The names of Israel's twelve tribes were written on the gates. - The city's wall had twelve foundations, with the names of the Lamb's twelve apostles on them. . . .

The city had a square layout: its length was the same as its width. The city was measured with a measuring rod and found to be 12,000 stadia [1,379 miles]: its length, width, and height were equal. Its wall was measured to be 144 cubits [216 feet] by human standards of measurement, which an angel was using.

The wall was made of jasper, but the city was pure gold, like pure glass. The foundations of the city's wall were made out of every kind of precious stone. - The twelve gates were twelve pearls - and the city's highway was pure gold, like transparent glass.

God's radiance gave light to the city, and its lamp was the Lamb. - The nations that have been rescued will walk toward its light, and the world's kings will bring their magnificence and dignity to it. (Revelation 21: 1, 2, 12-24)

When we read this passage, we understand it only literally. According to this interpretation, the sky and land we see now are going to disappear. Then a new sky will come into existence, and the holy city Jerusalem will come down onto a new land. This city will have the dimensions given in the description.

But angels have a completely different way of understanding all of this. Every detail that we interpret on a physical level, they interpret on a spiritual level. The angels' way of understanding it is what it symbolizes: it is the Bible's inner, spiritual meaning.

Here is what the details of this passage mean according to the angels' inner, spiritual understanding of it:

"A new sky and a new land" refer to a new religion in heaven and on earth.

"The city Jerusalem coming down from God out of the sky" means this religion's philosophy from heaven.

"Its length, width, and height," which were equal, refer to all the good qualities and true ideas in this philosophy, seen as a whole.

"The city's wall" means the true ideas that protect it.

The measurement of its wall, "144 cubits by human standards of measurement, which an angel was using," refers to all this protecting truth seen as a whole and what it is like.

The "twelve gates" made out of pearls mean the true ideas that bring people into the religion.

The "twelve angels at the gates" mean the same thing.

The wall's foundations, "made out of every kind of precious stone," mean the concepts this religious philosophy is based on.

"Israel's twelve tribes" mean everything about the religion, seen as a whole and in all its different aspects. The "twelve apostles" mean the same thing.

The "gold like pure glass" that the city and its highway were made of means the good qualities that come from love, which make the true ideas in this philosophy shine through.

"The nations that have been rescued" and "the world's kings" who will "bring their magnificence and dignity to it" refer to all religious people who do good things and have true ideas.

"God" and "the Lamb" refer to the Lord as the divine itself and as the divine human.

This is what the Bible's spiritual meaning is like. The physical-level meaning, which is the literal meaning, serves as a basis for it. These two meanings, the physical and the spiritual, work together through correspondences.

The city of Jerusalem has a special meaning for Jews, Christians and Muslims. This place has always been a symbol of God's presence on earth. From the history of the Jewish people and the prophecies of the Bible, Jerusalem has become a symbol of our inner destiny, and a state of spiritual peace, which may feel like a long-lost home. (Isaiah 43:5-7; Jeremiah 31)

The New Jerusalem is a symbolic image found in the Christian Bible, in the Book of Revelation, Chapter 21. Here the city New Jerusalem is described as a place of peace and happiness, the goal both of human history and of individual human life.

Many people have interpreted the prophecy of the New Jerusalem as a literal, historic event. Others have seen that this story contains a deeper meaning, that it represents the spiritual peace and happiness that God wants to give each of us.

Emanuel Swedenborg described this spiritual meaning of the New Jerusalem in his prolific writings. He describes them in such a way that people see God's hand at work, and find a promise of happiness and peace to come, not as a literal 'end of the world,' but as a new presence of God in the hearts and mind and lives of all people within themselves.

Thus the New Jerusalem is really a new spiritual time during which God works and re-creates the world, not through terrible and dramatic intervention, but using mankind's own free choices and rational/logical thinking.

~~~~~~~~~~~~~~~~~~~~~~~

Joe Mason comments:

The New Jerusalem Plan. It is similar to diagrams of the Zodiac and to the symbol of the heart chakra. The Four Living Creatures trace back to the camp positions of the Twelve Tribes in Numbers 2 of the Bible. The four major Tribes correspond to the Living Creatures, and to the Zodiac signs of the solstices and equinoxes during the

Age of Taurus. In each quarter is a major Tribe and two other Tribes for a total of Twelve Tribes. In the center of the encampment is the Tabernacle. The camp arrangement is a reflection of 'heaven', that is the circle of Zodiac signs in the sky above.

It is probably not a meaningless coincidence that The Tree of Life appeared as a crop circle in 1997, or that the Menorah appeared as a formation in 1999. The Tree of Life stands in the center of The New Jerusalem in Revelation 22:2. The Menorah, the lampstand with seven lamps, is in the Tabernacle. The son of man stands in the midst of the seven lampstands in Revelation 1:12-13. The two olive trees, the two annointed, stand on each side of the Menorah in Zechariah 4, and stand up after 3 1/2 days of being dead in Revelation 11:11.

~~~~~~~~~~~~~~~~~~~~~~~

Many people are speculating about 'where' the New Jerusalem will be, all the way from 'on top' of the Old Jerusalem, to Great Britain and various places in the United States. None of those places will bring what the New Jerusalem signifies and that would be 'a place of peace'. The only place that could possibly be is 'within each individual'.

AFTERWORD
WHAT IS A CONSPIRACY?

The most common definition of a conspiracy is two or more people secretly planning a criminal act. But a conspiracy doesn't always have to be 'criminal' or punishable by a court, trial, and prison. A conspiracy can be so outrageous that nobody or at least few people even recognize it for what it is.

Synonyms: plot, intrigue, machination, conspiracy, cabal mean a plan secretly devised to accomplish an evil or treacherous end. Plot implies careful foresight in planning a complex scheme. Intrigue suggests secret underhanded maneuvering in an atmosphere of duplicity. Machination implies a contriving of annoyances, injuries, or evils by indirect means. Conspiracy implies a secret agreement among several people usually involving treason or great treachery. Cabal typically applies to political intrigue involving persons of some eminence (a cabal among powerful senators).

Synonyms: Plan, plot , cabal, covin, intrigue, machination, practice, scheme.

Related Words: sedition, treason; disloyalty, faithlessness, falsity, perfidiousness, perfidy, treacherousness, treachery.

How does this fit into the context of religion? I suppose it depends on what religious beliefs you profess and how strong your beliefs are in that religion.
Some religious groups are so strict that normal people don't even get to speak to members of that group unless you are seriously looking for membership or born into the group. Other groups are so loosely knit, anyone can walk into the church (usually a store-front), be welcomed warmly and immediately feel right at home like you are with family.

Some religious groups, you meet at airports and on the street, given brochures and invited to meetings and once you are in the group, you are told you have to give up all your worldly possessions and even your family.

There is a wide range of groups - ranging all the way from so much love you can't believe anyone could be that loving - to raging hatred towards anyone who isn't like you, or who doesn't think like you.

Knowing this, how can the whole world become members of the same religion. It sounds impossible unless it is mandated by law. Even then, some people will secretly have their own religion. That's the way society has always been, and I believe will always be.

I have my doubts that 100% of the people will ever believe the same thing, but the way society is heading, more and more people are starting to think similarly enough to plan for a One World Religion.

UN Secretary General Kofi Annan said "the future of the world depends on women."

Women, for the most part - especially in the Western World are more religious than the men. In the Middle East it appears to be that men do all the worshipping - that's what we see in public. Older religions have always been patriarchal. Women have always been subservient, but that is changing in the Western Cultures particularly.

In Geneva, Switzerland, hundreds of spiritual and religious leaders met at the United Nations for a peace summit. And although all the major faiths were there, including those claiming to represent Christianity. However, it was apparent that Jesus was not invited to the meeting.

This meeting was the first UN sponsored summit of women religious leaders. One of the meetings had more than 500 women from more than 70 countries came to talk about achieving world peace. Most of these women were from "Eastern religions" - Buddhists, Taoists and Hindus.

There was a wide range of personalities at the meeting. For example, a woman named "Amma," known as the "hugging saint," came with her own followers. By hugging people, she claims to be able to impart "divine love and wisdom". She said, "It's not only hugging but it is also imparting that spiritual principal into people, so to have them know who they are, so once you know that, peace will spontaneously happen."

A lot of people believe that these days, it seems.

The Honorary Chair Shirley MacLaine, known for her New Age books, movies, and videos was not there, but other celebrities attended including Linda Evans, Lindsay Wagner and Linda Gray.

Linda Gray said, "I was raised Catholic, I bless that base, I think if you have a strong religious base where, whatever it is, then you branch out from there, or expand on it."

Bawa Jain, one of the organizers and one of the few men present, said, "And behold the power of women, look at that, the rain stopped, this is the power of women, a true demonstration here." Bawa Jain then led the women in a chant for peace. "Say it with me three times, 'No more violence, No more violence, No more violence,'" he said.

Co-chair of the Global Peace Initiative, Rev. Joan Brown Campbell said, "The thunderclouds of war gather around us, the sky grows dark but it never does envelope us. In a few moments we will light a single candle, and from that candle many will receive the light and that light will shine in the darkness."

A participant named Hanna Strong said, "The only way we're ever going to have peace is by people being peaceful inside, no aggression, no hatred, we have to transform these negative emotions that are creating situations for war."

There was a lot of talk about peace and how women can harness their "feminine energies" to bring peace to planet earth, there was no mention of the Christian Prince of Peace, Jesus Christ. There were no evangelical Christians speaking at or attending this world religious summit.

Does this mean that Christians don't want peace? I'm certain that is not the case. Christians have their own organizations working on this project, not in conjunction with the U.N..

When asked about the lack of evangelical Christians at this event, Rev. Brown Campbell said, "That's not a purposeful intent. This is a meeting, of course, of people of all religions. And I think what we've all tried to do is to call on the common deity that everyone will say... I mean everyone here would say there is a God, this is not a group of Atheists, this is a group of people of faith, and for everyone there is a god-person by whatever name." When asked whether evangelical Christians were not invited on purpose, Rev. Brown Campbell said, "No, no, no, not at all...the attempt to be broad-scale means there are not too many of any, and this is a first effort, identifying people was not simple."

Two years ago, honorary chair and CNN founder Ted Turner endeared himself to the crowd at the U.N. in New York City, by promoting the New Age concept that there are many ways to heaven. The Geneva summit was a direct outcome of the Millennium World Peace Summit of religious and spiritual leaders. "The thing that disturbed me was that my religion, the Christian sect, was very intolerant, not of religious freedom, but we thought we were the only ones going to heaven," Turner said.

Completely against Christian beliefs, here is a huge problem: The belief that there are many ways to heaven was also part of the New Age gospel at the Geneva summit. Strong said, "I'm very close to the Buddhists, the Taoists, the native Americans and uh, peace to me is being one with the source." When asked if she was referring to God "the Creator," she said, "Well, I don't necessary call it Creator, but, it's one name."

"The Nephilim were on the earth in those days, and afterward when The Sons of God came into the daughters of men and they bore children to them. These were the mighty men who were of old, men of renown." Genesis, chapter 6, verse 4.

Continuing studies to determine emotional and intellectual understanding, and attitudes—and successive alterations of them if any—regarding the possibility and consequences of discovering intelligent extraterrestrial life.[34] [**]
Historical and empirical studies of the behavior of peoples and their leaders when confronted with dramatic and unfamiliar events or social pressures.[35] Such studies might help to provide programs for meeting and adjusting to the implications of such a discovery. Questions one might wish to answer by such studies would include: How might such information, under what circumstances, be presented to or withheld from the public for what ends? What might be the role of the discovering scientists and other decisionmakers regarding release of the fact of discovery?

EXCERPT - PAGE 216 OF THE BROOKINGS REPORT ON EXTRATERRESTRIALS

The most influential of the early contactees was George Adamski, a California occultist. Adamski made physical contact with his first Venusian on November 20, 1952 in a California desert. Adamski later wrote several popular books, which detailed his contact experiences and included drawings of aliens and spacecraft. Adamski's books borrowed heavily from the works of the Theosophist Madame Blavatsky. The Theosophical interpretation of alien contact is an approach used by most flying saucer religions.

George Adamski, had this to say to C.A. Honey who published some of his writings and opinions:

Quote: "I wish to make an apology - I did not sanction The Origin of Religions, which C.A.Honey published in the Newsletter. For the space brothers that I work with did not come here to impose a new religion upon us or to change the one we may have. The publication was contrary to the Brother's wishes." Signed - Sincerely Yours, George Adamski. Unquote.

C.A. Honey writes: "At no time have I ever said, or even hinted, that the "space people" were trying to change our religion or establish a new religion. The fact remains that the government keeps secrecy imposed due to conclusions published by the Brookings Institute as discussed in my other Publication # 249, entitled GOVERNMENT SECRECY ABOUT UFOS. . I will reproduce five paragraphs of that article here and will supply the complete article free to anyone requesting it. Most followers of the "flying saucer" situation over the years are aware of the Brookings Report issued by the Brookings Institute in regard to the effects of releasing space information of certain types to the public at large. The essential part I am concerned with at this time is partially explained and found on pages 225 and 226 of their report.

Quote: "The positions of the major American religious denominations, the Christian sects, and the eastern religions on the matter of extraterrestrial life need elucidation. Consider the following:

The Fundamentalist (and anti-science) sects are growing space around the world and, as missionary enterprises, may have schools and a good deal of literature attached to them. One of the important things is that, where they are active, they appeal to the illiterate and semi-literate (including, as missions, the preachers as well as the congregation) and can pile up a very influential following in terms of numbers. For them, the discovery of other life--rather than any other space product--would be electrifying....

Additionally, because of the international effects of space activities and, in the event of its happening, of the discovery of extraterrestrial life, even though space activities are not internationalized, it is very important to take account of other major religions.

These quotes are only a brief portion of the entire Brookings Report, consisting of a few paragraphs from pages 225 and 226 of the entire report. They do make it plain that in their opinion major upheaval would occur around the world if the real truth about the reality of "flying saucers" was made public. The religious implications were also made plain.

Note also their poor opinion of the public at large, especially the religious public, considering them to be illiterate and semi-literate, including in this category the preachers as well as the congregation. I don't agree with those statements. Most religious people and their ministers are intelligent though misinformed.

So basically we find that the government, taking the Brookings Report seriously, has kept the true facts about "flying Saucer" origin and their pilots completely secret because of certain religions and their viewpoint that only they (the religious) know the truth. In all likelihood they will continue to keep UFO facts secret from the world public at large. "

EZEKIEL - CHAPTER 1

"Now as I looked at the living creatures, I saw a wheel upon the earth beside the living creatures one for each of the four of them. As for the appearance of the wheels and their construction, their appearance was like the gleaming of a chrysolite, and the four had the same likeness being as it were a wheel within a wheel. The four wheels had rims and they had spokes, and their rims were full of eyes round about. And when the living creatures went, the wheels went beside them and when the living creatures went, the wheels went with them, for the living creature was in the wheel." Ezekiel, chapter 1, Versus 15 thru 21. Revised Standard Version

ZECHARIAH SITCHIN

And Abram said unto himself 'Surely these are not gods (Enki and Enlil) that made the earth and all mankind, but these are the servants of Yahweh!

Book of Jasher Chapter IX: 19.

Note that the book of Jasher is NOT in our current Bible, but is quoted several times within it:

Chris Ward, D. Min, writes:

"Zecharia Sitchin is a brilliant author and contemporary Ufologist. He has authored eight books reporting his polytheistic interpretation of Sumerian, Biblical, and Egyptian history. He states that the Sumerian account of the origin of civilization predates that of the Biblical record and implies that it is therefore a more accurate report of our origins.

He implies in his book, "Divine Encounters", that the Hebrew account in Genesis of the creation of man is an inferior record of the origins of man and was copied by Moses from the Sumerian cuneiform clay tablets and the Epic of Gilgamesh.

He suggests that Yahweh may be interpreted as the Hebrew expression of the gods of Sumeria Enki or Enlil. He maintains a polytheistic view of the gods of Sumeria and the Jews. He further goes on to attempt to establish that Yahweh may be in fact Enlil the Sumerian demigod.

"And the story of Man's Divine Encounters, the subject of this book, is so filled with parallels between the biblical experiences and those of encounters with the Annunnaki by other ancient peoples, that the possibility that Yahweh was one of 'them' must be seriously considered." P. 347.

"The question and its implied answer, indeed, arise inevitably. That the biblical creation narrative with which the Book is beyond dispute." p. 347.

"That the biblical Eden is a rendering of the Sumerian E.DIN is almost self evident. P. 347.

"That the tale of the Deluge and Noah and the ark is based on the Akkadian Atra-Hasis texts and the earlier Sumerian Deluge tale in the Epic of Gilgamesh, is certain." P. 347

"That the plural 'us' in the creation of The Adam segments reflects the Sumerian and Akkadian record of the discussions by the leaders of the Anunnaki that led to the genetic engineering that brought Homo sapiens about, should be obvious. p. 347.

"Indeed, in the very tale--the tale of the Deluge--where the identification of Yahweh with Enki appears the clearest, confusion in fact shows up. The roles are switched, and all of a sudden Yahweh plays the role not of Enki but of his rival Enlil.

In the Mesopotamian original texts, it is Enlil who is unhappy with the way Mankind has turned out, who seeks its destruction by the approaching calamity, and who makes the other Annunaki leaders swear to keep all that a secret from Mankind." P. 350 & 351.

While claiming to have drawn his conclusions that Yahweh was one of the Sumerian Gods by having read the Book of Jasher, then he states that the Sumerian history substantiates his view that Yahweh is the "b'nai Elohim".

"Joshua 10:13 refers to the Book of Jasher, which is also listed as a known source text in II Samuel 1:18. These are but passing references to what must have been a much more extensive trove of earlier texts." P. 5.

"The Books of Nathan and Gad have vanished, as did other books--the Book of the Wars of Yahweh, the Book of Jasher, to mention two others--that the Bible speaks of...They all provide a wealth of insights into the nature and identity of Yahweh." P. 330.

The Book of Jasher contains a detailed account of the life of Abraham, the Father of the Hebrew nation. Abram was the son of Terah who was a prince, priest, and sorcerer for Nimrod.

Chapter VII, verse 49-51: *And Terah the son of Nahor prince of Nimrod's host, was in those days very great in the sight of the king and his subjects, and the king and princes loved him, and they elevated him very high.*
Terah was seventy years old when he begat him, and Terah called the name of his son Abram, because the king had raised him in those days, and dignified him above all his princes that were with him.

At the birth of Abram an omen appeared in the sky that suggested that the child would replace Nimrod as king. An attempt was made to kill Abram but Terah gave up a child of one of his slaves to the king's men to be slain and then sent Abram to Noah to be raised in secret.

Chapter IX verse 6: *And when Abram was in Noah's house thirty-nine years, and Abram knew Yahweh from three years old*
He went in the ways of Yahweh until he the day of his death as Noah and his son Shem had taught him.
And all the sons of the earth in those days greatly transgressed against Yahweh
And they rebelled against Him
And they went after other gods (Enki and Enlil),
For they forgot Yahweh who had created heaven and earth;
And the inhabitants of the earth made unto themselves, at that time, every man his god; Enki and Enlil
And the sons of men served them and they became their gods (polytheism).

It is very clear as in the Biblical account that the Watchers (the Annunaki) made an attempt to get the whole world to worship the Sumerian gods Enki and Enlil and to supplant Yahweh as creator God.

The Geneva Conference Continued

A former director of the Family Research Council, Robert Maginnis, said of the summit, "Well, I can see the possibility that it's the globalization of world religion."

Maginnis said that it appears the hidden agenda is to unite people under one religious umbrella so they will peacefully accept the UN's radical political goals. "I would submit that the United Nations is very anti-life, they are anti-faith, anti-family, they're anti-national sovereignty, but they are pro one-world government," he said.

Christian scholars say the Bible warns of a time when all the world will unite under a false global religious and political system. Maginnis says, it appears the UN could be taking the first steps in that direction.

"You're taking the Muslim community, the Christian community, the Hindus, the Confucians and all the many hundreds of religious groups, trying to identify key leaders, and you are basically trying to co-opt them into cooperating with you," he said.

Christians believe there is one way to heaven, because Jesus said, "I am the way, the truth and the life and no man comes to the Father except by me."

CROP CIRCLES, ETS, AND RELIGION

People who have personal contact with extraterrestrials for a period of time know that the extraterrestrials have a high sense of spirituality that is greater than that of humans.

Those contactees who join 'abductee' groups for the purpose of understanding what is happening to them, start out with great fear and confusion. A few years later, these same 'abductees'/contactees express an entirely different attitude about their contact, their fear is gone, and know that nothing bad is going to happen to them. They also know that they are part of large program to help earth. No specific religion is ever expressed, but their sense of spirituality is great and extraterrestrials know that their is a God/higher source of creation above all of us.

That said, the extraterrestrials' God is not the God of our earthly Bible, and even though Jesus has been said to be seen on UFOs, Jesus is not considered to be Divine like our earthly religions make him out to be.

These particular problems of religion in the Christian community cannot be eliminated, but it is apparent that the more Christians who are abducted/contacted, a different understanding comes to these contactees about the realities of spiritual life. Many remain Christians, but gain a greater spirituality through their contacts.

Some have said that this change, which comes over contactees, is some kind of mind-control. Mind-control is a possibility, but for someone to feel 'good' about their life doesn't seem to be a bad thing, especially when their relationship to God is improved.

If our government is hiding the evidence of UFOs and extraterrestrials from the population in general, as a reality, they are still allowing movies, TV shows, commercials, and hundreds of books to be published on the subject.

People themselves are coming to grips with the evidence of UFOs and abductions/contacts all alone. Many times it is a rough road to take, to feel alone with this kind of knowledge. However, eventually, help is found through psychiatrists, psychologists, friends, family, and through the internet, which has been a fabulous educational tool for people who feel that they might be being abducted/contacted.

The media in the United States is still in the dark-ages of education about important topics like this, though some cable/satellite stations are coming around and showing the truth here and there.

Here and there, some of the television news stations in the United States are showing crop circles for a moment or two. Hopefully, as more crop circles appear in the United States there will be more. How can the media hide what is in our own back yards. Hopefully by then, the truth of the matter will be more apparent and people will no longer blame all the crop circles on hoaxers.

Speaking of hoaxed crop circles, of course there are some. There is always someone who has to joke around and try to get away with something to fool other people. But no matter, even extraterrestrials know that whatever design a hoaxer chooses to make, it will be inspired to teach people something.

WHAT RELIGION ARE CROP CIRCLES TEACHING?

The chapters of our book rather outline which religious ideas are noted by crop circles. THE WAY GOD CREATES, SRI YANTRA, NEW JERUSALEM AND CHAKRA, YIN YANG, TAO, FENG SHUI , TRINITY, TREE OF LIFE , MENORAH, MANDELBROT SET, THE BUILDER SQUARE, T - TAU, THE OPENING EYES, THE APERTURE, FLOWER OF LIFE, METATRON'S CUBE , DNA, NEW JERUSALEM PLAN, WHERE WILL THE NEW JERSALEM BE LOCATED?

Within those titles include the religions of Buddhism, Christianity, Gnosticism, Judaism, Hinduism, Kabbalism, Sufi, Egyptian, Toaism, and offshoots of these religions as well.

306

Within those disciplines, so-called New Age teachings pick up on crystals, acupuncture, acupressure, chakra energies, other healing modalities, DNA repair, Masonic building trades and design, and sacred geometry. Actually, none of these disciplines are New Age; they've been known for thousands of years and are just now being brought back into knowledge that is more wide-spread than it ever was.

The New Age religion is about the total person; Mind-body-spirit as one whole entity. The physical body is not separate from the mind or spirit. It does not have a formal name, no holy texts, organization or membership roles. There are no clergy schools or universities, no dogma or creed one has to follow.

About a quarter of the New Age believers, believe in a non-traditional concept of the nature of God. Within the New Age spiritual groups that may gather, some believe that God is 'a state of higher consciousness that the person himself may reach.' Others believe that God is the 'total realization of the self-human-potential.' Some believe that every person is God.

Other forms of religion and beliefs are:

Monism: All that exists is derived from a single source of divine energy.

Pantheism: All that exists is God; God is all that exists. This leads naturally to the concept of the divinity of the individual, that we are all Gods. They do not seek God as revealed in a sacred text or as exists in a remote heaven; they seek God within the self and throughout the entire universe.

Panentheims: God is all that exists. God is at once the entire universe, and transcends the universe as well.

Reincarnation: After death, we are reborn and live another life as a human. This cycle repeats itself many times. This belief is similar to the concept of transmigration of the soul in Hinduism.

Karma: The good and bad deeds that we do either adds and subtracts from our accumulated spiritual record - our karma. At the end of our life, we are rewarded or punished according to our karma by being reincarnated into either a painful or good new life.

Personal transformation: Many people are having intense personal spiritual experiences which lead them to look for others who have had similar experiences outside their normal church, which they grew up in.

They are led to use meditation in several forms, even hypnosis to try to find out who they were in past-lives. Others even use illegal drugs to induce higher states of consciousness. One may find these New Age practices within the formal churches these days as well, though drugs are not recommended by the major religions - one will find small groups here and there that do.

What is a Universal or World Religion? Once one accepts the concept that all paths eventually get you to God, and since all is God, all people will feel comfortable and accepting of everyone elses' beliefs even if they do not profess them personally. It will be expected that a One-World religion will bring about a Utopia, within which there will no longer be wars, disease, or hunger. Everyone will care for everyone else - there will no longer be poor or starving people. Rather than feeling an allegiance to one's own state or nation, one will concern oneself with all the peoples of the world. No one could say that is a bad thing. Could one?

RECOMMENDED BOOKS

Bible

The Zohar - See http://www.kabbalah.com/k/index.php/

The Sign of the Serpent Ken to Creative Physics.
Mark Balfour, Prism Press, UK, 1990.
Paperback: ; Dimensions (in inches): 0.75 x 8.75 x 5.50
Publisher: Prism Pr Ltd; (December 1994)
ISBN: 1853270628

Mark Balfour, Metavison Research Consultants, 1/1/ Richmond Avenue,
Cremorne, Sydney2090, Australia. Tel: (02) 953-4660
http://www.abel.net.uk/~sayer/cereol.htm

Seth Speaks - Jane Roberts
Paperback: 445 pages
Publisher: Amber-Allen Publishing; Reprint edition (June 1994)
ISBN: 1878424076

The Nature of Physical Reality - Jane Roberts
Paperback: 446 pages
Publisher: Amber-Allen Publishing; Reprint edition (June 1994)
ISBN: 1878424068

Channeling - Jon Klimo
Paperback: 474 pages
Publisher: North Atlantic Books; 2nd edition (April 1998)
ISBN: 1556432488

Tantric Way: Art, Science, Ritual, by Ajit Mookeajee and Madhu Khanna.
Paperback: 208 pages
Publisher: Thames & Hudson; Reprint edition (April 2003)
ISBN: 0500270880

The Inner Reaches of Outer Space - Joseph Campbell
Hardcover: 160 pages
Publisher: New World Library; (February 9, 2002)
ISBN: 1577312090

The Book of Knowledge, The Keys of Enoch - J.J. Hurtak
Hardcover: 619 pages
Publisher: Academy for Future Science; 3 edition (December 1982)
ISBN: 0960345043

Secrets in the Fields - Freddie Silva
Paperback: 332 pages
Publisher: Hampton Roads Pub Co; (September 2002)
ISBN: 1571743227

The Lost Continent of MU - James Churchward
Paperback: 424 pages
Publisher: Brotherhood of Life Books; Reprint edition (October 1995)
ISBN: 0914732196

The Lost Covenant - Joan Sckrabulis - Privately published
Now in e-book form:
http://home.earthlink.net/~eclipseproductions/eclipse.html

Chaos: Making a New Science - James Gleick
Paperback: 368 pages
Publisher: Penguin USA (Paper); Reprint edition (December 1988)
ISBN: 0140092501

Lost Tribes of Israel Study Maps - Daniel Walsh
Privately Published
See: http://www.geocities.com/Eureka/3401/C1st.html

Pole Shift I - Dee Finney
Paperback: 236 pages
Publisher: Great Dreams Publications; (November 2001)
ISBN: 0971427240

Pole Shift II - Dee Finney
Paperback: 392 pages
Publisher: Write To Print; (April 2002)
ISBN: 0971427275

Great Dreams - Quest for Truth - Dee Finney & Joe Mason
Paperback: 230 pages
Publisher: Great Dreams Publications; (July 2001)
ISBN: 097026304X

Egyptian - Book of the Dead
E. A. Wallis Budge
ISBN: 048621866x
Paperback 533 pages

The 12th Planet - Zechariah Sitchin
Mass Market Paperback: 448 pages
Publisher: Avon; Reissue edition (February 1, 1999)
ISBN: 038039362X

Divine Encounters - Zechariah Sitchin
Mass Market Paperback: 400 pages
Publisher: Avon; Reissue edition (January 1996)
ISBN: 0380780763

Genesis Revisited - Zechariah Sitchin
Mass Market Paperback: 352 pages
Publisher: Avon; Reissue edition (October 1, 1990)
ISBN: 0380761599

When Time Began - Zechariah Sitchin
Mass Market Paperback: 416 pages
Publisher: Avon; Reissue edition (October 5, 1999)
ISBN: 0380770717

Chariots of the Gods - Erich Von Daniken
Paperback: 248 pages
Publisher: Berkley Pub Group; Reprint edition (January 1999)
ISBN: 0425166805

Jesus Christ, Sun of God - David Fideler
Paperback: 430 pages
Publisher: Quest Books; (November 1993)
ISBN: 0835606961

City of Revelation - John Michell
Mass Market Paperback
Publisher: Ballantine Books; (June 12, 1977)
ISBN: 0345258754

The New View over Atlantis - John Michell
Paperback: 224 pages
Publisher: Thames & Hudson; Reprint edition (May 2001)
ISBN: 050027312X

The Dimensions of Paradise - John Michell
Paperback: 216 pages
Publisher: Adventures Unlimited Press; (May 2, 2001)
ISBN: 0932813895

Time-Life book, Indians of the West
Hardcover
Publisher - Time-Life Books - 1973
See: http://www.3sacharm.com/si/7075076.html (used book seller)

Deity, Cosmos and Man - Geoffrey Farthing
available in full on the internet
See: http://www.theosophical.ca/DeityCosmosMan-Book1.htm

Isis Unveiled - H.P. Blavatsky
Paperback: 1471 pages
Publisher: Theosophical Univ Pr; (November 1999)
ISBN: 0911500030

777 - And Other Qabalistic Writings of Aleister Crowley-
Israel Regardie and Aleister Crowley
Paperback: 336 pages
Publisher: Red Wheel/Weiser; (October 1990)
ISBN: 0877286701

Other Great Books by
Dee Finney

An intriguing and detailed look at how information came to Dee Finney that directed her to start a community designed to help people survive the 'end times' referred to in the biblical book of Revelation.

Included in this first volume are details of how extraterrestrials are helping people to know what to do to survive the impending Pole Shift, without coming forward themselves in a physical manner such as humanity is expecting.

Dee gives the reader more than her extensive experience. She details maps that show how the Earth will be tilted after the Pole Shift occurs and more.

Her amazing insight into what is to come will not only fascinate readers, but may also give them the clues they need to gather their own tool and find a safe place to face the changes in store for planet Earth.

Pole Shift Vol 11 continues the directions given to Dee Finney in dreams and visions to start a community of like-minded people to survive the 'end times' referred to in the biblical book of Revelation.

This volume of Pole Shift details the various extraterrestrials who communicated with her along the way. Dee has drawn their pictures, some of whom posed for her for this purpose.

It gives the reader instructions for saving the planet from man-made destruction, as well as maps of the danger zones on the earth where cracks may open up and create new volcanoes,but also swallow the ocean water that will fill the 'hollow-earth' below.

Only from Great Dreams Publications
Available in all bookstores, including Amazon.com and
Barnesandnoble.com

Printed in the United States
18160LVS00002B/125-126